FORGOTTEN TEXAS LEADER

Number Two
THE CANSECO-KECK HISTORY SERIES
JERRY THOMPSON, GENERAL EDITOR

But none was more brave than McLeod. He was seen alternately in every part of the field dashing from rank to rank, like a meteor glancing through the murky clouds of battle, as heedless of the balls that were flying around him as if it were the mere pattering of rain.

—*Houston Telegraph and Texas Register,* July 28, 1841

Forgotten Texas Leader

HUGH MCLEOD AND THE TEXAN SANTA FE EXPEDITION

PAUL N. SPELLMAN

Foreword by Stanley E. Siegel

TEXAS A&M UNIVERSITY PRESS
College Station

The paper used in this book meets the minimum requirements
of the American National Standard for Permanence
of Paper for Printed Library Materials, z39.48-1984.
Binding materials have been chosen for durability.
∞

Frontispiece of Hugh McLeod from *Hood's Texas Brigade: A Compendium*,
by Col. Harold Simpson. Courtesy Hill College History Complex.

LIBRARY OF CONGRESS CATALOGING-IN-PUBLICATION DATA

Spellman, Paul N.
Forgotten Texas leader : Hugh McLeod and the Texan Santa Fe
expedition / Paul N. Spellman. — 1st ed.
p.   cm. — (Canseco-Keck history series ; no. 2)
Includes bibliographical references (p.   ) and index.
ISBN 0-89096-896-9 (alk. paper)
1. McLeod, Hugh, 1814–1862.   2. Texan Santa Fé Expedition, 1841.
3. Soldiers—Texas—Biography.   I. Title.   II. Series.
F390.M526s64   1999
976.4'04'092—dc21
99-18341
CIP

[b]

Contents

Illustrations

Foreword

A full-fledged biography of Gen. Hugh McLeod is long overdue. While biographical studies of McLeod's contemporaries—Sam Houston, Mirabeau B. Lamar, Anson Jones, and others—abound, Paul Spellman's is the first account of Hugh McLeod's life and times. Most scholars have relegated McLeod to that second tier of Texans, just below Thomas Jefferson Rusk, David G. Burnet, and Albert Sidney Johnston. Spellman makes a very effective case for elevating McLeod to the pantheon where his peers—friend and foe—placed him.

Born in New York City and raised in Georgia, and a graduate of the United States Military Academy at the bottom of his class, McLeod was posted to Fort Jesup on the Texas-Louisiana border. Here the excitement of the independence struggle against Mexico proved too strong for the young soldier, who resigned his commission in the U.S. Army and volunteered under the emblem of the Lone Star. Deeply involved in the new republic, McLeod built a law practice in Galveston, married, and devoted himself to family pursuits. Critical of President Sam Houston's policies, he linked his political fortunes to those of Houston's successor, Mirabeau B. Lamar. After three diplomatic missions failed to achieve true peace with Mexico, Lamar turned to the sword. By the terms of the 1836 Boundary Act, the Republic of Texas claimed the Rio Grande as its boundary, "from source to mouth." The incorporation of Santa Fe was essential to validate that claim.

General McLeod's command of the Santa Fe expedition dwarfed every other aspect of his career. Ill-conceived and poorly planned from the beginning, the expedition lost many of its volunteer soldiers long before reaching its destination. The straggling survivors limped into New Mexico, where they were betrayed by one of their own and compelled to surrender under false assurances. American citizens among the Pioneers were promised amnesty, a pledge soon broken. The prisoners were marched to Mexico City under barbaric conditions, and many died along the way.

Others perished in Mexican prisons. Those who eventually returned home bore the indelible imprint of the tragic event for the rest of their lives.

McLeod's name will always be associated with this disaster, but the greater blame lies with Lamar. He badly misjudged the sentiment among the Santa Fe population for union with Texas. In addition the venture was authorized by Lamar without the approval of the Republic's congress. Because haste was at a premium, lest Congress refuse the endeavor, planning and preparation suffered. Although there is plenty of blame to go around in the Santa Fe calamity, McLeod should not bear the greatest portion.

McLeod rounded out his career in political and military service to Texas and the United States, and finally, to the Confederacy, in a public life that spanned more than three decades. He was a witness to and a participant in some of the most decisive events in Texas history: independence, annexation, the Mexican War, and secession.

Spellman has succeeded brilliantly in giving Hugh McLeod his just due.

— STANLEY E. SIEGEL
UNIVERSITY OF HOUSTON

Acknowledgments

Library staffs and research centers across the country provided consistent and invaluable service to me. I am grateful for the deliberate work of Donely Brice and his staff at the Texas State Archives in Austin, and to the staff at the Center for American History (the Barker Texas History Center) and the Perry-Castañeda Library at the University of Texas at Austin. The Galveston and Texas History Center at the Rosenberg Library in Galveston contains a treasure trove of materials that provided a foundation for chapters on the McLeod family and Hugh McLeod's business dealings in Galveston.

For the military research, I am indebted to the staffs at the United States Military Academy in West Point, New York, the United States Navy Yard in Pensacola, Florida, and the adjutant-general archives at Camp Mabry in Austin. The archives at Tulane University, the San Jacinto Battleground Museum, and the Huntington Library in San Marino, California, provided significant materials, as did the Nacogdoches Archives at Stephen F. Austin State University. Historical societies in Del Ray Beach, Florida, and Van Zandt and Henderson Counties in Texas helped me make connections to the McLeod family.

I received help from research personnel in Savannah, Macon, Atlanta, and Augusta, Georgia; insight from Bill Walraven in Corpus Christi, Texas; and constant support from the library staff at the University of Houston. Thanks to the staffs at Hollins College in Roanoke and the Hollywood Cemetery in Richmond, Virginia, for helping in my search for information about R. J. and Caz McLeod in their later years. I also want to acknowledge Craig Slein and Joseph Stang for their technical support.

In my research on the Pioneers' trail from Brushy Creek to San Miguel, I learned a great deal from interested townsfolk in Turkey, Tulia, and Quitaque, Texas, and in tiny Anton Chico, New Mexico.

I wish to thank Stanley Siegel for his support and encouragement over the past four years. He lent his experience and expertise to me in order that I might succeed, and I am grateful for his friendship. I would also be remiss if I failed to thank those who read the manuscript critically, including James Kirby Martin, who helped at several stages along the way; Linda Reed, whose insight was so helpful; and Barry Wood, who helped me refine my work.

My gratitude to members of the McLeod family who provided me with key personal information on the general and his descendants. I especially want to recognize the late Sarah Mathews McLeod, who passed away before I could show her the results of my work, and Philip LaMarche in California. I wish to dedicate this book to Sarah.

And to each member of my family, a word of thanks for your unflagging emotional support. My father, Lou Spellman, helped with some of the digging; my mother-in-law, Tuleta Boatman, never let me give up; my children, Matt and Paula, rooted for me; and my wife, Tudy, read and listened and never gave up on me.

FORGOTTEN TEXAS LEADER

Hugh McLeod and Charles Berger walked into the Galveston tavern feeling worn around the edges. It was Monday, August 22, 1842, and the two had been off the ship from Mexican imprisonment for less than twenty-four hours. A drink sounded especially good. As Berger reached into an empty pocket to buy the first round, McLeod insisted on paying, as he still had a doubloon given him by a Mexican guard at Vera Cruz.

The two men, joined by several others, enjoyed the first relaxing moment in months, gathering an audience with their tales of battle, desert marches, and the horrors of Castle Perote. When it came time to pay the tab, McLeod could not find the coin and groaned in embarrassment. A crew member from the ship that had delivered the Santa Fe prisoners home reminded the general that he had given it to his friend Col. William Cooke earlier, when Cooke needed it to board the ship. The tavern owner gladly tore up the bill, and Berger wrote later, "McLeod's hand and heart were ever open to the necessities of his friends; the Good that the one prompted and the other performed was forgotten in the impulse of the next moment, and passed forever from his mind."[1]

Such was the prevailing opinion of Hugh McLeod, even grudgingly admitted by his political enemies, for few if any carried personal animosities against him. He was ever in good humor, quick to come to the aid of an ally, and just as quick to engage in bombast against what he perceived to be an injustice. His generosity and his opinions tumbled from him easily and often. He sought the limelight not only out of vanity, of which he bore his full share, but as a stage from which to promote the causes he was so well known for during his public career. If anything, he may have been a rebel with too many causes.

McLeod came to Texas at the height of its revolution against Antonio López de Santa Anna's dictatorship and died preparing to fight the Union on behalf of slavery and states' rights. In between, he marched against the Indians of Texas, led an expansionist expedition toward Santa Fe, for which he is best known, and supported the Rio Grande republics of Antonio

Canales and José Maria Jesus Carbajal. He raised money and recruits for the filibustering William Walker in Nicaragua and spoke on behalf of George Bickley's Cuban enterprise. He barely escaped disaster by walking away from Charles Warfield's abortive expedition to control the Santa Fe Trail and encouraged his friend William Cazneau during the secret filibuster in the Dominican Republic.

Along the way, McLeod served officially in four armies and held a full epaulet of ranks. He marched as a 2nd lieutenant in 1835 and as a lieutenant colonel in 1861 in the U.S. Army, as major and colonel in the Texas Revolutionary Army, and as adjutant general, inspector general, and brigadier general in the Texas Republic forces. He assumed the ranks of major, lieutenant colonel, and colonel in the Confederate army, the last his commission at his death. Throughout most of his Texas years, he was known as General to the populace and Mac to his friends.

Hugh McLeod (1814–62), born in New York City, raised in the countryside of central Georgia, and a Texan for twenty-five years, lived and died unabashedly seeking success for his causes and glory for himself. In his own time, he was mentioned in the same breath as Sam Houston, Mirabeau Lamar, Thomas Jefferson Rusk, and Albert Sidney Johnston. He was acclaimed as an orator and a soldier, and as a friend of Texas and the South. He served in the Texas Republic's Seventh and Ninth Congresses but fell short in campaigns for higher office. McLeod remained loyal to the Southern Democratic Party, except for a side excursion with the Know-Nothings. He represented Galveston at two significant national commercial conventions and traveled extensively in search of funding for the many causes in which he ardently believed.

As adjutant general under Presidents Sam Houston (1837–38) and Mirabeau Lamar (1838–41), he organized the office itself, wrote key reports of historical events such as the Kickapoo War and the Council House Fight, and repeatedly left his desk and his home to engage enemies on the Neches River, San Antonio's Main Plaza, and later Matamoros and the Potomac River. He made key contributions to his adopted home of Galveston nearly from its inception as a Texas port. He dabbled in law, the cotton press industry, education, the railroads, and the newspaper business.

McLeod married Rebecca Johnson Lamar, a cousin to the Texas president; raised a son who became the city manager of Richmond, Virginia; and buried an infant daughter. Mac and "R. J." lived in a beautiful mansion on the main streets (Broadway and Twenty-sixth Street) of Galveston, owned eight slaves, and immersed themselves in civic opportunities and the Presbyterian Church. The couple proudly displayed original portraits of two great heroes, George Washington and Stephen F. Austin.

Hugh McLeod, ca. 1840, photograph of portrait.
COURTESY TEXAS STATE LIBRARY & ARCHIVES COMMISSION.

They fought for a public school system on the island and made at least one trip together to New York City to raise funds for the Republic of Texas. McLeod belonged to the fraternity of Masons and was a charter member of the Philosophical Society of Texas. Throughout the 1850s the couple hosted galas and dignitaries in their home, where McLeod usually entertained with his humorous anecdotes and flair for the dramatic. He was one of the most sought-after keynote speakers in the state.

When the aging Sam Houston declared that he would make one last defense of his antisecessionist views in 1861, he chose Galveston as his

5

podium and named McLeod as his principal political adversary. Unfortunately for both men and the Galveston crowd that came that April day, McLeod missed the affair while bargaining in Alabama for a commission in the Confederate army. That Houston placed McLeod in a category of political enmity speaks to the reputation McLeod had garnered by the end of his life.

Yet history has relegated McLeod to the often repeated single line, "commander of the ill-fated Santa Fe expedition." There is hardly more than a mention, or at best an occasional paragraph, of any other contribution or adventure that set McLeod alongside the great early Texans. The failure of the Santa Fe Pioneers to achieve their expansionist objectives has fallen, not entirely unfairly, on their military leader. To be sure, the ex–West Pointer made several poor decisions, but on balance he proved to his men that he was more than able, as evidenced by those same men months and even years later.

The misfortunes of this 1841 enterprise were manifold, and the brigadier general fell victim to the foibles of a poorly conceived, poorly executed march across the wilderness of western Texas. The group started off too late with too little; they got lost not once but several times; and the officers squabbled along the way. They misjudged the route and the distance to Santa Fe with tragic consequences. Worse, the Pioneers surrendered without a fight to the Mexican troops that awaited them. Marched deep into Mexico, the expedition again became lost, this time in the mire of Santa Anna's offensive against Texas: Salado Creek and the Dawson Massacre, the Somervell and Mier campaigns, and the ignobility of Castle Perote.

Upon his return to Texas in 1842, McLeod lost little time in doing whatever he could to redeem his tarnished name. For the next twenty years, until he succumbed to the ravages of exhaustion and fever, the Texas warrior strove to vindicate his belief in his own leadership and to feel deserving of the continuing respect that followed him in spite of the accusations that haunted him.

This biography of the life and times of Hugh McLeod presents his attributes as a true Texas hero and his frailties as a man who never quite had the stuff of which great leadership is made. If greatness were measured by desire and self-confidence alone, he would be hallowed in the history texts. But his ability to lead and inspire generally fell just short of the necessities of the moment. He graduated from West Point, but he was last in his class. He defended the people of Nacogdoches, but they abandoned their homes anyway. He fought with distinction against Caddoes, Cherokees, and Comanches, but the laurels of those engagements went to men such as Albert Sidney Johnston, Kelsey Douglass, and Thomas J. Rusk.

McLeod took on the complex job of leading 320 soldiers and merchants across an unknown frontier, but he could not overcome the brutalities of the summer heat, the Kiowas, and his officers' lack of confidence. He made critical decisions that saved lives, but most backfired. His decision to surrender his forces was made contingent on the honorable assurances of his enemy, and history has castigated him for it. He bravely withstood the indignities and the physical abuses of imprisonment, often to protect his men, but he was blamed for poor leadership.

McLeod stood firmly behind grandiose enterprises for liberty and democracy, but all of his causes failed. He campaigned for the high offices of his republic and his state, but he lost. He found himself second-in-command at many junctures along the way and accordingly received secondhand notice. He tied his political fortunes to the Lamar faction, which generally found itself bested. Perhaps most significantly, McLeod took on Houston again and again, often face to face. And while many people who witnessed those entertaining confrontations considered the outcome a draw, history has reported otherwise.

Would history have been kinder to McLeod if he had taken on lesser giants, smaller challenges? Would the textbooks write glowing remarks about the Galvestonian if Santa Fe had become a part of the expanding Texas Republic after all? Would McLeod have established a far different place for himself had he won the U.S. congressional seat in 1849 or 1851, and had he been in on the Washington debates concerning the Compromise of 1850? What if the Republic of the Rio Grande had achieved independent status from Mexico, or Bickley's Havana empire had seen reality? And, finally, if McLeod had recovered from the pneumonia that took his life in Virginia, would the most famous, embattled regiment of the Civil War be known as McLeod's brigade, not Hood's?

History does not presume nor assuage. This in-depth study of the so-called ill-fated Texan Santa Fe Expedition of 1841 will reveal the strengths of its commanding officer in balance with the mistakes he made. Perhaps McLeod's moments of bravery on Bexar Road and the Neches River bottom, at Caddo Lake, and inside the Council House will reserve a more notable place in history's ranks of the courageous. A more detailed look at the life of Hugh McLeod, soldier and statesman, will provoke a kinder perspective and at last reveal the man who sat in that tavern, bedraggled but not defeated, "his hand and heart ever open to the necessities of his friends."

The first four chapters of this biography examine McLeod's early life, his problems at West Point, his heroics at Nacogdoches in 1836, and his years as adjutant general of Texas. They also give the most detailed account

written of the Council House Fight of 1840. By the end of that year Mc-
Leod was as well known across Texas as any other and associated with the
larger-than-life heroism of the frontiersman. In this period he had been
described on a battlefield as "a meteor glancing."[2]

The middle chapters take an in-depth look at the Santa Fe expedition.
Relying on the primary sources of the diaries of George Wilkins Kendall,
Thomas Falconer, George W. Grover, and Peter Gallagher, the account
also acknowledges two excellent compilations, Horace Bailey Carroll's *The
Texan Santa Fe Trail* and Noel M. Loomis's *The Texan–Santa Fe Pioneers.*
Carroll painstakingly reconstructs the geography of the land which the Pi-
oneers crossed on the march, and Loomis offers details on individual men.
Typically, even Claude Elliott's 1952 review of Carroll's book fails to men-
tion General McLeod, the commander of the expedition.[3]

These chapters also draw on records of the commander himself, later
newspaper accounts, reminiscences of several expedition survivors (dis-
crepancies notwithstanding), and an assessment of reasons for the enterprise's failure. Kendall offered his own evaluation in *Narratives of the Texan
Santa Fe Expedition and Capture of the Texans,* and these narratives serve as
the outline for chapter nine. Although the expedition skews the pace of the
book's time line, it is the most significant topic here, for it has characterized McLeod over 150 years of meager historical references. By following
the Pioneers on an almost daily basis, for the first time through the eyes of
its commander, these chapters offer a detailed and comprehensive account
of the expedition.

The final chapters deal with the last twenty years of McLeod's life, including his marriage and family, his Galveston career, and the myriad attempts he made to link his name with the causes of his day. He came close
to standing atop the political mountain. Had he not twice lost to Volney
Howard, McLeod would have spent 1849 through at least 1853 in Washington, D.C., where his booming voice would have been heard on issues
that soon divided the nation. Had he stayed in the Democratic fold instead
of switching to the Know-Nothings, his 1855 speech in Austin might have
carried him to the governor's office. When he died of pneumonia on January 3, 1862, he was next in line for the command of the Texas regiment that
ultimately marched under John B. Hood.

The key to his life, however, was the Santa Fe expedition. He reached
the brink of greatness in June, 1841. A victorious march to the upper Rio
Grande would have dramatically changed Texas' history and McLeod's future. Instead the ignominious surrender to Mexican forces laid waste the
plans for an empire reaching to the Pacific and haunted its commander
beyond his own life and into the textbooks. This biography by no means

intends to belittle McLeod's responsibility for the enterprise's failure. Rather, it places that failure in the context of the courage McLeod displayed throughout the ordeal and, for that matter, throughout his life. If the life and times of Hugh McLeod come alive for the reader, this biography will have achieved its objectives.

CHAPTER I

West Point

The *James Madison* sailed out of New York Harbor on January 5, 1818, bound for Savannah, Georgia. On board, the McLeod family looked forward to a new world, a new life, a new start. With the freezing temperatures and falling snow, thirty-seven-year-old Hugh McLeod likely understood the irony of the moment. The bitter weather had gotten the best of the Scot native, and his physician had suggested a warmer climate. Uprooting family and career, McLeod must have hoped for a better and longer life as he watched the city fade in the distance.[1]

Born on the Isle of Skye across the Atlantic, McLeod was the great-grandson of Daniel and Elizabeth, and the third surnamed Hugh. His parents moved to New York at the end of the American Revolution with him and their daughter, Margery. By the age of sixteen the young man had moved out on his own, to Schenectady and then east to Boston. There he met and married Isabella Douglas in 1806, and the couple moved to New York Island—what would become Manhattan. Their four children accompanied them on the packet: Isabella, age nine; Daniel, age seven; Christianna, age five; and Hugh, age three.[2]

New York City had been good to Hugh and Isabella. They arrived after the terrible yellow fever epidemic of 1805 had passed and survived the fire of 1811 that destroyed blocks of wooden homes and buildings. Out of the ashes rose a new city and a construction fervor that continued unabated through the war years. McLeod and a partner, Joseph "Alec" Clark, established an architectural firm near Broadway and enjoyed several years of prosperity.[3]

But the harsh winters took their toll on Hugh, and the decision to move south was ameliorated only by the fact that Savannah needed builders to alleviate its own growing pains. The arrival in Georgia signaled a fresh beginning. Alec Clark would soon follow his partner to renew their business together that summer. The family settled into the friendly Savannah society, and by the end of 1818 they seemed well ensconced in their new surroundings.

On February 14, 1819, Hugh McLeod died, never having fully regained his health. The widowed Isabella set out to care for the four children, and her eldest daughter helped with baby-sitting and other household chores. On January 11, 1820, a fire raced through the streets of Savannah, leaving dozens injured or dead and hundreds homeless. The fire destroyed thirty blocks of the downtown area, including more than four hundred structures. Only five months later, yellow fever raged through the rebuilt city, taking 695 lives by November.[4] The family suffered in Savannah what they had avoided in New York City. Only strength of character and resolve saw them through the disasters. Alec Clark helped as he could. He became a surrogate father for the four children and made it official when he married Isabella on May 22, 1823, in Savannah's Presbyterian Church. Catherina Clark was born in 1825 in Macon, to which the family had recently moved.

The new village of Macon, on the extended Federal Road and the west bank of the Ocmulgee River across from Fort Hawkins, offered business opportunities for Alec and a healthy rural environment for the children. In January, 1826, Macon had more than 750 citizens on the edge of Creek Nation lands. As a center for the growing cotton industry, Macon prospered, building a new river ferry and establishing its first school, the Bibb County Academy. Rev. Lot Jones became its first rector, and the McLeod boys were some of his first students. Daniel and his younger brother, Hugh, took quickly to farm life. Several members of the Georgia Lamar family moved their businesses to Macon, and Gazaway Bugg Lamar opened the first bank later that year. Charles Augustus Lafayette Lamar, a cousin, and John T. Lamar, Gazaway's brother, invested in the cotton business, with access to mills and markets east along the road to Augusta or to the coast via the river barges.[5]

Tragedy struck the McLeods again on July 28, 1826, when Alec Clark died at age thirty-seven. Hugh, who turned twelve four days later, must have felt this loss more acutely than the death of his father, whom he barely remembered. But, as was typical in central Georgia, the townspeople rallied around the family and helped ease the pain. Hugh's sister Isabella, now eighteen, moved back to Savannah and married Robert Brower in 1827. The Land Lottery of 1827 allowed Isabella McLeod Clark to claim property in both Chatham and Washington Counties on behalf of the orphans of Hugh McLeod. Through the Lamar family, which had befriended her, she was able to make wise investments that ensured a comfortable future for her children.[6]

Daniel McLeod left for the University of Pennsylvania in Philadelphia, graduated from medical school in 1832, and entered the U.S. Navy as an assistant surgeon. He may have been inspired to serve when the famous

British seaman Capt. Basil Hall and his wife, Margaret, passed through Macon in March, 1827. Their stopover on the way to the Creek Indian Agency stirred up interest among the townspeople, for Hall's reputation as one of England's most decorated naval officers preceded him. Three months later a traveling exhibit of naval munitions and memorabilia passed through Macon, becoming the centerpiece for a huge Fourth of July celebration. Such impressions would not have been wasted on Daniel.[7]

For Hugh, only thirteen that summer, the world still revolved around school and the rustic farm life. He had probably met Rebecca Lamar, his future wife, by this time. Three years older, she may have made an impression on the adolescent farm boy. In 1828 her brother John was elected town commissioner of Macon, and a cousin, Henry G. Lamar, went off to Washington, D.C., to represent the Chatham District of Georgia in Congress. John Lamar seems to have become something of a father figure for Hugh during this period, and a much-needed one at that. His behavior in and out of school was drawing attention and began to concern his mother. The establishment of the Macon Presbyterian Church on Fourth Street in 1829 may have been an answer to her prayers, and she took her two youngest regularly, accompanied by many of the Lamars.

In 1829 Bibb County Academy reorganized as Macon Academy and hired Rev. C. B. Elliott as its headmaster; forty-five pupils attended the academy.[8] The year Hugh turned fifteen, John Lamar hired him to work in his cotton warehouse on the river. Hard work, long hours, and school changed Hugh's carefree life and forced him to do some growing up. During this time Lamar brought the subject of military school to Hugh and Isabella's attention. Southern tradition often included military academy life, where discipline and honor were inculcated, as part of the maturation of a gentleman. With the Lamar family's political connections, Hugh had a good chance of being admitted to the United States Military Academy in West Point, New York. With Isabella's permission, John Lamar procured letters of recommendation from his cousin Henry, who had just been reelected to Congress, Judge John MacPherson Berrien of Savannah, and Maj. Oliver H. Prince, author of the *Digest of the Laws of Georgia*. Later that year Berrien was appointed U.S. attorney general in the Andrew Jackson administration, further ensuring Hugh's acceptance to West Point.[9]

In December, 1829, Isabella signed an affidavit "to certify that my son Hugh McLeod is now in his fifteenth year and was born on 1st August 1814 and that Macon is now his home." McLeod himself wrote a letter of application, probably under the tutelage of John Lamar, noting "that the Academy appointments are to be made equally throughout the States according to the number of Representatives of that State in Congress. And I believe there has never been a single appointment made in Macon or the adjoining counties—and also that there is no preference given on account of priority—as such my application ought at least to receive a fair consideration." He added that "this letter may stand as a specimen" of his penmanship. Headmaster Elliott attached his own recommendation, writing that McLeod had "a good knowledge of English Grammar, Arithmetic and Geography. He is an excellent scholar, and will, I have not the least doubt, satisfy, in any Literary or Scientific course of Education, the most sanguine expectations of his friends and the best wishes of those to whose charge he may be committed."[10]

McLeod, still two years away from the generally accepted age for first-year, or Fourth Class, students at West Point, continued his studies at Macon Academy and work at the Lamar Cotton Warehouse. More than 39,000 bales of cotton passed through the town for the second year in a row, and commerce picked up further when the Federal Road extended to Columbus, on the Alabama border. John and Rebecca Lamar lost their mother that year, two years after their father had passed away. Eighteen-year-old Rebecca took primary responsibility for her two younger siblings.[11]

In the summer of 1830 McLeod received a letter of inquiry from Congressman Henry Lamar: Would he be attending the U.S. Military Academy the next fall? Apparently McLeod hesitated. In a February 3, 1831, letter he wrote: "You say I must tell you unequivocally whether I will accept the commission or not—I say I *will*. The only reason for the indecision that I evinced last Summer was this—I conceived that my obligations to John T. Lamar were very great and that in order to repay them I ought to lay aside every self consideration, and sacrifice *my* interests to forward his. After I had spoken with him he concluded that I had better go—My Mother said 'Go'—So I came to the conclusion and have never changed it since—I am ready to go—and have nothing to detain me after this time arrives."

He added that a Mr. Seymour would tutor him in algebra that spring, and that "I will endeavor to conduct myself in such a manner as not to reflect discredit upon the Person who interested himself in my behalf." The well-spoken youth promised Lamar to "curb my every loose passion and endeavor to conform to Rules however rigid. If the discipline is strict my propensities shall be found. If a constant Fear of the disgrace which expulsion would bring upon me, will restrict my former looseness of conduct—I *think* it will be done." Whatever the looseness of conduct he referred to, McLeod clearly understood the consequences: "It would overwhelm me to meet the angry repulse of a doating [*sic*] Mother—the disdainful sneer of enemies triumphing in my downfall! And above all the reproachful glances of insulted friends who expected me to conduct myself with propriety. These things when I think of them make me shudder." Concluding, McLeod wrote, "I sincerely hope that the knowledge that my future good fortune must depend entirely upon my good conduct will be a sufficient barrier against the intrusion of Vulgar propensities & inclinations."[12] Fine words soon forgotten, for McLeod's four years at West Point would be rife with troubles, both academic and social.

On March 29, 1831, McLeod wrote Secretary of War John H. Eaton acknowledging receipt of his September 1 appointment. "I will repair to West Point at the time prescribed," he wrote, "to undergo the requisite examinations." Isabella Clark added her parental consent, "by which he may bind himself to serve in said appointment for five years unless sooner discharged from the time of his admission into the Military."[13]

McLeod, seventeen on August 1, departed his Macon home and family by the American Mail Stagecoach Line to Augusta and Savannah, and then sailed by packet to New York City. His next four years would be a misadventure all its own.

Cadet McLeod's classes at West Point began September 1, 1831. The opening days included traditional initiation rites of the seventy-three Fourth Classmen and the opportunity to meet new friends. Oliver Prince's son, Henry, and two other Georgians were in his class. George W. Morell of New York would eventually finish first in the class of 1835. Another cadet that fall, George G. Meade of Pennsylvania, would make his mark in American military history three decades later. McLeod and James M. Wells built a friendship that would endure for years and reunite them in Galveston in the 1850s.[14]

McLeod's classes and instructors that fall included Ethan Allen Hitchcock (infantry tactics), Zebina J. D. Kinsley (artillery), Charles Davies (mathematics), Dennis H. Mahan (engineering), and Claudius Berard (French). Later that year he would take chemistry with W. F. Hopkins, drawing with Charles Leslie, and a course in geography, history, and ethics taught by Rev. Thomas Warner.[15]

Although grade records no longer exist, McLeod seems to have passed his courses for the first three years. He may, however, have spent more time at Gridley Tavern near the campus than in the library. With 200 demerits per school year sufficient for expulsion, McLeod ranked 62nd in his class in 1833 with 170 demerits and 183rd overall in the 211-member student body. Five of his classmates were expelled. By the end of his second year he had fared little better, ranking 202nd with 193 demerits. In the summer of 1834 he stood 230th of 242, and, with 170 demerits, last in his Second Class, now whittled down to 60 cadets.[16]

With the heated standoff between President Jackson and Academy Superintendent Sylvanus Thayer, controversy swirled around the cadets in 1833 and 1834. Thayer's association with Vice President John C. Calhoun, now resigned and back in South Carolina over the issue of nullification, galvanized Jackson against what he called the "eastern elitists who run West Point."[17] In McLeod's second year Thayer dismissed three of Jackson's personally appointed cadets, whereupon the president reinstated them over the superintendent's authority. When Cadet Ariel Norris defiantly planted an old hickory stick on the parade grounds and was summarily expelled by Thayer in 1834, the pot boiled over. Thayer resigned when Jackson ordered an immediate inspection of the entire school, and Col. René de Russy replaced him. Many believed that Jackson would have closed the school down had he not needed graduating engineers to work on the frontier roads.[18] Years later McLeod spoke of Jackson's personal attention as instrumental in his staying at the academy.[19]

When the school settled down, McLeod and his fellow cadets turned their attention to one more year of school and a June, 1835, graduation. McLeod's growing reputation among the faculty and administration, however, made him a marked man, especially for those still angry with Jackson. McLeod's conduct tally slipped once more, with 196 demerits, and his school ranking slid to 231st of 240.[20] Still, those numbers would allow him to graduate if he passed his spring classes. But he and his friend Henry Prince failed the final examination in Maj. John Fowle's course on tactics. On June 13 a special review committee refused to allow a reexamination for the two petitioning cadets, noting only that "if this examination is requested for satisfaction of the Board of Visitors, the Academic Board cheerfully grants it, and will be happy to have it take place at any time which the Board shall see fit to designate."[21] On July 1 the class took to the parade grounds for graduation, but McLeod and Prince could only watch from the sidelines.

Whatever intervention took place, two members of the biannual Review Board of Visitors received personal letters from Secretary Eaton in August, and Fowle was asked by the Academic Board of Professors to reexamine the two cadets. On September 3 the board reported that "cadets Prince and McLeod, who were found deficient in Infantry Tactics at the last June examination, were examined on the said subject by Major Fowle, and were found qualified to receive their diplomas."[22]

On September 18, 1835, McLeod graduated last in his class of fifty-six with a rank of brevet 2nd lieutenant, assigned to Company B, Third Infantry, U.S. Army, stationed at Fort Jesup, Louisiana. He was ordered to report for active duty within ninety days.[23]

In late September, 1835, McLeod returned to Georgia. His mother and his two sisters still at home, Christianna and Catherina, had corresponded with him while he was at the academy, and they may have come as far as Augusta to greet him. He probably renewed his gentle relationship with Rebecca Lamar and several members of her family in Savannah before returning home. Rebecca's brother Thomas had died at age seventeen, but new cousins had been born to brothers John, Zechariah, and George.[24] Hugh's brother, Daniel, three years into his service in the U.S. Navy, was stationed at Pensacola, Florida. In 1834 he personally directed a medical unit for civilians suffering from an outbreak of yellow fever, receiving accolades as a hero of that city.[25]

But the news of the day was from Texas. The Macon *Messenger* exclaimed, "The cries of our fellow countrymen of Texas have reached us calling for help against the Tyrant and Oppressor." Front pages of papers in Savannah and Augusta detailed the exploits at Gonzales against Gen. Martín Perfecto de Cos's Mexican army. A public meeting was announced in the *Messenger* "for all who are disposed to respond to the cry, in any form, to assemble at the courthouse, on Tuesday evening next, at early candle light."[26] Journalists reported a packed courthouse on November 10. A. P. Powers spoke, as did John Rutherford and Samuel Strong. But the highlight of the evening came near the end: "Lieutenant Hugh McLeod, recently from the Military Academy at West Point, addressed the meeting in a spirit-stirring appeal, pledging himself to resign his commission, and embark as a volunteer, in the cause of liberty; that the struggle in Texas needed Soldiers, not resolutions; that we should tender them our selves and our arms on the contested fields; that these would best express our sympathies on their behalf."[27]

At age twenty-one, McLeod displayed an oratorical prowess that would energize crowds and troops in the decades ahead and a propensity to take a stand for liberty. Volunteering to forsake his commission, a rash statement at best, he already exuded the self-confidence that would win him allies and create lifelong enemies. His experiences at West Point had taught him only that he needed no more than the rudimentary disciplines in order to establish himself as a leader of men. The effusive Macon crowd lifted his spirits and sent his ego soaring. A personal letter the next day tendered the city's gratitude "for the very able and feeling manner" of his address.[28]

John and Henry Lamar, men who had guided McLeod in his not so distant youth, stood in the audience that applauded his stirring vow; now they looked to him, not after him. William Ward joined the adulation, as did Jared Groce, a prominent cotton grower and slave owner whose immense Texas plantation would serve as an army camp just five months later. If there was ever a momentous transformation in McLeod's life, this dramatic night in central Georgia may have been it.

Twenty-nine men signed up for what they called the Georgia Brigade that night, and a collection took up more than $3,000 for the cause. Ninety more volunteers agreed to journey to Columbus a week later, gathering recruits for a heroic march to Texas.[29] McLeod joined the trek. The growing town of Columbus, on the Chatahoochee River across from Fort Benning and on the extended Federal Road, was the home of Mirabeau Buonaparte Lamar, poet, philosopher, and editor of the Columbus *Enquirer*.

Twelve days after the Macon meeting, Ward and McLeod called another rally, this time outside of Columbus, for everyone who would fight and those who would see them off. Hundreds heard the West Pointer speak again. At a poignant moment at the close of his speech, Colonel Ward presented a special gift to the brigade from Miss Joanna Troutman: a flag to carry into the glorious confrontation. On white silk, it bore a blue lone star on one side with the words "Liberty or Death"; on the other side were the words, *"Ubi libertas habitat, ibi nostra patria est"* (Where liberty resides, there our country is). McLeod wrote to "Miss Joanna" on behalf of the brigade: "Col. Ward brought your handsome and appropriate flag as a present to the Georgia Volunteers in the cause of 'Texas and Liberty.' I was fearful from the shortness of the time that you would not be able to finish it as tastefully as you would wish; but I assure you, without an emotion of flattery, that it is beautiful, and with us its value will be enhanced by the recollection of the donor. I thank you for the honor of being made the medium of presentation to the company, and if they are what every true Georgian ought to, your flag shall yet wave over fields of victory in defiance of despotism. I hope the proud day may soon arrive, and while your star presides, none can doubt of success."[30] The flag next unfurled over the Velasco fort at the mouth of the Brazos River in January, 1836, and last over the walls of Goliad in March.

The Georgia volunteers left Columbus in two units led by Ward and William A. O. Wadsworth. The editor of the *Messenger* pined sardonically: "The Texas fever has treated us worse than the Cholera! Our office is completely swept! Journeymen and apprentices, men and boys, devils and angels all are gone to Texas. If our readers get an empty sheet or no sheet at all, don't blame us!"[31] The volunteers went on to Montgomery, where they boarded the steamboat *Benjamin Franklin* for Mobile. Waiting for them on the coast, the schooner *Pennsylvania* would bring them to Velasco on Sunday, December 20. There, met by Columbus's own James Fannin, the Georgians combined with the Texas Brazos Guards, their destination Goliad.[32]

Lieutenant McLeod, however, parted company with the Georgia volunteers at Montgomery and headed west for Fort Jesup. At the Neutral Ground of the Sabine bottomlands, McLeod briefly assumed command of Company B in mid-December, 1835. But on December 31, he wrote,

> To Genl. Sam Houston
> Comdr. in Chief Army of Texas
>
> Sir—
> I have the honor to inform you that I have this day resigned my commission in the United States Army with the intention of joining the Patriot Army of Texas of which you are Commander in Chief—for some months past I have been traveling under orders, or I should have been in your Country at the commencement of the struggle.
>
> Do I claim too much, Sir, when I say that my commission in the U.S. Army should entitle me to rank in that of Texas? Will it, or not?
>
> I do not come to your country as "a summer soldier or a sunshine patriot." I embark my all in its cause, and am prepared to stand or fall by it.
>
> The acceptance of my resignation will be here in time to allow me to be at St. Felippe [*sic*] by the opening of the spring campaign. Will you have the kindness to write me on the subject?
>
> I am Sir with the highest regard, Yr's & c,
> Hugh McLeod[33]

CHAPTER 2

On to Texas

The muster rolls of the Third Regiment, Company B, indicate that Lieutenant McLeod arrived in Louisiana as per his orders in December, 1835. In the January, 1836, rolls, McLeod had been placed "in temporary command of the company." This was a military courtesy to the academy graduate, and the February rolls report that McLeod was on duty at Fort Jesup.[1] For many of the soldiers in Louisiana, reports from Texas indicated that the war might have come to an end. James Gaines wrote on January 9 that "from St. Philip to Nacogdoes [sic] one Entire Kind of Independence pervades all Class of Men. At Nacogdoes [sic] Much Canvas was flying with Liberty and Independence wrote on It in large Letters."

But many knew better. One wrote, "I am Too well acquainted with the Mexican character To Place any Confidence in their Joining us in the support of the Constitution of 24 or anything else Further than their private Interest may Dictate—Some Rumor had made the Rounds that Coss has had his Runners acting Among the Cherokees." He added, "David Crockett delivered one of his Corner Speeches yesterday at San Augustine and is To Represent them in the Convention on the first of March. So much for the Times."[2]

The threat of an uprising by the Indians, supported by Mexican agents around the Nacogdoches area, was considered real enough by the local council. As early as the previous October there were signs that unrest among the native nations along the Neches and Sabine Rivers could escalate. Although William Goyens, a free black and the informal spokesperson for several tribes, indicated that any problems would be minor and none would be related to Mexican activity, Gen. Sam Houston and Stephen F. Austin expressed concern.[3]

The nations in closest proximity to Nacogdoches—the Cherokee, Shawnee, and Coushatta—remained calm after Houston promised that land grants would be guaranteed and representatives of the tribes would be welcomed at the meeting. On the other hand, rumors persisted that trouble brewed in East Texas. Instigators such as Mexican agents Manuel Flores and Juan Cortina continued to travel in the area.[4]

On February 22, the day before General Santa Anna's arrival on the outskirts of San Antonio, Col. James Fannin informed James Robinson of the situation across Texas and called for more recruits from the United States: "I well know I am a better company officer than most men now in Texas and might do with Regulars &c for a Regiment. . . . We have none fit for it now in the country. . . . I think you can get several first-rate officers from the United States." Fannin recommended "Captains William G. Cooke and N. R. Brister, both of the New Orleans Greys, John S. Brooks and Joseph M. Chadwell, both having received a military education; also Joseph Cardle and Thomas Barton, the first a regular graduate at the Point." He added, "If possible, also Lieut. McLeod, U.S. Army, now waiting at Ft. Jesup, and his horse ready and resignation written."[5]

Two more weeks dragged by. Unbeknownst to the soldiers on both sides of the Sabine, Santa Anna had attacked the Alamo and killed all 188 men inside the Spanish mission's walls. As General José de Urrea marched toward Fannin and his Georgians, still holding at Goliad, Gen. Antonio Gaona moved across the Rio Grande to reinforce Santa Anna. More than ten thousand Mexican troops invaded Texas. In Nacogdoches, Texas Quartermaster A. J. Houston wrote Houston: "I have received advises from the Col. at this place advising me to return to San Augustine & try to urge & assist on Volunteers from that quarter. Lieut. [Henry] Teal's command moved from this place yesterday. I shall lose no time in doing all in my power to bring on Volunteers, or in case they do not turn out I shall be on immediately."[6]

Teal headed out of East Texas during the first week of March, followed by a company of Nacogdoches volunteers commanded by Capt. Hayden Arnold. The city had been left almost entirely unguarded. Garrison Greenwood wrote Houston "deeply impressed with a sense of the dangers in which the Frontier is exposed from the Indians. . . . There has never been the practice of the savage when the times and circumstances afforded a more favorable opportunity. . . . An abandonment of the place and perhaps of the country will probably be the result."[7]

On March 7, unable to stand it any longer, McLeod requested a ten-day leave of absence from his command of Company B. He never returned. Fort Jesup muster rolls list him in April, May, and June as "absent without leave." Approximately thirty other names, most of them privates from Company B, are likewise noted.[8] McLeod had gone to Texas for good, headed for the cause of liberty he had spoken of so eloquently at Columbus. At San Augustine McLeod met briefly with Andrew Hotchkiss and J. D. Thorn, members of the vigilant Committee on Safety. From there, the trail crossed the Atoyac River, past the Mast Ranch and into Nacogdoches. Henry Raguet and Frost Thorn would have met McLeod and his volunteers outside the town.[9]

The population in and around Nacogdoches numbered some 3,500 Anglo and Mexican citizens, although many had departed out of fear of an Indian attack. An old stone fort stood near the center of the town. Col. Juan Almonte's inspection only one year earlier had noted a scattering of homes built of wood, brick, or stone, and "no hostile tribes"; he listed Coushatta, Choctaw, Cherokee, Caddo, Creek, Shawnee, Tawaconi, Keecheys, and Kickapoo, as well as "very honorable and highly cultured families who have begun to establish themselves there."[10] These families would have included Irion, Raguet, Mason, and Sam Houston, who had opened a law office upon his arrival in Texas. Thomas and Mary "Polly" Cleveland Rusk moved to Nacogdoches only weeks before McLeod had situated himself at Fort Jesup. Rusk had journeyed to Texas earlier in pursuit of two men who had embezzled funds, and he had returned to Georgia to uproot his family and head for the frontier. When he left for the war, his brother David watched over the family, which included Polly and her three sons. Polly and David Rusk invited McLeod to reside at their home when he arrived in town. The friendship that grew from this kindness lasted twenty years.[11]

McLeod coordinated his efforts with the Committee on Safety, and his volunteer company cooperated with the handful of men still left in town to establish a perimeter of guards and defense for what most believed to be an inevitable assault. From Mobile, Alabama, John T. Lamar offered to raise an army of five hundred volunteers. Ira Ingram of the Committee on Safety arrived in Nacogdoches on April 5 with news of the fall of Goliad and the Palm Sunday Massacre of Fannin and his Georgia soldiers; he brought orders from Houston to prepare to evacuate the area. At the same time Col. John Darrington recommended to Texas President David Burnet that the capital be removed to the East Texas town, not only for safety but so "rumors being spread to the United States can be put down."[12]

Robert Irion sent three representatives to speak with Capt. Juan Cortina, a Tejano who had placed himself in charge of guarding the few Mexican families left in the area. Rumors persisted that Cortina was a double agent and that he had been seen visiting in the Indian villages. Menard reported to Irion in mid-April that Mexican agents were in fact dealing with Cherokee Chief John Bowl, a statement verified by two brothers who claimed to have witnessed the negotiations. John T. Mason rode to Fort Jesup to inform the U.S. Army. "All will be massacred there [Nacogdoches]," he reported, "without instantaneous relief." Another rumor spread that 1,700 Indian warriors were massing nearby.[13]

The terrifying news proved too much for most citizens of the town. By April 12 a full-scale panic and runaway had begun, with families carrying what they could eastward toward the Sabine River and safety. Polly Rusk gathered up her children, following the advice of McLeod, but remained calm amid the surrounding hysteria as she packed their few belongings for the trip. At the edge of town, she responded to a man who screamed, "Hurry up or the Indians will scalp you," by saying in a level voice, "You will save your scalp if your horse holds out." Later she wrote that "as long as the brave McLeod or one of his men is living, we have nothing to fear."[14]

Judge John A. Quitman, governor of Mississippi, arrived with a company of soldiers during the panic and offered his assistance to McLeod: "As travelers in Texas only, we are tolerably well-armed men ready to assist in the retreat of your women and children." They posted themselves on the outskirts of the abandoned town. By April 14, Ira Ingram reported, "Nacogdoches was safe, but deserted." Ingram recommended that "wandering forces here and at San Augustine need to be a part of a main army instead of causing alarm here." At the same time, Robert Irion received news that Mexican agent Manuel Flores had been spotted among the Indians to the northwest. Subsequent reports indicated that the effect of Houston's earlier treaties with the Indians remained more substantive than any of Flores's promises.[15]

By April 21, as a battle ensued far to the south at San Jacinto, McLeod and his volunteers spread their defense posts east and west along the main roads out of Nacogdoches.[16] At Fort Jesup, Gen. Edmund Gaines, just arrived from Florida to assume command, received a letter from Secretary of War Lewis Cass that "any action necessary to protect American citizens from Indian outrages" would be considered within the realm of his orders, but that "under no circumstances was a station to be taken beyond old Fort Nacogdoches." But one week later the news from San Jacinto indicated an end to the hostilities in Texas, and the five companies that had moved to the Sabine on the site of Wilkinson's former camp stood down. On May 1, with reports that the Cherokees had "returned to their fields," Gaines believed the danger had passed.[17]

That same day Gaines ordered an investigation of the mass desertions of his camp since the first of the year. Between 150 and 200 soldiers had left Fort Jesup, and many had made it to San Jacinto in time to oppose Santa Anna. Gaines sent one officer to Nacogdoches, but his report did not list any deserters there. By mid-June a handful of courts-martial had taken place, but McLeod and his volunteers escaped the proceedings.[18]

A second scare spread across Texas in mid-June. Rusk wrote Gaines that a renewal of Mexican hostilities was imminent. Meanwhile, Sterling Robertson sent messengers to warn Texans of Indian depredations occurring up the Brazos River. An interrogation of the Shawnee warrior Spy Buck on July 15 turned up the possible alliance of Shawnee, Waco, and Tawaconi tribes camped at the three forks of the Trinity River. Menard and Indian agent Isadore Pantallion headed north to verify the report.[19]

Families that had just returned to their homes began to pack for a second runaway. Gaines called for reinforcements along the Sabine on June 28. In Nacogdoches, McLeod, Quitman, and Irion stepped up their defenses once more. On the Red River, U.S. Army Lt. Col. William Whistler ordered his troops battle-ready for an immediate march south. He led three companies of dragoons and six of infantry out of camp on July 11, four days behind a caravan of more than 17,000 rations and other support supplies. On the morning of July 31 McLeod ordered an honorary cannon salute at the old stone fort as Whistler's troops marched into town.[20]

McLeod received his discharge from the U.S. Army on June 30 while preparing defenses for Nacogdoches. The next reports include his rank of major in the Republic of Texas army, although it is not clear when the commission became official nor who administered it. When a wounded General Houston arrived in Nacogdoches on August 1, however, it was Major McLeod who greeted him.[21]

Menard returned to the stone fort to report no activity among the Indians. Pantallion, meanwhile, indicated that Chief Bowl and the Cherokees continued to "act suspiciously."[22] To the north at Fort Towson, U.S. Army Gen. Matthew Arbuckle sent word that the Indians along the Trinity and Red Rivers would be no threat to Texas. Nevertheless Gaines called for additional troops from camps in Tennessee and Mississippi to be posted at Fort Jesup, just in case. By early October, when Gaines was recalled to a hearing in Frederick, Maryland, fear of Mexican and Indian trouble had subsided in East Texas. In the Nacogdoches area four hundred American soldiers prepared to fall back across the Sabine, the last of them marching east on December 19, 1836.[23]

McLeod left Nacogdoches in late September. In service to his new country, whose first elections had placed Houston in the presidency, McLeod answered a call to assist Maj. Gen. Thomas Jefferson Chambers in his continuing efforts to raise an army in reserve from the United States. Chambers left Texas in February, 1836, and headed for his home in Lexington,

Kentucky, assuring interim President Burnet that he would return with more than 1,500 troops.[24] In July the loquacious Chambers called on the "magnanimous and chivalrous sons of the West" to come to aid Texas "in her conflict, and in return, homes and rich estates, in the most beautiful region and delicious clime on the face of the earth." The volunteers were to congregate in Louisville on August 20 for the journey.[25]

In addition, Chambers hoped to raise funds for munitions and supplies with his rallying speeches up and down the Ohio River valley that summer. On August 4 he even put up his 25,000-acre estate for sale to arm the volunteers. Word of his activity spread to Texas by the end of August, and a few eager recruits crossed the Sabine around that time. In correspondence between Chambers and Samuel P. Carson, Texas Secretary of State, the suggestion of loans from the Kentucky state government prompted renewed hope that Chambers might be able to pull off his grand enterprise.[26]

The Texas government made arrangements, through Chambers, to order six cannon from the munitions company of McClung & Wade in Pittsburgh, Pennsylvania. The monies would be delivered by a special courier from Texas, and Chambers would prepare for the shipping of the artillery pieces. By September the process had begun.

McLeod, the special courier, accompanied by Col. Charles Harrison and Capt. James Austin Sylvester, departed from Nacogdoches, traveling up the Mississippi and Ohio Rivers by steamboat.[27] They met with Chambers in October before continuing to Pittsburgh, where the cannons were delayed and the three men were forced to wait through the cold winter months. Chambers noted in his diary on January 8, 1837, that McLeod remained in Pittsburgh. McLeod wrote on February 9 that the cannons were ready, but delays continued. On March 16 Chambers wrote McLeod to "come on with or without the cannon and in this case to bring the funds placed in your hands."[28] By April 1 the cannons had been loaded onto a steamboat and started downriver. McLeod wrote Chambers on April 13 that they would be leaving Frankfurt, Kentucky, on the following day aboard the steamer *Kentuckian* bound for New Orleans.[29] The entourage, which now included Chambers, completed the trek by May 1, and the cannons were eventually carted into Texas.

But McLeod did not accompany the delivery to its final destination. Instead he met his friend Mirabeau B. Lamar, vice president of Texas, in New Orleans. Lamar had taken a leave of absence from the new capital of Houston in January and had been in New Orleans for five months. Many believed that his political conflicts with Sam Houston had prompted the cultured Georgia newspaperman to absent himself from the inevitable collapse. If and when the government crumbled, a distant Lamar could be called upon to rescue Texas. If not before, McLeod now established himself as a staunch Lamar supporter.[30]

Whatever the motive for Lamar's lengthy leave from his official duties, he and McLeod decided to travel to Georgia for the summer. The vice president remained in Columbus until September, when he answered the call of the growing anti-Houston faction. His calculated return to Texas in late October, and a speech in the capital on November 9, did not have the effect he had hoped for. Texas seemed to have weathered its first year of independence and was enjoying its first prosperity.[31]

In Georgia, McLeod enjoyed an extended reunion with his ailing mother, who had moved in with his sister Isabella and her husband, Robert Brower, in Savannah.[32] He also spent time with Rebecca Lamar, developing a serious relationship. On August 1 he turned twenty-three years old to her twenty-five, and the age gap may not have seemed as wide as when they were teenagers. Whatever else transpired in Savannah, McLeod left for Texas alone.

In September he resided temporarily in Galveston before heading to Houston, where he was the guest of Surgeon General Ashbel Smith before taking up residence at the Ben Fort Smith Hotel.[33] Moving quickly into the political and social circles of the booming capital city on Buffalo Bayou, McLeod, the hero of Nacogdoches, was welcomed back to Texas to stay. On December 5 McLeod joined twenty-five other prominent Texas Republic leaders as a charter member of the Philosophical Society of Texas, a political fraternity dedicated to concerns of the Republic and issues of the day. Mirabeau Lamar served as first president, David Kaufman as vice president, Burnet as secretary, and Augustus Allen as treasurer. Houston took part as a member, as did Ashbel Smith and Henry Smith, Anson Jones, Rusk, Irion, and Chambers, back from Kentucky without his heralded volunteer army. The society met infrequently and had dissolved by 1845, but its initial membership remains a directory of the great names of the early Republic years.[34]

On December 19 McLeod was initiated into the newly organized Holland Lodge No. 1 of Freemasonry in Houston. Although he would be part of four Masonic lodges over the next twenty-five years, it is hard to determine the level of commitment he made to the fraternal order. He served in two minor offices in 1842 and 1843 and rose to the level of Master Mason shortly thereafter.[35] He made several keynote speeches at lodges in Austin, Galveston, and Houston over the years. The political advantages of the brotherhood likely assured his continuing participation. His involvement in the Philosophical Society and the Masons put him in touch with the most significant, influential leaders on the frontier. And it may have led to his first administrative position in the Texas government: the office of adjutant general.

McLeod's appointment as adjutant general of Texas in September was confirmed by the Texas Congress later that fall, and on December 21, 1837, he took office.[36] For the next four years his life and contributions to Texas would revolve around this position in the administrations of both Houston and Lamar.

CHAPTER 3

Adjutant General

The adjutant general of Texas was charged "with the safekeeping of the monthly returns of regiments and posts, and muster-rolls of companies; the annual returns of the militia; the proceedings of general courts-martial; and the records of the War Department which relate to the personnel of the army." In addition, the adjutant general was "the channel through which are issued all orders emanating from the headquarters of the army, and all regulations necessary to be communicated to the troops. He is charged with the details of the service—with the record of all military appointments, promotions, resignations, deaths, and other casualties, as well as the inventories of the effects of deceased officers and soldiers, with the registry, making out, and distribution of all commissions of the army and of the militia of the Republic."

The office was responsible for "the duties connected with the recruiting service, and the enrollment of all enlisted soldiers, showing the descriptions, date of enlistment, discharge, desertion, death, and everything connected with their military history—with the examination of all applications for pensions, previously to their being sent to the Pension Office," and finally, "with the making out of the annual returns of the army, and of the militia of the several districts, and the publication of the annual register."[1]

Col. Edward Morehouse served as adjutant general during the interim government of the revolution. McLeod now accepted that position, charged with developing its procedures and administration. He went to work immediately. On April 18, 1838, he reported his progress to President Houston. The Texas Third Brigade had been formed and its officers elected, he wrote. Two days later he sent an addendum indicating his intention to "withhold commissions of several of the officers" as a result of unsettled disputes.[2]

Already, trouble brewed between McLeod and Houston. Their political disagreements surfaced in 1837 with the increasing separation between Houston and his vice president, Mirabeau Lamar, who was McLeod's close friend. As the adjutant general sided with the western faction, his frustration with the president grew. For his part, Houston thought little of military academy officers. "You might as well take dung-hill fowl's eggs and put them in eagles' nests and try to make eagles of them," he once remarked, "as to try to make generals of boys who have no capacity, by giving them military training."[3]

When Secretary of War Albert Sidney Johnston grew impatient with the lack of supplies and reinforcements on the Texas frontier, he received no help from Houston. Resigning his commission, Johnston continued to scout the western perimeter and grouse about the poor conditions at several outposts. His successor, Barnard Bee, was sympathetic but declined to send provisions or soldiers. "The nakedness of the land you are by this time stuck with," he informed Johnston. In San Antonio, Johnston described the garrison as no more than "a few broken down sorry jades which serve to drive in cattle." If the Mexican army should invade Texas, Johnston believed they would have little difficulty capturing Bexar and the surrounding countryside. "Fortunately," Bee responded, "our Enemy are not disposed to humble us."

In February, 1838, McLeod wrote Johnston after his own unsuccessful attempt to pry reinforcements out of Bee or the president: "It is with great regret that I have to inform you that our hopes of seeing a force upon the western frontier are for the present frustrated . . . and no further orders will be issued to reinforce you with militia." In a revealing postscript, he added, "But I am in hopes that the Enemy will soon releive [sic] us from this embarrassment, and enable us to 'go it alone.'" J. Pinckney Henderson told Johnston, "I hope that the Mexicans have ere this given you an opportunity of breaking a lance with them."[4]

On May 26 McLeod departed the capital for an official tour of the defenses of Texas. He rode to San Antonio, then turned north across the Colorado River to the Falls on the Brazos River. He made a pass northeast toward the Red River, skirting the Cherokee territory, and headed over to the Sabine River, finally stopping in Nacogdoches in July. The extensive tour in the summer heat left McLeod exhausted and feverish. Thomas and Polly Rusk took him into their home, where he stayed for nearly a month.

On a side trip from Nacogdoches to San Augustine in June, McLeod wrote a long letter to Vice President Lamar. The occasion was a speech "on St. John's day, & the Masonic festival has brought in a large concourse of citizens." Apart from scouting the territory, McLeod was also paving the way for Lamar's summer campaign for the presidency. "Your personal friends are numerous & influential," McLeod wrote, "but inert. They are sanguine & unsuspicious, while our enemies are active, vigilant, and untiring. . . . The truth is, General, your presence is needed in the Red lands to fix the popular feeling, and give it a permanent direction. . . . It was truly gratifying to find that all the opposition to you was cold, crafty, & calculating—Wherever I found a burst of honest feeling it was for you— By all means come. The people ask for you everywhere."5

Events would interrupt the political campaigning, for Johnston's wishes had come true. Vicente Cordova, a Mexican agent who lived in Nacogdoches, was in contact with the Cherokee Nation, stirring up a revolt against the Republic of Texas. Cordova's attempt to ally the Mexican forces with Chief Bowl's warriors in 1836 had been preempted by the sudden end of the war. Now, with the Texas Constitution allowing for slavery and Mexico intent on some kind of reprisal, Cordova made plans for a combined effort to bring down the government. When his plans were discovered, Cordova fled up the Angelina River to join one hundred Mexican soldiers and the Cherokees. Gen. Kelsey Douglass arrived in East Texas to deal with the crisis, meeting with McLeod and other officials in Nacogdoches around August 1.

On August 5 a bedridden McLeod reported, "The town has been in an uproar since dusk last night on account of a fight between a party of Americans and Mexicans which occurred about six miles from here in the afternoon." Returning from a search for stolen horses, the Americans "were ordered to halt and immediately fired upon by a party of Mexicans and Anadarco Indians by which one man was killed. . . . The Mexicans are assembling in considerable numbers and moving toward the Cherokee Nation, Douglass in rapid pursuit and Genl. Rusk moves immediately with a detachment to cut them off. He has dispatched the Indian agent Wright with [William] Goyens to warn the Cherokees of the consequences of the slightest movement."

McLeod's postscript alludes to the continuing frustration of inadequate provisions on the frontier: "The orders enclosed are a requisition for 150 mounted men from your county & 100 from Shelby to be raised and in readiness to march to this place should they be necessary. I hope you will use all your influence which I know is powerful to see it promptly done."6 Later that month McLeod ordered Maj. Jacob Snively to raise two companies of cavalry for three months' service, noting that the quartermaster "will furnish the requisite subsistence, and such equipment *as the service is able to command*"7 [emphasis added].

Meanwhile, up the Angelina River a rebel force of nearly six hundred Mexicans and Indians sent a letter to Houston disavowing allegiance to the Republic and declaring themselves aligned with Mexico. When Rusk and Douglass arrived in the vicinity of the camp in mid-August, however, the

Cherokees had dispersed and Chief Bowl had sent his own message denying any participation in the rebellion. Cordova escaped into Mexico, but several of his officers and a hundred soldiers were captured.[8]

Houston rode to Nacogdoches during the insurrection, and according to McLeod the two "never did or could agree well." Like most frontiersmen, McLeod had little affection for the Indians, and this conflicted with the empathetic nature of Houston's kinship, especially for the Cherokee Nation. In this situation Houston gave the benefit of the doubt to Bowl, refusing to believe that the old Indian warrior would betray the 1836 treaty they had signed. To Bowl, Houston wrote, "I hope to the Great Spirit that my red brothers will not make war nor join our enemies, for if they gain a little now they must soon lose it all." McLeod wrote Lamar that Houston "cramped Genl. Rusk in every way, with his orders, written here, where we could not judge what was the true state of affairs at Hd. Qtrs."[9]

In Nacogdoches, Houston delivered an order to McLeod regarding treatment of the "peaceful citizens"—the Cherokees. "The army and soldiers of the Republic will in no case molest those who remain at their homes and should it be proper to obtain from them anything, they must be paid a fair valuation for the same. And property of every kind is to be respected and protected when found in the hands of peaceful citizens. The families, and the women and children of Mexicans and Indians will be treated with the greatest humanity and kindness, and will be special objects of the soldiers' care and protection. Acts of humanity always characterize the brave man and the soldier."[10]

McLeod informed Lamar that "but for the accidental explosion of [Cordova's] plot before it was matured, every tribe of Indians in Eastern Texas would have been engaged in this. . . . Genl. Rusk's movements prevented, I have no doubt, a general Indian war." He added, "As it is, the Mexicans are dispersed, and captures are made every Hour. . . . The jail and a guard house in town are crowded with prisoners. None of the mainsprings of the affair, however, are yet taken. Our Militia, as you are aware, have never been commissioned by the President, a Court Martial therefore cannot be legally organized for the trial of the prisoners. To wait for the tedious process of the evil authorities, will destroy nearly the whole effect. *Example, to be powerful, should be prompt*" [emphasis added].

McLeod's frustration with Houston showed in other comments he made to Lamar, including rumor of "the President drunk they say . . . dealing Billingsgate most lavishly upon a little man, whom he happened to underestimate, for the little fellow bucked up, and in reply told his Excellency some of the most unwelcome truths he has heard for many a day." Feeling additional aggravation about "our financial schemes all knocked in the head," McLeod complained to his friend, "Damn 'em can't the President [-Elect] of a Republic and the Adjutant General get credit for a paltry 20,000? No matter, we'll be rich some day without their aid."[11]

McLeod did receive accolades for his efforts that summer in the Kickapoo War. Isaac Burton of Nacogdoches updated Lamar in late August regarding "the Rebellion of the Mexicans and their attempt to let loose the Indians on the frontier. . . . It is over now and we are daily catching the poor devils and I suppose we shall have a fine hanging frolick shortly." Burton commended Rusk and Douglass and noted, "McLeod is an able officer."[12]

McLeod remained in Nacogdoches through August. An urgent message from Georgia through John T. Lamar in Mobile caused great concern and temporarily distracted him from the crisis at hand. He wrote Lamar that he had "heard of the shipwreck, and that Rebecca and Gaz were all right as far as I know." The tragedy of which he spoke had, however, taken the lives of several Lamar kin.

The *Pulaski,* a ship owned by Gazaway Bugg Lamar, sank on the night of June 14, 1838, off the coast of North Carolina. More than seventy men, women, and children drowned. The maiden voyage of the rebuilt packet steamer had been billed as "two days of travel between Savannah and Baltimore," an excursion that Gaz and most of his family had boarded. Rebecca Lamar went along as a nanny for the younger children. The ship broke in half in the middle of the night, and Rebecca spent most of the next twenty-four hours rescuing and comforting the survivors. But four of the seventy-seven dead included her nieces and nephews and Gaz's wife. Rebecca was later hailed as the heroine of the *Pulaski* and wrote a lengthy recollection of the tragic story. The relationship between Hugh and Rebecca seems clear after his words of fear for her in his letter to Lamar: "When I first saw the account of the loss of the *Pulaski,* the fever had only been broken one day and I came very near a relapse. . . . But a dreadful load was removed from my mind when I heard of the safety of Rebecca."[13]

In East Texas bad news quickly followed good. In the September, 1838, elections Lamar was elected the next president of Texas; he would take office in December. Unable to get to Houston on election day, McLeod cast his ballot for Lamar in Nacogdoches as "a citizen of the Republic at large."[14] The bad news for McLeod, Douglass, and Rusk was this: although Chiefs Bowl and Big Mush (Gatunwali) had apparently moved their Cherokee villages away from trouble, Mexican agents Cordova and Flores were again organizing renegades for an assault against the settlers.

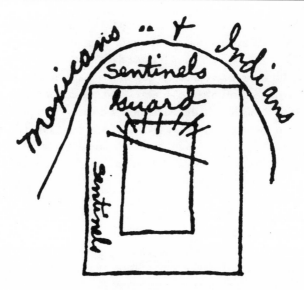

Sketch in McLeod's report to Lamar.
THE [MIRABEAU B.] LAMAR PAPERS, 1838 VOLUME, #846, P. 282.

On October 5 a band of marauding Shawnee and Biloxi warriors, supported by Mexicans, attacked the Killough family at the edge of Indian lands and butchered eighteen people. Within a week another attack occurred, this time at Fort Houston on the upper Trinity River.[15]

General Rusk, joined by McLeod, mobilized two hundred troops and headed into Indian territory. Bowl and Big Mush immediately sent messages disclaiming any involvement in the attacks and announced their intentions to withdraw from the area. Rusk gathered provisions at Fort Houston; McLeod described the action that followed: "On the morning of [October] 16th just after day break at the Kickapoo Town, we were attacked. Our camp was an oblong square, with the horses at the center. The attack was made principally on the head of the square within forty yards of the guard, but they displayed around three sides as marked and compelled us to maintain the square. For this reason the troops at the head had to bear the brunt of the action." McLeod inserted a sketch in his report to Lamar, then continued,

The woods were very open and the trees large, affording an admirable opportunity for their favorite tactics of fighting behind a cover, and the morning was very misty. . . . General Rusk, with a view to draw them out, advanced about 20 paces and shouted, "You damned cowardly ———, come out and show yourselves like men." They made no reply except the yell and their rifles. . . . In about 15 minutes their fire began to slacken, and a charge was ordered. They were pursued for half a mile.

Their force was variously estimated at from 150 to 300. My own opinion is at least 250. It was a motley gang—Mexicans, negroes, Coshattees, Caddoes, and some thought Keechies. Among the dead and the nearest man to our camp was a Cherokee named Tail. Bowl says he was a bad Indian, that he could never manage him, and that he was well killed. They left on the ground 11 killed, and the grass full of trails of blood; we have since heard they lost about 30. On our side we had 11 wounded, one badly, but the surgeon thinks he will recover. Nearly every man in the head of the square had his clothes cut; it was the closest shooting I ever saw to do so little execution. We also lost about 35 horses.[16]

Within the week Bowl came in to parlay with Rusk and McLeod, assuring him of peaceful intentions and agreeing to talk with Big Mush and other chiefs about a proposed council talk. Houston sent Alexander Horton, a surveyor and unofficial Indian agent, to speak with Bowl and assure him of efforts to leave the Cherokee Nation out of the escalating hostilities. To Rusk, Houston ordered a boundary line marked to protect the Cherokee: "If it is not immediately done, all future calamities must be attributed to its omission. I am satisfied if it is not done there will be another runaway scrape and Eastern Texas will be desolated. . . . If it is not done an Indian war may ensue which may cost more blood and treasure than ought to purchase twenty such Indian countries."[17] Frustrated by Houston's interference, Rusk and McLeod nevertheless averted involvement with the Cherokee during the October 16 fight, which came to be known as the Kickapoo War.

McLeod also reported to Lamar the gist of a conversation he had with Houston earlier that fall. "Houston said that officious men, and the enemies of both you and him, had fomented angry feeling between you. He was charged, he said, with being your enemy; it was false. . . . He scorned such a course, if his own [term in office] had been clogged by unprincipled men, it would afford him no gratification to see you suffer from the same cause." This olive branch had impressed McLeod, who told Lamar he "could not repress the emotions of admiration such sentiments were calculated to arouse. . . . I rose and gave him my hand, saying that I felt proud of being the organ of such sentiments. I hope for his own sake as well as yours he is sincere."[18]

On October 25, with reports of Mexican subversion calmed for the moment, McLeod wrote again to Lamar, this time on behalf of Rusk, "to give you an outline of his views in relation to our Indian policy. . . . The time he says has arrived for a general, prompt and vigorous campaign against the Indians. Temporizing will only weaken us among ourselves, and render us contemptible to the enemy. Every hour we hear of fresh depredations, and each petty success leads to bolder efforts. It may do for those at a safe distance who have no interest at stake, to prate the sickly sentiments of a mistaken humanity, but the man whose cabin is in ashes, whose family are wanderers and himself hunted down like a wild beast, must answer blow by blow, and take blood for blood. . . . The time has come . . . to exterminate the race; with the exception of those who are unequivocally friendly, to wit: the Shawnees, Delawares, Cherokees, Kickapoos and Choctaws."

McLeod complained about Houston's refusal to support the frontier army: "The General [Rusk] is making every exertion to bring this force into the field, but he is crippled for want of means. The act passed at the last session 'for the protection of the frontier' appropriated $100,000 for the purpose. And yet we have never seen one dollar from the Treasury. . . . For God's sake cannot the money that is lying idle, and which can only as fast as law is concerned be used for this purpose, be sent to us? Genl. Houston has been called upon for it several times."[19]

In mid-November McLeod picked up where he had left off a month earlier. "Since I last wrote, another Army has been in the field, a few trifling Indians killed, but nothing done. The Cherokees were thought from some suspicious appearance, to have begun hostilities upon the settlements below us. . . . The General feared the worst, and moved down to Bowl's house. There we found everything quiet." He noted that they had been unable to raise an adequate force for lack of funds or available commissions: "The damnable Indian policy has produced all these difficulties."[20]

McLeod traveled to the Shawnee village to investigate the atmosphere. Rusk headed for the Red River, McLeod wrote, "to make an effort to carry a force from there, and cripple them sufficiently to give breathing time for the adoption of a permanent means of defense," referring to Lamar's administration due to be inaugurated in three weeks. "You will perceive the dangers that *may* beset you, and God grant the Congress may give you the means to avert them." After his visit to the Shawnees, McLeod sent a brief message to Lamar: "They talk fair, but they will *act* fair when a permanent force is here, to demonstrate the folly of acting otherwise. The Shawnee Chief, Elanie, is a famous warrior." He added, "The thermometer is at zero, and fingers frozen."[21]

Cordova continued to prowl the Indian territories in late November. A sighting of the Mexican agent eighty miles north of the Trinity River spurred McLeod and Rusk on a chase with a force of 450 volunteers. After meeting up with Capt. Edward H. Tarrant and combining forces, Rusk marched to the Caddo camp at the headwaters of the Trinity and Brazos Rivers, at Caddo Lake. McLeod wrote on November 23 that the Caddoes had been spotted. "They have retreated to a cane brake, and are awaiting an attack, fully prepared for it. They are on U.S. ground, but something must be done at once. . . . If they are attacked, General Rusk you know might as well lead it, as remain here—He has resolved to go—It will be a bloody affair, as the numbers are about equal, & the Indians well armed & desperate." He concluded, "If I fall, please write to my mother, & send her the year's pay that is due me."[22]

The Caddoes asked for a parley after only a few shots had been fired, "which however passed harmlessly over us," McLeod wrote. Rusk and McLeod met two Caddo chiefs at the edge of the lake, and McLeod later wrote of the conversation and a surprising development: "The chief stated his ostracized condition in being bought out and expelled by the United States, and in being denied a right to hunt or live in Texas. Rusk acknowledged the hardships of his case and offered to support his people in Louisiana until the two governments could act, if he would give up his guns to the agent in Shreveport. The chief agreed, but, his horses and families being on the other side of the lake, he could not go at once . . . . Rusk exchanged hostages with him, taking a Caddo chief and leaving me in the Indian camp. The next day Rusk and the Chief met at the agency in Shreveport, and after some discussion and a great deal of opposition by the Agent and some citizens of Shreveport the arrangement was concluded. . . . This is the only case of unquestionable reclamation against the United States for Indian depredations that I recollect."[23]

In Shreveport McLeod learned that the Indian agent had been subsidizing the Caddoes, a violation of the reconstructed Treaty of 1833 between the United States and Mexico that now included Texas. The angry adjutant general minced no words: "That you should furnish these Savages with the means of murdering the defenseless women and children of Texas is a matter of the greatest astonishment." McLeod sent a copy of this stern letter to Lamar on November 21, noting "that [Agent Charles A.] Sewell has not only furnished the Caddoes arms, but had been heard by respectable men to say, that he did not care if they murdered every woman & child in Texas, and that he would arm them & push them across the line."[24]

With this Caddo band taken care of, Rusk and McLeod continued their march across northern Texas: "These are not all the Caddoes," he informed Lamar on December 1. "By far the largest portion of the tribe are under Tarshar, or the Wolf, among the wild Indians of Texas. . . . We start immediately for Three Forks, the 4th Brigade will have 400 men ready to march as soon as we get there at Clarksville. . . . I say if the U.S. is faithless enough to refuse to remove them We must await a more auspicious moment than the present, to exterminate them." Angered by a legislature slow to respond to the crisis, McLeod continued, "Great God! In the defence of a bleeding frontier a matter of such doubtful policy that grave Senators must appeal to the feelings & imaginations of the people to give them succor? Is there not a Law far more imperative and sacred surely than Senatorial opinions and appeals 'for the protection of the frontier'? Let [men] go to the front with the Sober certainty of privations & dangers, not with the pseudo patriotism of a stump speech or the self erected heroism of a boy. Then we may have men that will do the country service."[25] The Texas troops moved on for ten days, from November 21 to 30, following signs of the Caddoes west along the Trinity.

At a camp twenty-five miles west of Clarksville, McLeod took a bad fall from his horse during a night march, "rupturing me severely," he wrote Lamar on December 20. "I have been at this place, on that account, for nearly three weeks." But hearing of another uprising, McLeod informed the president, in spite of his injuries: "I am starting now. We have a good pilot, plenty of provisions, and stout hearts. The weather is bitterly cold, and our force is too small (30) to camp with fires. So we must watch the moon and 'ken our horn'—resting in the day. If we are not in time for the main battle, we may pick up a 'chunk of a fight' with a straggling party." In the margin of the letter McLeod wrote, "I can scarcely regret the death of the murdered men, they were killed by only an equal number, and never fired a gun—Everybody above here is fated."[26]

No such main battle occurred. Even so, after McLeod caught up with the main force, they trudged through the winter cold to the edge of the eastern Cross Timbers, destroying abandoned Caddo villages along the way. In Red River country, as McLeod described it on January 9, 1839, they "saw large droves of Buffalo, & wild horses . . . but the weather was so severe, we could not enjoy the sport." Given to hyperbole, the tiring McLeod announced, "We are recruiting our broken down horses, and equally exhausted selves, after a march, in my opinion, unparalleled since De Soto's."[27]

On January 17, 1839, McLeod returned to Nacogdoches, "so 'used up' now, that I cannot undergo the fatigue. I've been riding so long, that I have almost become a centaur." He reported to Lamar that the Kickapoo guides had misled the army away from the marauders, but the campaign at least had the "one great effect, which amply compensates for its expense, [that] the Indians never knew they had an enemy beyond their *neighborhood*, nor did they believe a white man could go to the prairies. And when they find a wide road made from Clarksville to the Brazos, and learn from the Kickapoos that *five hundred men* made that road, they will perceive the hopelessness of such a contest. They will soon scatter into small parties, and being deceived by the representations of the Mexicans, they will probably kill them."[28]

By late February McLeod had recovered sufficiently to make his way to Houston, where he, Johnston, and Lamar instigated a secret recruitment scheme in the United States. In a letter marked confidential and dated March 23, 1839, McLeod ordered Capt. William Redd of the First Texas Infantry "to proceed forthwith to the United States and as soon as possible recruit men for the Regiment to which you belong. But it will be necessary to observe great caution and not violate the laws of the United States. The men must nominally be emigrants, but at the same time, they must understand perfectly the terms on which they are sent out, and that they will be required to enlist at Galveston, at which place, they will receive their bounties, the term of service three years."[29]

Unbeknownst to the Texas government, during the spring of 1839 Mexican General Valentin Canalizo, stationed in Matamoros to defend against a presumed invasion by France, sent word to Cordova through Flores to create an Indian alliance against the Republic of Texas. Cordova and Flores were to enlist the Indians in establishing a line of defense from the Red River south to Bexar and on to the Gulf coast, and "not to cease to harass the enemy for a single day—to burn their habitations, to lay waste to their fields, and to prevent them from assembling in great numbers." The offer of an alliance, "and peaceable possession of your lands" as a reward, made its way to the Caddoes, Kickapoos, and Shawnees, as well as to Bowl and Big Mush in the Cherokee Nation.[30]

On May 17, while crossing the San Gabriel River above Austin, Texas' new capital, Flores was routed by a Ranger patrol commanded by Lt. James O. Rice. Rice recovered letters, plans, and the alliance offers from the Mexican agent and forwarded them to Johnston. Lamar sent Maj. B. C. Waters with a force to occupy the Neches River at the edge of Cherokee lands, to which Bowl strenuously objected. But Lamar saw his opportunity to carry out the final removal of the Indians from Texas, and he sent agents Martin Lacey, W. G. W. Jowers, and John H. Reagan with an ultimatum for the chief: "This Government is looking forward to the time, when some peaceable arrangements can be made for [your] removal, without the necessity of shedding blood. . . . Whether it be done by friendly negociation [sic] or by the violence of war, must depend upon the Cherokee themselves."[31]

Bowl asked for ten days in order to speak to the council. In mid-June he returned to say that although many of the council had agreed to the removal, the younger warriors had not. He insisted that the removal could take place only if the Cherokee Nation was allowed to harvest their crops in the fall and then leave unescorted. Lacey and Reagan refused the conditions, and negotiations abruptly ended.

On June 27 Lamar appointed Burnet, Rusk, Johnston, James Mayfield, and J. W. Burton as special commissioners charged with "the immediate removal of the Cherokee Indians, and the ultimate removal of all other *emigrant* tribes now residing in Texas."[32] He sent McLeod back to Nacogdoches to effect the necessary military support. On July 9 McLeod rode to Bowl's camp with a message from Rusk informing the Cherokee chief of Lamar's orders. "Come and see us and we will talk more fully on the subject," read the message from the commissioners. "Colonel McLeod will give you and as many of your head men as you choose to bring, safe escort to our camp." The next day Bowl met with the commissioners. He was accompanied by the Shawnee Spy Buck but refused to discuss the orders until Big Mush could be present. A meeting the next day also ended without negotiations. On July 12, with Big Mush and the Delaware Chief Harris present, Bowl responded at length to Rusk's warning that if the Cherokees persisted in being "friendly with the wild Indians and Mexicans, we will be forced to kill your people in defense of our frontier. You are between two fires and if you remain you will be destroyed." Once more, and without success, Bowl asked for a delay.[33]

The two sides met twice more, on July 14 and 15, but the opportunity for peaceful settlement had long since disappeared. Bowl indicated a desire to sign the deal in the last moments, but he was prevented from doing so by the other council members. The Indians rode back to their camps in late morning, and the Texas army prepared for an assault on the village. Rusk's forces marched along the north banks of the Neches while McLeod and Col. Edward Burleson crossed the river to head off the Indians' retreat. At dusk on July 15 Rusk and Douglass rode into the abandoned village, and a hunt for the runaways ensued. Three miles north of the campsite the Texans engaged the rear guard of Bowl's people in a brief firefight that left eighteen Indians and two Texans dead. After Burleson and McLeod arrived, the night was spent collecting provisions left behind by the fleeing Indians, including five kegs of gunpowder and 250 pounds of lead. The next day the Texans picked up a trail that led through an empty Delaware village, which they burned.[34]

The Texan force numbered 250 to 300 and included a remarkable array of the leaders of the Republic: Burnet, Burleson, Douglass, Rusk, Johnston, Reagan, Kaufman, and McLeod. The combined Indian forces were probably twice that number, with Bowl, Big Mush, Harris, and other chiefs leading Cherokee, Shawnee, Delaware, and Kickapoo.[35] The Indians took up a position in the Neches River bottom about five miles from the previous night's confrontation. When the Texans caught up with them just after dawn, a fierce two-hour battle raged. Twice the Texans charged down into the river bottom, and twice the Indians repulsed them. Burnet was wounded, as was Johnston. Big Mush died alongside his warriors. Douglass and Burleson led one unit in a third attack while McLeod led another from a flanking position. When Lt. James McNeely lost his horse, McLeod gave him his own and continued the battle on foot. The fighting became hand-to-hand in places, and both sides battled courageously. A later newspaper account from several eyewitnesses noted: "But none were more brave than McLeod. He was seen alternately in every part of the field dashing from rank to rank, like a meteor glancing through the murky clouds of battle, as heedless of the balls that were flying around him as if it were the mere pattering of rain."[36]

In the last moments of the battle, a warrior's arrow lodged in McLeod's thighbone. Bleeding profusely, he continued to engage the enemy. A few minutes later the firing stopped. The surviving Indians escaped, leaving trails of blood through the nearby woods. "They must have suffered severely," Rusk reported.[37] A hundred warriors lay dead and dying in the Neches valley. Three Texans had been killed in the fray and thirty wounded, including Burnet, Johnston, and Kaufman.[38] Reagan later wrote of the battle's closing moments:

Chief Bowl displayed great courage. . . . He remained on the field on horseback, wearing a military hat, silk vest, and handsome sword and sash which had been presented to him by President Houston. He was a magnificent picture of barbaric manhood and was very conspicuous during the whole battle, being the last to leave the field when the Indians retreated. His horse, however, was now disabled, and he dismounted, after having been wounded himself. As he walked away he was shot in the back and fell. Then, as he sat up with his face toward us, I started toward him with a view to secure his surrender. At the same time my captain, Bob Smith, with a pistol in his hand, ran toward him from farther down the line. We reached him at the same instant, and realizing what was imminent, I called, 'Captain, don't shoot him.' But he fired, striking Bowl in the head, and killing him instantly."[39]

The Cherokee Wars had come to an end, although there would be a series of cleanup operations in the following months. Cordova continued to range between San Antonio and the Rio Grande through early 1840. Some Texas Cherokees traveled to Indian Territory, in Oklahoma, to live with the Eastern Cherokee Nation that had been placed there by President Andrew Jackson, and others headed for Mexico. The wounded McLeod would carry the piece of arrowhead in his thigh for the rest of his life. After receiving medical attention in Nacogdoches, he returned to Austin and to his responsibilities as adjutant general. His dealings with Mexico and the Indians of Texas, however, had not ended.

CHAPTER 4

The Council House Fight

With an apology up front, McLeod began his official report to Secretary of War Johnston for 1838–39: "In consequence of my detention with the troops, ordered to be drafted by the President beyond the time anticipated by my orders, I have been unable to furnish the report of this Department at an earlier date. The most important Military operation of the year, however, having been conducted under your own eye, will, I presume, diminish any difficulty that might otherwise result from the delay."[1]

He left little doubt about the situation he had inherited, including the initial organization of the office itself, the term spent in frustration under Houston, and the transition to the Lamar administration amid the Indian conflicts: "Much embarrassment has been experienced in organizing this Department, in consequence of the deranged condition of the records of the Army, and also of the officers of the Department having been employed, for a considerable portion of the year, on active duty." He added, however, "I have the honor to inform you, that it is now completely organized, and all information required by the different Departments, to facilitate individuals holding Military claims against the Government or respecting the present Military operations of the country, can be promptly and correctly finished."

McLeod also noted that the recruiting system under Lt. Col. William S. Fisher "has been successfully continued up to the present time," although the records were delayed due to the Cherokee campaign. One thousand copies of "Rules and Regulations of the Army" had been written, printed, and distributed at a cost of $3,400, of which $2,000 had been paid to the printer, Maj. Samuel Whiting. McLeod recommended the use of a "uniform system of tactics for the Army and Militia" patterned on the U.S. Army system and described in the pamphlet by Capt. Samuel Cooper, adjutant general since 1818. Regardless of whether Cooper's work was part of the course McLeod failed at West Point, he did not feel qualified to create the necessary set of regulations on martial law. A closing recommendation, which spurred debate in Congress, was "the propriety of substituting the draft for the Volunteer System in calling into service," McLeod argued. "It ensures greater promptness and equalizes the burdens of war over all classes of citizens. Experience enables me to say that troops thus brought into the field, harmonize better, and feel a stronger interest in the result of the campaign, than the floating chivalry which generally compose our Volunteer Corps."

The report included a document listing the formation of companies across the Republic and muster rolls for 111 companies in twenty-four of the thirty-one counties, totaling more than five thousand troops. The largest military presence was in Victoria (642 soldiers), with ten companies formed in Nacogdoches (533) and five in Montgomery (493). The distribution shows Texas' interests against the Indians to the northwest and to the south and southwest, in Mexico.[2]

McLeod's report concluded, "In all our contests with the enemy, the arms of the Republic have been victorious." The Texas Congress approved his report, and it was filed in his office's newly organized records among a multitude of individual reports from the regiments and copies of requisitions and receipts from the Indian wars. McLeod added to them the papers confiscated from Flores a year earlier, including a detailed document in Spanish outlining the alliance and plans for attacks against the Republic.[3] He reported later that the office also had papers from Delaware Chief Harris's wagon, taken during the withdrawal in August.[4] A letter from McLeod confirmed for the congressional records that Paymaster General Jacob Snively "acted in my capacity, as Adjutant General, after the 16th July, 1839, in the Cherokee Campaign," taking over the duties of the office while McLeod recuperated from his serious wound. The embedded arrowhead caused a fever that pestered McLeod for the rest of his life. He was forced to take off the month of February, 1840, because of it, leaving P. Hansborough Bell in charge and nearly missing the activities that occurred the next month.[5]

On December 3, 1839, during a congressional session in Austin, McLeod took the opportunity to launch another political assault against Houston and his "Easterners." Vice President Burnet had retrieved Bowl's silk hat from the battleground on the Neches in July and passed it on to Burleson, who allowed McLeod the privilege of making a mocking presentation of the article to Houston. This turned out to be no laughing matter, and Houston came within a breath of challenging the perpetrators to a duel, demanding in a January 8 speech that McLeod be dismissed from office for this "personal indignity, not only to himself but to Congress." Congressman Thomas Jack responded in defense of the adjutant general, and no action was taken.[6]

If there had been any friendly competition between the two men, it ended here. Their political animosity grew vitriolic in the years that followed, and the two were barely able to speak civilly to each other. Any hopes for a middle ground of political differences evaporated in the ill-advised presentation. Houston had been attacked in what he believed was a personal manner. For his part, McLeod never apologized. Bitterness would characterize their relationship from that day forward.

As 1839 came to an end, McLeod surveyed the exciting year he had come through—not unscathed. His first full year in Lamar's administration gained him a growing reputation across the Republic. He was part of the social and political elite. His heroics on the Neches battlefield gained him additional fame, and he had laid his political future on the line clearly alongside Lamar and against the Houston faction. He owned land in Texas, a 640-acre bounty grant in Galveston County, although he had not made a decision about establishing a permanent residence. Nacogdoches had been home for part of the year, as had Houston before it, and now Austin would be after the capital's move in October.

McLeod had made a significant investment in the San Saba Colonizing Company, but it appeared to come to nothing. The promise of German immigrants to Texas intrigued him, and in April he became a stockholder in the fledgling plan along with other notables: Andrew Briscoe, William G. Cooke, Thomas G. Western, and George Hockley. But by the end of August, despite the valiant efforts of their agent Henry Francis Fisher, the operation flagged badly. Eventually the stockholders cut their losses as the Germans headed to Texas through the auspices of the *Adelsverein*,[7] a society established in Germany to foster mass emigration to Texas.

McLeod's best friend in Texas was William Cazneau, a thirty-two-year-old Bostonian he had met on staff with General Chambers in 1837. The two bachelors traveled together, fought side by side against the Indians, and now worked together following Cazneau's appointment as commissary general of the Texas army. Other confidantes included the Rusks in Nacogdoches, President Lamar, Captain Redd, Secretary of War Johnston, and General Douglass.

Another acquaintance, Reuben Ross of Gonzales, had come into Texas with Judge Quitman at the defense of Nacogdoches in 1836 and joined McLeod on Bexar Road that spring and summer. It may have been Ross's influence that directed McLeod's attention to the Federalist Rebellion along the Rio Grande in 1839. Ross joined forces with other Texans to form the Texas Auxiliary Corps, more than 225 mercenary soldiers allied with

Antonio Canales, José Maria Jesus Carbajal, and Antonio Zapata, in an attempt to liberate the northern Mexico provinces from Santa Anna's Centralist government.[8] A key ingredient to the revolution's success would be the support, or at least a strong neutral stance, of the Republic of Texas.

The campaign had begun in November, 1838, in Guerrero, Tamaulipas, with Canales's declaration against the Centralists. One month later he wrote Lamar asking for approval or even recognition of the insurrection. In a comment before Congress on January 16, 1839, Lamar could "perceive no benefit in communicating with the writer of this letter, or with any official personage of that Republic, who may be in open revolution against the government." After a week of debate, however, Congress authorized trade with the rebel villages along the Rio Grande.[9]

By summer Canales and Zapata had moved their insurgent army across the upper Rio Grande in a series of raids, incurring dramatic newspaper headlines but little success. Their Texas allies joined the revolution soon after the end of the Cherokee campaign in East Texas. In addition to Ross, Samuel W. Jordan, who had been wounded on the Neches, and Richard Roman of Refugio County commanded companies that participated in a victorious battle at Mier in November. Visits to San Antonio by Francisco Vidaurri, Juan Pablo Anaya, Carbajal, and Canales himself helped their recruiting efforts.[10] One of the enlisted was Col. Henry Karnes, commander of three companies of the Texas army in San Antonio. He sent word to Lamar in Austin that the Federalists were in the vicinity soliciting assistance.[11]

Lamar ordered McLeod to contact José Ramos, the alcalde in Laredo, for more information on the filibuster. McLeod wrote: "President Lamar especially desires to know if there are any considerable number of Texans in the expedition, the names of the leaders, both of Mexicans and Americans. I am not sure that I understand what it proposes to accomplish. The President regards such an expedition, at this time, unfortunate for Texas, as it will tend to further excite envy and hatred among the Mexicans who have recently given assurance of a better understanding of our people and our government."[12] When Canales declared the independence of the Republic of the Rio Grande later in the year, Laredo was designated as its capital.

As the revolutionary army faltered at Matamoros in December and Canales began to lose his Texans' support, Lamar disengaged from any relationship to the rebels, "warn[ing] and admonish[ing] all citizens of Texas to abstain from all attempts to invade the territory of Mexico," and also from participating in "marauding incursions, and other acts of hostility."[13] Lamar intended to dispatch McLeod to the Rio Grande to make contact with the Texans, but McLeod had fallen ill. His assistant, Col. Benjamin N. Johnson, went instead, with an entourage of five Texans and two Mexican servants who were guides and interpreters. On their way back from Mier, the six Texans were butchered by a party of Caddo Indians, their mutilated bodies left hanging in a tree.[14]

McLeod, intrigued by the cause for which his friend Ross fought, learned just after Christmas that the revolutionary officer had been killed in a separate dispute involving Ben and Henry McCulloch.[15] In spite of the setbacks and the official ban against participation, McLeod continued to keep abreast of the activities of the Republic of the Rio Grande. He held at least one private meeting with Carbajal, who had lost the use of his right arm in the December battle at Matamoros, and came away impressed.[16] Even as the revolution slackened in the summer of 1840, Canales continued to correspond with Lamar and even met with him in Galveston. In midsummer Carbajal wrote Lamar that he "expected Karnes and McLeod at any time" to join the filibuster along with a company of Texas recruits, hoping "that Col. Kernes [sic] will take enough artillery."[17]

McLeod did not join the rebellion, although he considered the possibility. He wrote, "I will determine in a moment whether I can or not, and if so, send my resignation on at once—I do not think there will be any difficulty."[18] But when he heard of the Federalists' plunder of Laredo—"they took it, friends and foes," he wrote—it dampened the glory of the enterprise.[19] Instead, he concentrated his efforts on preventing the frontier army from deserting to the Mexican forces or assisting in the recruitment visits. He discharged one entire unit, the Pitkin and Border Guards stationed at San Antonio, reporting that they "were worthless and complaining. . . . They have done and would do nothing. . . . They are now out of service."[20]

At the same time, McLeod never lost his respect for Carbajal, nor for the idea of an independent republic along the Rio Grande. In the summer of 1846 he would put his own name beside such a title, and six years later he would accept the privilege of standing next to the proud freedom fighter and introducing him to a cheering audience. The cause of freedom had brought McLeod to Texas and would always be a motivating force behind his actions.

During the months he was involved in the Canales movement, the frontier and Indian trouble never strayed from McLeod's mind, especially with the Texas capital's move to Austin. Now Lipan Apache and Penateka Comanche had wandered into the picture. Raids along the Brazos and Colorado Rivers caused a frontier officer to write the War Department that he was "convinced that speedy relief must be had, or depopulation will necessarily soon ensue. The whole country is literally swarming with redskins."[21] Of main concern were the Comanche raids in and around San Antonio and as far east as Gonzales, where in 1838 four children had been kidnaped, two from the Putnam family and the two Lockhart children, John and Matilda. Despite the best efforts of posses and Rangers, the marauders snuck back to their Comanche territory with plunder and the children.

Distracted by the Cherokee campaign through the summer months and the chase by General Burleson that led to the Christmas Day attack on the last of the Texas Cherokees on the San Saba River, McLeod and Lamar's administration left the western frontier to the militia. Colonel Karnes, commander of the forces at Bexar, organized his meager, poorly provisioned troops into roaming companies with only minimal effect. A chase up the San Saba in 1839 led to a confrontation with a band of Comanches at their winter camp. Ranger John H. Moore and a hundred volunteers took the village by surprise but did not succeed in recapturing any of the kidnaped children spotted during the battle. During the fight the Texans lost their mounts and were forced to walk back to Austin in the February cold.[22]

Despite repeated forays into the settlements and inadequate response by the outposts, a Comanche council decided in January, 1840, to negotiate a peace treaty with the Texans. Karnes reported in a message to Johnston that the Comanches "refused to treat with the Cherokees, who, along with Mexican agents, solicited them with large presents to enter with them in a war against the Republic." The representatives of the Penateka assured Karnes that they would sit with his people to talk whenever he suggested. Karnes agreed to contact his government but stipulated that no negotiations would take place "without the release of the American Captives, and the restoration of all stolen property; besides giving guarantees that future depredators on our property should be delivered up for punishment." The Comanches agreed to his terms and promised to return within thirty days.[23]

Secretary of War Johnston appointed McLeod and Cooke as special commissioners for the negotiations and sent additional companies of soldiers to Bexar under the general command of Colonel Fisher and his First Regiment. McLeod wrote Lamar on March 17 from San Antonio that the army was preparing for the negotiations, but no word had yet come from the Comanches. "The troops are in fine condition," he wrote, "well satisfied, and both men & officers delighted with the Country, and their quarters."[24]

Fisher designated the old stone Council House in San Antonio as the meeting ground. Situated on the corner of Main Plaza and Market Street, it adjoined the city jail and provided a strategic location for controlling the situation. The council room was large enough to accommodate both parties, but there was only one entrance. With soldiers stationed all around the square, an outbreak of violence could be managed.

Mary Maverick, George Howard, and Hugh McLeod were eyewitnesses to the events that day. On March 19 two Comanche scouts arrived in the city and informed McLeod and Cooke that the peace party was on its way. Soon the citizens and soldiers saw sixty-five men, women, and children riding and walking casually toward the plaza. Twelve of the Penateka principal chiefs, led by Muk-wah-ruh, greeted the commissioners stoically and were led into the Council House. Several women accompanied them inside and stood against a back wall while the rest of the party waited outside.[25]

A handful of Comanche boys began to play on the street while Bexar citizens watched, fascinated. Lt. Edward Thompson's brother, a judge from South Carolina residing in Houston and visiting his kin, soon engaged the boys in a game. Seeing their small bows and arrows, he challenged them to shoot at coins and paper money that he leaned against a nearby fence. From across the street, Mrs. Mary Maverick and her neighbor, Mrs. Higginbotham, watched the boys shoot the targets with remarkable accuracy. Cordoning the Council House as soon as the chiefs went inside, Capt. George Thomas Howard's company waited near the entrance while William Redd's men stood at ease around the back. Bexar Sheriff Joseph Hood visited with Redd from the front porch of the jailhouse.

Inside their home, Samuel Maverick sat at the dining table with his eldest son Andrew and their guest, Capt. Mathew "Old Paint" Caldwell, in from Gonzales. George W. Cayce, a young man in his late teens who had delivered some papers to Maverick from his father in Matagorda County, was also there. When the Comanches appeared at the plaza, Cayce and Caldwell wandered into the yard to watch. Jinny Anderson, the Mavericks' black cook, worked in the kitchen house out back and kept an eye on the four children in her care. Dozens of Anglos and Mexicans wandered around the plaza.

Inside the large council room, McLeod and Cooke stood facing Muk-wah-ruh, with Lt. Col. Fisher at the doorway. A handful of soldiers stood at wary attention with their rifles resting in their arms. Lt. William M. Dunnington stared at Muk-wah-ruh throughout the proceedings. One of the women threw back the long blanket around her to reveal the tiny shape of a young white girl, weakened by starvation and physical abuse. Her nose had been cut and burned to the bone, and she had scars on her shoulders and legs. Fifteen-year-old Matilda Lockhart looked half her age and was in a pitiful state. She had been a captive and slave for two years.

Fisher, barely able to contain himself, stepped forward and demanded to know where the other captives were. "We have brought in the only one we had," replied Muk-wah-ruh through an interpreter. "The others are with other tribes." Fisher knelt and spoke quietly for a moment to Matilda. In a shaky voice she told him that many other captives were in the camp where she lived; she had seen some of them that morning.

Fisher stood up and silence filled the room, interrupted by the flippant voice of the principal chief: "How do you like answer?" he said. Fisher responded: "I do not like your answer. I told you not to come here again without bringing in your prisoners. You have come against my orders." At this moment McLeod turned toward the door and motioned for a company of soldiers to come inside. Captain Howard led his men in, and they arranged themselves in a line facing the chiefs. Fisher continued: "Your women and children may depart in peace, and your braves may go and tell your people to send in the prisoners. When those prisoners are returned, your chiefs here present may likewise go free. Until then we will hold you as hostages." The interpreter refused to translate Fisher's words. Fisher demanded that he do so, his eyes never leaving Muk-wah-ruh. Haltingly, the interpreter mumbled the Penateka translation.

Instantly and as one, the eleven chiefs behind Muk-wah-ruh strung their bows. Fisher ordered the soldiers inside the Council House to "Fire if they do not desist." Most of the rifles had already been raised into position as he spoke. The Comanches made the first move. One of the chiefs lunged for the only door out of the room. Howard grabbed the man by his shirt collar. The chief stabbed him in the side but was shot down at the entrance. The first shot brought a firing of arrows and rifles at nearly point-blank range. Smoke filled the room, and the officers shouted orders as the firing continued. Dunnington was shot through by an arrow, but he turned before he fell and fired his pistol into the face of the closest Comanche. "His brains bespattered the wall; he turned around and exclaimed, 'I have killed him, but I believe he has killed me, too.'"[26] The twelve chiefs and three women lay dead inside in a matter of seconds. Dunnington died twenty minutes later.

On the plaza, the sounds of gunfire and shouting from inside the building spurred others to action. Two Indian boys strung their bows and shot Judge Thompson through.[27] Another turned and killed young George Cayce where he stood. Caldwell ran across the plaza unarmed, grabbed a rifle from a warrior, shot him, and beat another to death with the gun until it splintered into pieces. He fell when a rifle ball pierced his leg, but he propped himself against the Council House wall and threw rocks at the enemy as they ran by.

The warriors outside made a break around the back of the building and ran right into Capt. Redd's company. The fighting was hand to hand for several minutes, and four Comanches were killed. Pvt. Frederick Kaminski died in the pitched battle. Sheriff Hood started down from the jailhouse porch and was shot in a hail of arrows. Some of the warriors broke through Redd's line and made for the river several blocks away.

Back in the plaza Pvt. Robert J. Whitney lay dead near the entryway of the Council House. Across the street Thomas Higginbotham ran from his house and was severely wounded before he could get to the street. His wife knelt in shock nearby. Next door, Mary Maverick stood transfixed as bullets and arrows passed her. Two Indian boys lay dead in the street; one was the son of Muk-wah-ruh. Gunfire sounded as the Comanches rushed inside buildings around the square. When two warriors headed toward the Maverick house, Mary turned and raced them to the door, pulling down the heavy bar lock just ahead of them.

Sam and Andrew Maverick sat serenely at the dining room table, oblivious to the noise. Mary yelled, "Here are Indians!" Sam grabbed his rifle and headed for the front door as Andrew joined his mother in a race to the backyard. At the rear exit they saw Jinny standing in the backyard with the four children crouched behind her wide apron. She held a large rock overhead and screamed at the Comanche a few feet away, "If you don't go 'way from here I'll mash your head with this rock!" The Indian disappeared behind the kitchen house before Andrew could get off a shot with his pistol, but he chased the Indian and killed him before he reached the riverbank.

Mary hurried to the front of the house just in time to see Col. Lysander Wells riding into the plaza. Unaware of the action, he had stumbled into the middle of the battle. As he pulled up his mount, an Indian leapt onto Wells from the shadows of a building, and the two struggled on horseback. Wells managed to pull his pistol from its holster and shot the Indian point blank. Then he rode toward the river, firing his pistol at straggling Indians and shouting orders to passersby and soldiers.

Mary saw three Indians lying at the edge of her lawn, two not moving. Higginbotham's journeyman walked over to the wounded Comanche and pointed his pistol at the Indian's head. Mary cried out, "Oh don't, he is dying!" The man laughed, said, "To please you, ma'am, I won't, but it would put him out of his misery," and walked away. From across the plaza,

McLeod hollered at her, "Are you crazy? Go in or you will be killed." But Mary went looking for her children.

At the river, the Texans fired into the water as the Comanches retreated. Only one, later identified as a "Mexican renegade," managed to escape. On the square McLeod, Fisher, and Capt. James C. Allen coordinated the fight that continued. A number of Comanches had hidden in buildings, and a house-to-house search resulted in the deaths of another half-dozen warriors and the capture of twenty-nine, including two old men. One survivor hid in a stone kitchen house off Soledad Street and refused all attempts to be captured. Hours later, as night fell, two Texans crawled onto the structure and dropped a burning candlewick ball soaked in turpentine down the chimney. The fiery weapon struck the warrior on his head. He threw open the door and was killed instantly by gunfire.[28]

The Council House Fight ended with thirty-five Comanches dead, including the twelve principal chiefs who had entered the meeting room. Seven soldiers and citizens had died, and eight were seriously wounded. It was thought that Higginbotham and Thompson, the latter shot through the lungs, would not live, but both survived. Medical care was extended through the night by several volunteers under the direction of Dr. Eduard Weidemann, a Russian-born physician who lived in San Antonio.[29]

McLeod wrote his official report the following day and sent it to Lamar. The report appeared on April 4 in the Richmond *Telescope and Texas Register*. In San Antonio, McLeod declared a twelve-day truce against the Comanches in the area. He sent one of the captured squaws to take the news to their camp and prepare for an exchange of prisoners. Chief Piava came to San Antonio on April 3, and the next day seven children were exchanged for some of the Comanche prisoners. The children told of the horrors at the camp when word of the fight came and how the Indians "howled and cut themselves with knives, and killed horses for several days. And they took the American captives, thirteen in number, and roasted and butchered them to death with horrible cruelties." The rest of the jailed Comanches were moved to Mission San José. By the end of April nearly all had managed to escape.[30]

In retaliation for the Council House Fight, a large band of Comanche warriors drove down through the Texas settlements in July, almost to the coast, where they burned the town of Linnville before turning around. With captives and a mile-long caravan of plunder, the Indians headed for the safety of their Comancheria, but they were surprised at Plum Creek on August 12 by two hundred Texans. The decimation of the war party effectively brought an end to the hostile presence of the Penateka inside the Texas frontier.[31]

On August 19, 1840, McLeod wrote Johnston from Austin, "I got here a few days just in time to be too late for the skirmish with the Linnville plunderers." He noted that several adjustments would be made to the frontier defenses as a result of the fighting, and that "the military will make a campaign from San Antonio against the Comanches." He informed Johnston of Cooke and Fisher's resignations and of the pending resignation of several other officers. The letter then becomes personal, with notes about common acquaintances and the illness of Felix Huston, among other items. Near the end of the missive, McLeod wrote, off by itself, "I think of resigning and running for Congress from Bexar."[32] Instead, another chapter awaited him: the expedition of the Santa Fe Pioneers.

CHAPTER 5
Background to Expansionism

Both the United States and Texas coveted Santa Fe in the early nineteenth century. Even as the first of Stephen F. Austin's colonists, the "Old Three Hundred," made their way across the Sabine River into the northernmost Mexican province of Coahuila-Texas, U.S. President John Quincy Adams appointed Joel R. Poinsett as minister to Mexico with express instructions "to sound the authorities upon the possibilities of fixing a new boundary line somewhere between the Sabine and the Rio Grande." Poinsett's journey to Mexico City in 1825, and again in 1827, resulted in little more than the aroused suspicions of the Mexican government and its refusal of a $1 million offer for the purchase of territory spanning the southwest. Continuing negotiations between the two nations over the next several years failed to change any of the boundaries or land claims established by the Adams-Onis Treaty of 1819.[1]

Additional suspicions were aroused in 1827 when Haden Edwards's Fredonian Rebellion attempted to lay claim to the Rio Grande in an alliance with the Indian nations. Mexico's suppression of this uprising reinforced a growing concern about Americans' migration into Texas and was a factor in the firm restrictions of the Law of April 6, 1830.

Recognition of the upper Rio Grande in the jurisdiction of the Coahuila-Texas government occurred in 1829, when two English promoters received a land grant for colonization between the Nueces River and the Rio Grande. In August, 1829, Stephen F. Austin drew a map of Texas that included Santa Fe and wrote Henry Austin a proposal that would eventually divert Santa Fe trade away from the Midwest and through Galveston.[2]

In the United States, President Jackson brought up the subject of the Southwest again, replacing Poinsett with Anthony Butler and increasing the offer to Mexico to $5 million. Unfortunately for Jackson, Butler proved a greater diplomatic failure than his predecessor, compounding the already delicate situation. Jackson was encouraged again early in 1833, when his close friend Sam Houston, now of Texas, informed him that a proposed separation between Coahuila and Texas would likely include the Rio Grande ter-

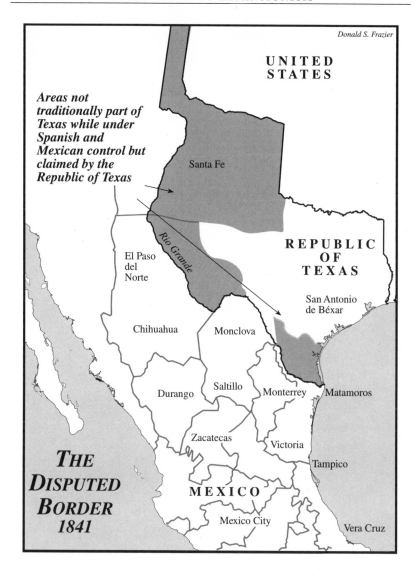

Donald S. Frazier

UNITED
STATES

*Areas not
traditionally part of
Texas while under
Spanish and
Mexican control but
claimed by the
Republic of Texas*

Santa Fe

Rio Grande

El Paso
del
Norte

REPUBLIC
OF
TEXAS

San Antonio
de Béxar

Chihuahua   Monclova

Durango   Saltillo   Monterrey   Matamoros

Zacatecas   Victoria

*THE
DISPUTED
BORDER
1841*

MEXICO

Tampico

Mexico City   Vera Cruz

ritory in Texas. When that plan failed and Butler's subsequent proposal fell on deaf ears in Mexico City, the possibilities of an American claim on Santa Fe appeared to evaporate.

As revolution stirred Texas in 1835, however, interest in boundaries, notably south and west, once again included Santa Fe, indicating renewed plans for a trade route that would benefit Texas commerce, a road from the state of Chihuahua across the Rio Grande and the Nueces River. Trade between Chihuahua and Santa Fe had increased over the years, and a connection to that commercial expansion meant prosperity for Texas, independent or not.

By the fall of 1836 an independent Republic of Texas struggled to identify its territorial limits between Mexico and the United States. Secretary of State Austin supported the idea of the Rio Grande as a western boundary that would include Santa Fe in Texas, but he also expressed fears that this boundary might renew hostilities with Mexico. Texas President Sam Houston had no such anxiety and signed a bill that read, "Such a work, extending to the doors of our birthplace upon the one hand, and to the verge of California on the other, will be not less magnificent in conception than useful in fact."[3] In October, 1836, Branch T. Archer and James Collinsworth sought congressional approval of a commercial corporation that would "connect the waters of the Rio Grande by internal navigation and rail roads with the waters of the Sabine." And on December 19 the Texas Congress finalized the boundary proceedings extending "the civil and political jurisdiction of Texas over this [Rio Grande] territory."[4] Still, uncertainty about the actual jurisdiction of the Texas government over Santa Fe led many to believe that the upper Rio Grande was under the administrative authority of Mexico.

In 1837, with diplomats from Texas and the United States considering annexation of the former, Texas merchant George S. Park urged that Santa Fe trade be diverted to Texas as a way to profit from the silver trade and to undergird the Texas currency system. He proposed the construction of a trade route from Bastrop on the Colorado River to Santa Fe, a journey he claimed incorrectly to be "no more than five hundred miles." He believed the route would open "to the enterprise of North Americans the valuable country of California on the shores of the Pacific Ocean." Although the Texas legislature took up the plan late in January, 1838, a bill in May to investigate the route was defeated.[5] As annexation plans disintegrated that year, fervor for territorial or trade claims on the upper Rio Grande likewise faded.

After Lamar was elected president of Texas in 1838, expansionist efforts came alive again. Lamar set aside talk of annexation and instead outlined a grand plan for the expansion of the Republic from the Gulf of Mexico to the Pacific. His inaugural address on December 10, 1838, left no doubt that the Rio Grande, and thereby Santa Fe, belonged to Texas by virtue of the resolution of December 19, 1836. Lamar had already instructed Secretary of State Bee to offer a compromise price of $5 million to Mexico for the disputed territory. Meanwhile Lamar sent Richard G. Dunlap to Washington, D.C., to ask the United States to mediate treaty negotiations that might result.[6]

Although Santa Anna, Mexico's president, refused to recognize Bee's mission, Lamar tried again in August, sending James Treat with additional instructions to "feel the authorities of Mexico out" about the possibility of a Texas boundary along the Rio Grande.[7] Although Treat received recognition and spoke to government officials in January, 1840, the talks had broken down once more by March. Complicating the situation, the revolutionary Federalist army under Canales succeeded in establishing a provisional government along the Rio Grande that month. Whatever hope the Texas government had of working out a treaty with Mexico now appeared useless.

Nevertheless, Lamar refused to give up hope that, if nothing else, he could persuade the people of the upper Rio Grande to pledge their loyalties to Texas rather than Mexico. When an American merchant, W. G. Dryden, arrived in Austin in the spring of 1840 and told Lamar of the perceived interest of Santa Feans to be part of Texas, Lamar leapt at the opportunity. On April 14, 1840, he prepared a message for Dryden to hand deliver to the citizens of Santa Fe, "friends and compatriots of Texas." The letter conferred equal privileges, religious toleration, and legal rights to them and promised to send trade commissioners who would explain "the interests which so emphatically recommend and ought perpetually to cement the perfect union between Santa Fe and Texas."[8]

Dryden's Santa Fe report underscored earlier information Lamar had received from William Jefferson Jones, who placed the value of annual trade with New Mexico at $20 million in gold, silver, and furs. Jones indicated that the lucrative fur trade would put Texas at the center of a world market and that "the trappers would place themselves under the protection of our government and gladly resort to the new Capital of the Western Empire of North America." Such hyperbole would only have reinforced Lamar's expansionist ideals. Jones likewise suggested that a trade route be established up the Colorado River to within three hundred miles of Santa Fe itself, yet another piece of deadly misinformation about the distances west of the Texas settlement line.[9]

Jones's letter of February, 1839, may have been the first suggestion Lamar received for "a politico-military mission to Santa Fe with a view to the introduction of the trade of New Mexico through the natural outlet within the limits of this Republic." Jones assured Lamar of success in throwing off the Mexican authority along the Rio Grande. "The revolutionary spirit is warm in New Mexico," he wrote, referring inadvisedly to a series of minor rebellions there in 1835 and 1838.[10]

On February 21, 1839, Lamar issued an official proclamation indicating his interest in "opening a trade with the Mexican citizens on the Rio

Grande, reciprocating the desire to establish and cultivate such friendly intercourse between the inhabitants of Mexico, disposed to peace and amity, and the citizens of this Republic, and believing that a free and liberal trade properly conducted will conduce to that end. . . . And I do hereby enjoin it upon all officers civil and military of the Republic of Texas, to afford all proper aid, countenance and protection to such of the peacible [sic] inhabitants." Caught up in the excitement of the venture, Lamar addressed the Harrisburg volunteers a month later, congratulating them on the prospect of working "under the command of Colonel Karnes in the anticipated expedition to Santa Fe." [11]

One year later Lamar's commitment to the expedition had not waned. On April 15, 1840, the *Texas State Gazette* voiced its support for him: "The inhabitants of Santa Fe desire Texan sovereignty, and on our side will there be no advantages gained? Most assuredly there will. . . . The Santa Fe trade would certainly tend to patch up [Texas'] dilapidated finances."

Despite the failure of the Treat mission to Mexico City in 1840, Lamar sent Dryden to Santa Fe, instructing him to cooperate with two Santa Feans, John Rowland and William Workman, in negotiations for changing the authority under which the people of the upper Rio Grande would live. Dryden departed Austin on April 29, although it is significant that his chosen route to Santa Fe was via New Orleans and St. Louis, not the route he was recommending. [12] He had arrived by September and proceeded to carry out orders, writing Lamar the next spring that "every American, and more than two-thirds of the Mexicans, and all the Pueblo Indians, are with us, heart and soul; and whenever they have heard of your sending Troops (!), there has been a rejoicing." Suspicions of Dryden's zeal might have been aroused when he added, "the Governor says he would be glad to see the day of your arrival in this country." His additional report in July, that "the Comanches have gone north . . . and those that attempt to make the trip to Santa Fe will be in no danger," only stirred the excitement. Later incidents showed these assertions to be patently untrue. [13]

The Dryden correspondence did not reach Austin until July, 1841, after the Santa Fe expedition had commenced. By then, unwilling to wait any longer and frustrated by an uncooperative Senate, Lamar had acted on his desire to expand the Republic across the continent. In November, 1840, the House approved a plan to fund a trade commission to Santa Fe, with a military escort to protect merchants against hostile Indians. Lamar tied the expedition to a colonization plan that included Santa Fe, and a House committee began work on a budget for the expedition. [14]

The proceedings were interrupted on December 12 when Lamar requested, and received, a ninety-day medical leave of absence. Accompanied to New Orleans by McLeod, Lamar left Burnet in Austin as acting president until his return late in February, 1841.[15] Burnet's militant attitude toward the upper Rio Grande territory may have affected the proceedings, for by the time Lamar and McLeod returned to Austin the expedition bill was dead. Burnet had railed in a December speech that "Texas proper is bounded by the Rio Grande—Texas as defined by the sword may comprehend the Sierra del Madre. Let the sword do its proper work."[16] Gen. Felix Huston had followed up with a Santa Fe colonization plan that included a military expeditionary force of one thousand men along the upper Rio Grande to establish the colony, situated at a point "that would greatly embarrass an invading Army."[17] Uneasy at the possibility that renewed hostilities with Mexico might be a consequence of such an expedition, Congress hesitated. Adjourning on February 5, 1841, it left appropriations on the table but no legislative support for Lamar's commission plans.[18]

Lamar, infuriated by the lack of support from what he had considered a loyal, expansionist legislature, resolved to proceed with the commercial qua political expedition without congressional consent. Encouraging letters in March and April from constituents across Texas convinced him to find a way around the dilemma.[19] Since Congress had not voted down the compromise bill and had agreed to the commercial appropriations of such an expedition, Lamar argued later that the spirit of the plan had survived, and since "there was left on hand a considerable supply of military equipage, and the means of transportation, it occurred to me that it was a favorable time to carry out this desirable and long contemplated expedition." Fully expecting more positive news from Dryden in Santa Fe, Lamar resolved to send an unofficial commercial expedition, with military escort, "without embarrassing the country, and at an expense altogether trifling, when compared with the objects to be achieved."[20]

On March 24, 1841, Lamar instructed Secretary of the Treasury John G. Chalmers and Quartermaster Gen. William Cazneau to put together an expedition of merchants and soldiers for the Santa Fe trip. Cazneau wrote to Robert S. Neighbors: "It is absolutely necessary that Six or Seven thousand pounds of dried Beef should be delivered in this place by the 15th of May. . . . The price is high, but the Beef must be delivered, without fail."[21] At the same time, Lamar sent Maj. George T. Howard to New Orleans to purchase supplies and perhaps recruit merchants and volunteers. Howard, twenty-seven years old and well known in the Southwest as an Indian fighter and a Texas Ranger, met George Wilkins Kendall in New Orleans. Kendall, owner and editor of the *Picayune*, agreed to accompany the expedition as an observer and independent journalist.[22]

In April newspapers printed a call for volunteers to come to Austin "for the purpose of opening a commercial intercourse with the people of Santa Fe; for which purpose troops are necessary to escort the merchandise through the Comanche wilderness."[23] By mid-May hundreds had responded. Because the Texas legislature had not sanctioned the expedition, more than a dozen soldiers in the Texas army resigned before heading for Austin. These included William Cooke, who was discharged April 30, and Howard, W. D. Houghton, John Holliday, J. C. P. Kenneymore, and C. C. Hornsby, all of whom resigned on May 8. All but Kenneymore would enlist as officers in the Pioneers.[24]

Lamar had already selected the man to lead the military escort and head up the expedition. Hugh McLeod had been a part of the conversations and planning for a year before the expedition began. In June, 1840, Lamar traveled to Galveston to meet with McLeod, Ashbel Smith, Albert Sidney Johnston, and others, outlining a timetable for the trek. A frontier excursion by Col. Cooke that summer for the establishment of up to nine military posts from San Antonio northward to the Red River would supply an updated analysis and map route for that portion of the journey.[25]

In October McLeod traveled up the San Marcos River to help lay out one of the posts. "I have examined the topography of the whole surrounding Country," he wrote Lamar. "You will find much to amuse you, in hunting & fishing & more to admire in the grandeur of Dame Nature's freaks." Waxing eloquent, he continued: "Fairy Land cannot excel it in the beauty of its landscape, nor will the Highlands of the Hudson compare with the bold, yet softened scenery of its mountain views—Towering hills arise on every side, but the bleak baldness that would chill the blood in a northern clime, is veiled here, in the perpetual verdure of the live oak."[26]

McLeod seemed the perfect choice to lead the expedition, but not everyone agreed. James Durst wrote Lamar of "a great objection to Col. McLeod [for] a want of courage, as Houston's friends have tried to impress it on the minds of the people that it is a very dangerous expedition." Despite the political chicanery, McLeod planned to quit his travels in late April and begin the march on June 5. He was ill when he arrived in Austin around June 1, however, and this delayed the start of the expedition by at least two weeks. On June 17 Lamar formally appointed McLeod brevet brigadier general, commissioned to lead the Santa Fe Pioneers.[27]

McLeod in turn appointed the redoubtable Valentine Bennet quartermaster of the expedition and Theodore Sevey as adjutant. Major Howard, returned from New Orleans, became McLeod's aide-de-camp as second-in-command, and John S. Sutton was next in command at the head of Company A. Four other infantry companies, and an artillery company pulling a six-pounder cannon under the command of Capt. William P. Lewis, completed the military escort of more than two hundred soldiers. Another one hundred merchants, teamsters under the supervision of wagonmaster Joseph Rogers, visiting journalists, guide Samuel W. Howland, and support personnel rounded out the expeditionary force of 320.[28]

The civil commissioners appointed to accompany the expedition and formally greet the people and authorities of Santa Fe were Colonel Cooke, Dr. Richard F. Brenham, and Tejano José Antonio Navarro, whose influence on the Mexican population would be important. Nineteen-year-old George Van Ness was official recording secretary to the commissioners, carrying a wagonload of pamphlets and flyers in English and Spanish to distribute along the upper Rio Grande.

Although Kendall would write extensively about the expedition, the official chronicler was Thomas Falconer, English historiographer and Royal Geographical Society fellow. Falconer had come to Texas the previous December, had been formally introduced to Lamar, and now carried with him a presidential commission "to give such an account of the intermediate country and its scientific capacities, as will enable the Government to form a correct estimate of its value and extent."[29] He enjoyed exemption from military orders and was accompanied by Tom Hancock, a scruffy twenty-one-year-old frontiersman hired in San Antonio who acted as Falconer's guide and bodyguard.[30]

Kendall arrived in Austin with adventurers from Houston including: Radcliff Hudson, captain of Company C; Volney Ostrander; Thomas Lubbock, younger brother of Francis Lubbock; and Franklin Coombs, seventeen-year-old son of the Kentucky governor. The teenager, one of more than a dozen volunteers under the age of nineteen, was very hard of hearing and kept close to Kendall and Hancock throughout the march.[31]

Upon his arrival in Austin, Kendall learned of the expedition's delay. He and Falconer rode south to San Antonio and stayed for several days, visiting the Bexar Archives.[32] They failed to grasp the importance of one item in the files: a 1788 map by Spanish army Col. José Mares showing the route, hazards, and correct distances between Natchitoches and the Red River, and the Red River west to Santa Fe, a journey Mares had made with Pedro Vial in 1787.[33] This map would have saved the expedition weeks of frustration and unnecessary tragedy.

On the way back to Austin, Kendall fell while walking near the steep banks of the Colorado River and severely sprained his ankle. Determined to make the journey, and with the aid of Lamar himself, Kendall rode in a specially fitted Jersey wagon for the first weeks of the trip.[34]

Mathew Caldwell came along for the adventure and brought his twelve-year-old son, Curtis. The forty-three-year-old Kentucky frontiersman had fought alongside McLeod and Cooke at the Council House in 1840; now he captained Company D to Santa Fe. Caldwell's bravery and experience would be called on several times in the weeks to come.[35] George Grover served in the artillery company under Lewis and kept notes that he transcribed, with the help of John Talk, into a diary the following spring. Besides Kendall and Falconer's recollections, the only daily diary during the march was that of Peter Gallagher, an Irish stonemason who brought a considerable amount of merchandise with him. Stephen Hoyle of the medical staff helped Gallagher rewrite the diary in Mexico.[36]

The arrival of more than three hundred men, along with the sizable equipment and supply train that had cost the government more than $78,000, made it impossible to camp in one location during the several weeks of delay.[37] McLeod organized three camps in the vicinity of the small capital city. Camps Bell and Cook set up quarters four miles east of Austin, where Walnut Creek spills into the Colorado. McLeod spent time at Camp Bell when he was not in the city. The third camp was about five miles up Walnut Creek, where the Military Road laid out by Cooke in 1840 crossed on its way north.[38] The six companies of soldiers spread out among the three camps along with the gathering of merchants, and the numbers increased daily from June 1 to June 19.

Trouble began long before the expedition was under way. McLeod's late arrival and continued ill health provoked concern and impatience among some of the men anxious to get started on the adventure. Although age meant little on the frontier, McLeod at twenty-six was younger than most of the officers he commanded, including Cooke, Caldwell, and Howard. These men, as well as guides Howland and Hunt, knew it was imperative to get a good start before the intense summer heat became a more formidable enemy than the terrain or the Kiowa. Assuming the journey would take about six weeks, an early June start meant arriving at the cooler New Mexico mountains before August.

McLeod's late arrival led to a dispute about command and authority that left bad feelings in Company A and some suspicions among the others. In the April newspaper announcement, Cooke had clearly indicated that each company would be allowed to elect its own officers.[39] When McLeod arrived from Galveston, unaware of that proclamation, he began to assign company commands. When Sutton's men objected to an assignment, McLeod reacted. "The commanding officer has been informed with surprise this morning," McLeod began his first special order of the expedition on June 1, "that Capt. Sutton's Company demand the right of electing their own officers. . . . They voluntarily agreed to serve under the officers appointed by the Government." Acknowledging that Company B's officers, under Houghton, had agreed to let their men hold elections, McLeod ordered Company A discharged because of a violation of the terms of their enrollment and for making "a demand so unreasonable." McLeod's relationship with soldiers and officers began poorly, as he unwisely continued: "Factious men and bad soldiers have seduced them from their duty. . . . If the Company return to a sense of duty immediately [and most of them did] they will be received and the past forgotten."[40] It is safe to assume that not everyone forgot. When John Doran of Company A was promoted to sergeant major of the expedition four days later with the admonition that "he will be obeyed and respected accordingly," what may have been an attempt at conciliation fell on deaf ears.[41]

Meanwhile McLeod had his own problems. He had exhausted his personal finances in Austin, and on June 10 he wrote Lamar: "I requested [Secretary of the Treasury] Dr. Chalmers to mention my private situation, with regard to my creditors, yesterday, and he returned with a reply, that I might disband my Troops—I hate second hand abuse—I owe money here, & there is at least the possibility of my being killed in this Campaign. . . . If it is not granted, I shall feel myself much lowered in my own estimation."[42]

Tragedy struck twice before the expedition got under way: the accidental shooting of two volunteers, Pvt. John C. Snow on the night of June 3 by a sentinel, and Pvt. Andrew Jackson Davis on June 12 at Walnut Creek when his own gun discharged. When E. B. Lockridge shot himself five days into the march, superstitious soldiers must have wondered at the advisability of continuing.

McLeod ordered the consolidation of the three camps on June 11, six days after the original departure date. Hudson and Company C left Camp Cook and joined the main body as it moved a few miles north to Brushy Creek; Caldwell and Company D were to catch up as soon as possible. Sutton, Houghton, Capt. J. H. Strain of Company E, and Lewis's artillery were on the trail.[43]

The preparations for reorganizing the six companies, organizing the twenty-three ox-driven (and overloaded) supply and merchant wagons, and herding the seventy head of beef cattle to Brushy Creek took several days more. Davis's death and his military burial two days later—a coffin had to be procured from Austin, delaying the services—postponed the plans yet again. By June 16, most of the 320 Santa Fe Pioneers, as they had been designated by Lamar, were bivouacked at a spot on the creek named Camp Cazneau by McLeod, less than a mile from the site of Fort Kenney, which had been built on a bluff three years earlier.[44]

The June 16 *Austin City Gazette* lauded the enterprise with a retort to an earlier letter criticizing Lamar and his "unconstitutional expedition": "We advocated [in April of 1840], as we do now the policy of planting the banner of the Lone Star of Texas in the public square of Santa Fe."[45] As if to underscore the Pioneers' commercial nature, a June 17 letter to the editor inquired "whether or not I can get some land located on this trip, as I presume selecting and locating land is the main object of the expedition."[46]

On June 18 the final party of Pioneers—including the Jersey wagon carrying the injured Kendall and Navarro in ill health, Coombs and Hancock in the entourage, Chalmers, and Lamar—headed for Brushy Creek to see the grand enterprise Lamar had anticipated as the star in his presidential crown. He impressed the soldiers at the creek when he sat with them around the evening campfire, cooked his own supper, and slept on a bedroll under the stars with the volunteers.[47] The next day, before he and Chalmers returned to Austin, Lamar delivered a stirring speech, reiterating his charge to the civil commissioners. The expedition's objective was to attach Santa Feans to the Texas system of government; to create in their minds a reverence for the Texas Constitution; and to spread among them a spirit of liberty and independence. The commissioners and the military escort were to conduct themselves with caution and not use military force to accomplish these ends. If successful, as Lamar knew they would be, the commissioners would appoint new leaders for the Santa Fe government with the aid of the military escort.[48] To the rousing cheers of an anxious, excited camp, Lamar championed his cause, McLeod and his fellow officers, and the future of Texas.

Inspired by the dramatic speech of the president, Kendall wrote later that "never since the discovery of America had such a journey been undertaken."[49] If Kendall's statement was laced with hyperbole, it could not have rung truer. The Santa Fe Pioneers prepared to embark on a great journey into a world more mysterious than they knew, in search of a place where an anticipated welcome would not, and could not, ever come. They could not imagine the trials of danger and uncertainty that awaited them, the betrayal and unmitigated failure that would transcend that of other expeditions on the American frontier.

CHAPTER 6

From Brushy Creek to the Brazos River

The Pioneers left Brushy Creek on Sunday, June 20, 1841.[1] "Heaven speed them! Success attend them!" declared the *City Gazette*.[2] But success had already abandoned them in many respects: the deaths of two volunteers; a two-week delay; some early tension between McLeod and several officers, not to mention the soldiers of Company A; a ponderous wagon train; and not a single map of the route among them.

Despite the ominous warnings, excitement for a genuine adventure compelled most to overcome uncertainty on the first days of the trek. Captain Caldwell and his fifty soldiers led the way, followed by the merchant wagons and the Jersey wagon with Kendall and Navarro. The others stretched over the prairie for a mile. The artillery company settled in as the rear guard, lugging the brass cannon, while the other four infantry companies established a rotation for herding the cattle and fatigue duty, clearing obstacles, cutting trails, and setting up camp ahead of the rest. A makeshift band of several musicians accompanied the expedition, playing brightly for the first days of the march at reveille and the evening campfires. "I ordered a parade & the appointment was read to the Troops," McLeod wrote to Lamar. "You Know me well enough Genl, to feel assured that I will carry out your wishes. My heart is full."[3]

The first objective was the crossing at Little River, a march of less than five days due north from Brushy Creek. These first fifty miles or so would be familiar to some frontiersmen, including McLeod, Cooke, and Howard. Cooke had traveled this ground a year earlier to locate frontier posts for defense against Indian attacks; McLeod had traveled as far as Bryant's Station; and Howard told some of the volunteers of his fight with Comanches in the area.[4] The prairie rolled lightly along the route, with creek and river crossings easily traversed. The Pioneers camped at the fork of the San Gabriel River and Opossum Creek on the first two nights of the journey and at Darrs Creek on June 23, leaving them only eleven miles short of Little River. On the morning of June 25, the party crossed Little River and made camp on the north banks. Nearby stood the remains of Fort Griffin, a

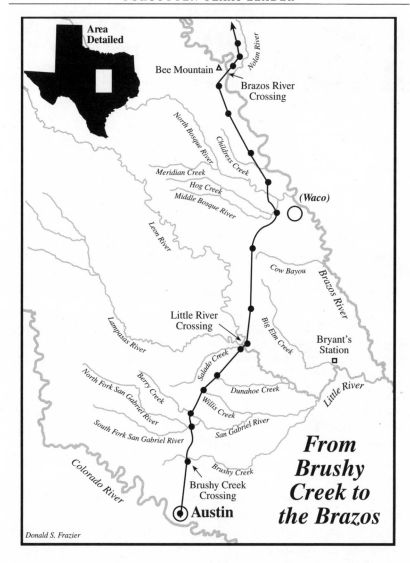

Area Detailed

Bee Mountain △

Nolan River

Brazos River Crossing

North Bosque River

Childress Creek

Meridian Creek

Hog Creek

Middle Bosque River

(Waco)

Leon River

Cow Bayou

Brazos River

Little River Crossing

Big Elm Creek

Bryant's Station

Lampasas River

Salado Creek

Dunahoe Creek

Little River

North Fork San Gabriel River

Berry Creek

Willis Creek

South Fork San Gabriel River

San Gabriel River

Colorado River

Brushy Creek

Brushy Creek Crossing

⊙ Austin

From Brushy Creek to the Brazos

Donald S. Frazier

picket stockade built in 1836 by Maj. George Erath but soon abandoned in favor of a protected settlement several miles downriver.[5]

In spite of an apparent smooth start, several incidents in the first days proved critical to the remainder of the journey. No sooner had the party stopped for their first night's camp on the San Gabriel—named Camp Archer by McLeod—than the commander realized the inadequacy of the wagon train and sent Maj. H. L. Grush, commissioner of subsistence, northeast to Bryant's Station for an additional wagon and oxen.[6] The over-loaded wagons, containing military equipment and merchandise, pulled by six oxen each, were proving slow and dangerously fragile. Breakdowns, expected on such a long trip, had to be minimized, and McLeod wanted to lighten the load as much as possible.

A second event foreshadowing trouble occurred the second day out from Brushy Creek, when bison were spotted to the west. Some Pioneers, especially the younger volunteers and several merchants and correspondents from the East, had never seen the shaggy creatures that roamed by the thousands across central Texas. Kendall indicates in his diary that the designated hunters rode off to bring back meat for the night's supper, but others soon accompanied them, enjoying the thrill of riding over the prairie and giving chase, "notwithstanding orders given the volunteers not to break their double-file ranks."[7] A disciplined military escort would have refrained from such antics unless ordered otherwise, and there is no evidence that McLeod permitted this break in ranks. Each time a soldier broke across the trail, another seemed to get carried away and follow, until dozens had joined in the merriment. Had McLeod maintained adequate control over his soldiers early on, much of the angry sentiment weeks later might have been averted. The moment could not have been lost on military men like Caldwell and Cooke. Some accounts mention that men had gone ahead to a campsite and were found "fishing and shooting alligators" when the others arrived, implying impropriety once more. A lead party instructed to locate a campsite would have been allowed such activities, however, once they had completed their duties.[8]

All of the diaries and later accounts mention a terrible storm that careened through the camp at Opossum Creek, "a tremendous storm of thunder, lightning, and wind, although but little rain fell." The late spring blast carried tents and equipment into the night, and many of the Pioneers "took plain without kiver" until the next morning.[9] The storm proved uncomfortable to Kendall and Navarro's leg injuries. More significantly, the fever that continued to bother McLeod worsened, leaving him barely able to lead the expedition to Little River over the next two days.

On the morning of the fourth day, at Camp Navarro on Darrs Creek, the ailing McLeod called the first court-martial of the expedition. He turned over the recording of the proceedings to 1st Lt. William Henry of Company D, with Captains Lewis and Houghton on the court. Thomas Gates, a Cornishman and private in Company E, had stolen bread from the hospital stores wagon while on fatigue duty. Apart from the bison-hunting, this incident would be the first to test McLeod's capacity as commanding officer. Gates pleaded not guilty to the charge, but he was found guilty by the court and sentenced to a month without pay. Then, in what must have been a surprising decision, Lewis and Houghton recommended a remission of Gates's sentence on the basis "that others of the same party set him the example, and that his disobedience appears to have resulted from an excitement gotten up after he had taken the bread from the wagon." McLeod disapproved of the clemency request and said so in the recordings; nevertheless, he bowed to the court's wishes by remitting half the sentence, "supposing there must have been some good reason for the recommendation." [10]

Setting a precedent for leniency may have seemed appropriate at the time, but it looked like weakness to some of the officers. McLeod's apparent inability to keep the troops under control did not sit well with men like Howard or Cooke, who would later criticize the brigadier general. Subsequent events surrounding Captain Lewis also may have raised questions about who was, in fact, in charge of the expedition. When McLeod had the recordings added to the Order Book two days later at Little River, he wrote a postscript that revealed his frustration and an attempt to regain control. "Hereafter," he ordered, "when the fatigue party is required for duty the officer who commanded it when on guard will turn it out, take charge of it, and see that the work which is necessary to be done is completed." [11] Placing blame on the officers did nothing to enhance McLeod's command of the Pioneers.

At the Little River encampment McLeod again assessed the materials and found them wanting. Kendall wrote later that from the outset the Pioneers had been "obliged to march unprovided with many necessaries," and this glaring truth surfaced in the first week. [12] The initial delays meant that many of the beef cattle were butchered before the expedition left Brushy Creek. Major Howard and Archibald Fitzgerald were sent northeastward to the Falls at the Brazos to purchase more cattle, a delay that necessitated a five-day wait at Little River. After only a few days' march, soldiers and merchants met this delay with grumbling. Only Navarro and Kendall appreciated the extra time to heal.

The delay afforded an opportunity for McLeod, whose fever had worsened in the first night on Little River, to take a brief leave and seek medical care. Bryant's Station was twelve miles downriver. Grush returned with oxen and a wagon that McLeod would ride back to the settlement. With Howard already departed for the Brazos, McLeod assigned Sutton temporary command of the expedition until he or Howard returned. [13] McLeod expected to fill the wagon with supplies before he rejoined the company. Sutton would inform Howard of the situation, and Howard was to resume the march as soon as he returned from the falls, regardless of McLeod's absence. McLeod left camp on June 26.

In the first week of the expedition, problems with discipline, supplies, leadership, and direction were signs of increasing trouble. On the second night at Little River two more incidents began to sour the excitement of the adventure. At about 10 p.m. on June 26, as most of the camp slept, a shot rang out from near the central campfire. E. B. Lockridge, a young lawyer from Louisiana who seemed disconsolate and had kept to himself, apparently upset over bad debts and the realization that the Texas frontier might not refresh his lagging fortunes, shot himself with his rifle.[14] Lockridge's suicide shocked many of the volunteers. Just after midnight, a second shot rang out at the edge of camp. A nervous sentry, not hearing a response to his challenge from a shadowy figure, had fired at—and missed—a Dutch servant to Commissioner Cooke.[15]

On the evening of June 28 Howard returned from the Falls on the Brazos with thirty head of beef.[16] At the time some thought the extra livestock was unnecessary and would only slow down the expedition. The area along the Little River, abundant with deer, javelina, and bison, meant plenty of meat and no shortage of clear, running water. Since most believed the entire journey would be like the first week, any waste of meat was largely ignored by most of the men and the additional duty of herding cattle seemed an unhappy circumstance.

When Howard learned of McLeod's absence, he assumed command and ordered the expedition ready to march the next morning. This was good news to most of the Pioneers, and for the next several days they made slow but steady progress north by northwest, eight miles along the Leon River and seventeen miles to South Cow Bayou, where they spent an extra day—July 1—repairing several of the wagons that were weakening with the heavy load and the rough-cut trail. At the Cow Creek camp, Howard presided over the second court-martial, which found Kentuckian Thomas Glass not guilty of stealing sugar from one of the supply wagons.[17]

Howard also organized the first "spy company" of the expedition, a scout party headed by Caldwell for the general purpose of laying out the trail over land that, after crossing the Brazos upriver—still two weeks away—would be foreign to any of the Pioneers. Since this was also Indian country, Caldwell's volunteers would maintain a vigilant watch for danger.[18] Although Howard had authority, as temporary commander of the Pioneers, to set up the spy company, it was a major affront to McLeod's authority. More than a concern for the safety of the Pioneers, Howard's action reveals growing tensions between the two leaders. Although Howard was only a few months older than McLeod and had no formal military training, his experience on the frontier had toughened him beyond his years. His scorn for McLeod's West Point education may have been exacerbated by what he perceived to be McLeod's weak leadership, evidenced by his illness and delays. Furthermore, if Special Order No. 12, placing the onus for the break-down of discipline on the officers, was at all directed toward Howard, his resentment would surface when the aide-de-camp was in charge. The spy company may have been a test between the two leaders for control of the Pioneers.

As the expedition resumed its march north from the Leon River on July 2, McLeod continued to recuperate at Bryant's Station. Benjamin Franklin Bryant, a forty-one-year-old Georgian who came to Texas in 1834 and fought at San Jacinto two years later, moved out to the edge of the Texas settlements with the Robertson Colony in 1838 and built a stockade not far from the ruins of Fort Griffin. On January 1, 1839, Anadarko Indians under Chief José Maria massacred a family in the vicinity, and Bryant's organized company fought the Anadarkos to a draw two weeks later at the Battle of Morgan's Point. By 1840 Bryant's settlement was a stop on the mail route north of Austin. The fort, on the south bluffs of Little River, afforded a protected stop for travelers and merchants and was soon a station on the stage line.[19]

McLeod received medical treatment at Bryant's Station and, more importantly, plenty of bed rest. But after five days the fever had not abated and he was forced to remain, knowing the Pioneers would be on their way without him. McLeod stayed two weeks, finally pronouncing himself well enough to depart early on July 10. He purchased enough supplies to fill the wagon and several head of beef and headed north along the mail route toward the Falls of the Brazos. He and his small entourage camped at Big Elm Creek on the first night, made Deer Creek the next evening, and pushed themselves up the south banks of the Brazos on July 12. Believing the expedition would be somewhere along the same river by that time, McLeod crossed Steele and Phelps Creeks, riding into the Pioneers' camp that evening.[20] He had been gone sixteen days.

Meanwhile the Pioneers continued toward the Brazos crossing, fording the South Bosque River on July 3 and camping, for the first time, without water. Much of the canteen supplies had been drained during the hot day, and the night proved particularly aggravating. A court-martial sentenced Michael Campbell, a sentry who had fallen asleep on duty, to two weeks of fatigue duty and two days of leading his horse. Even with the first real signs of Indians since Leon River camp, the punishment seemed excessive and may indicate growing discontent.[21]

The Fourth of July brought only tragedy for the tiring men. Samuel Flint, originally from New Hampshire, ingested too many wild berries along the march and died of severe cramps and colic the next day, despite the efforts of Charles Whitaker, the camp physician.[22] Grush's arrival with

the beef cattle did little to assuage many of the men's negative feelings. Another driving thunderstorm left equipment and clothing soaked, and several unwelcome rattlesnakes sought shelter in the night tents.[23]

Crossing the North Bosque proved one of the most difficult obstacles so
far. Thick clusters of trees had to be cut away from the steep banks. In the
July heat, a natural road discovered along a level limestone plateau was a
welcome relief for exhausted volunteers, who had trudged ten miles in
twelve hours to make a five-mile distance across the North Bosque. When
a prankster tied a large tree limb to his horse's tail and caused a massive
stampede of horses, mules, oxen, and cattle through the center of the main
camp, he was lucky not to be strung up on the spot.[24]

The Pioneers made eleven miles on July 6, ten on July 7, and only eleven
over the following two days due to wagon repairs. When a natural campsite near some springs was spotted along the south banks of the Brazos,
whose midsummer waters proved brackish, Howard ordered a two-day
halt for rest and repairs before crossing the big river. Late on the second
day McLeod arrived and resumed command.[25]

At the North Bosque camp the expedition made the first of several critical mistakes identifying the terrain's landmarks. Comanche Peak rises as a
flat-top mountain high above its neighboring hills and has a readily iden-
tifiable v-cut about two-thirds of the way across. Explorers, Indian fighters, and Indians who made their way through this country used the peak
to get their bearings. Reaching Comanche Peak would put the expedition
far enough up the Brazos that they could confidently continue to the forks
of the Trinity and Red Rivers, their midway destination. Following the
Red River due west to the mountains would lead any party right into Santa
Fe, according to previous travelers. The estimated distance of a march from
Austin north to the Red River and west to Santa Fe was six hundred miles.
If Comanche Peak rose up 150 miles north of Austin as supposed, one-
quarter of the trip could be marked.

Caldwell's spy company had spotted what they thought was Comanche
Peak to the west two days earlier, and now, near the confluence of Noland's
River and the Brazos, everyone could see the gray mesa rising up the river.
Crossing the Brazos on July 13, the Pioneers, McLeod, and Grush had renewed confidence that the march was back on track. Every account's entry
broadly recorded the sighting of Comanche Peak "some five miles up the
river." [26]

What they had seen was Bee Mountain, a singular mesa with a similar
flat top miles south of the more prominent Comanche Peak. They had
erred in the distance measured east to west, well as south to north. Bee
Mountain rises south and east of its fellow landmark, and a survey would

show that the Pioneers had just shortened their trip by more than fifty miles—about one week's travel time. This mistake, compounded by what they thought was the Red River two weeks later, would ultimately cost the expedition its very objective—Santa Fe.

Another foreshadowing disaster occurred on July 13 when the expedition was crossing the Brazos. They watched in amazement as a prairie fire engulfed the horizons from south to west to northwest. The swirling winds kept the fire from spreading toward the Pioneers, who stayed near the Brazos banks and only made two more miles that day.[27] The men seemed to dally in the area, making camp on July 15 at Ham Creek, one of the most picturesque campsites of the journey. There, near the Brazos where Noland's River spills in from the north, a limestone ledge hangs over a deep pool and water gushes over the ledge from a spring.

Finally McLeod ordered the march taken up again in earnest. On July 16, the twenty-seventh day of the journey, the Pioneers left the great turn of the Brazos, Kimball Bend, and struck out due north, aiming for the Red River and the march west. They made twelve miles on that day, ten more the next, then six and eleven and so on, never covering quite as much ground as they wished but steadily drawing near what they thought was the halfway point.[28]

None of the eyewitnesses nor later accounts mention the salient moment of the next few days. On July 16 or 17 the volunteers, merchants, chroniclers, soldiers, and teamsters should have seen—off to the northwest and barely discernible at first—a long flat-topped mountain rising above the other hills, with a v-cut two-thirds along its plateau. By July 18 they should have come parallel to it, though nearly forty miles to the east of its base, and by the next day it should have faded behind and to their left. No one would have mistaken the real Comanche Peak, yet no one recorded its sighting. The significance of its absence, no longer a hopeful landmark but a sign of a greater distance yet to go, shocked the Pioneers into an awkward silence. Sam Howland, the guide, and William Hunt, Cooke's surveyor, were forced to recalculate the journey.[29]

On July 18 the pioneers crossed the Clear Fork of the Trinity River, but they erroneously believed they continued along the upper Noland's. One of Caldwell's spies found the skull of a white female on the prairie, "but recently killed."[30] Deep into Comanche country, the wariness increased as each mile passed. Although they made eleven miles the next day, the bumpy plateau was littered with tiny, steep-banked creeks every mile or so that slowed them to a frustrating, exhausting climb and crawl on July 20. Wagons broke down frequently, and the oxen were used for dragging the merchants' supply carts out of mud pits.

Sixty-five discouraging miles past the Brazos crossing, the Pioneers camped at the edge of a deeply forested stand of elm, oak, and black jack, with briars entangled for miles in the woods. To continue north on the designated trail to the Red River would mean cutting and slashing their way through the dense belt of timber and brush. To detour east or west meant days and miles of treacherous hills and valleys. The officers' response was mixed, at best, to the July 21 decision to go into the western Cross Timbers and fight for every inch over the next eight days. But no better alternative presented itself.

The decision would be costly and ill advised. The thick timber belt was only ten miles wide east to west, and a detour to the left would likely have saved the expedition time, energy, and hope, all of which were much needed in the weeks that followed.[31]

CHAPTER 7

West to Camp Resolution

Looking north from the banks of the Clear Fork of the Trinity River, the Pioneers could see vast hills rolling past the horizon. "The growth of timber is principally small, gnarled, post oaks and blackjacks," noted Kendall, "and in many places the traveler will find an almost impenetrable undergrowth of brier and other thorny bushes. Here and there he will also find a small valley where the timber is large and the land rich and fertile, and occasionally a small prairie intervenes; but the general face of the country is broken and hilly, and the soil thin."[1] To have built a home there would have meant a breathtaking landscape in every direction, plenty of fresh, flowing water, and decent land for cattle and horses to roam. But the three hundred men who had endured 175 miles of often torturous travel in the last four weeks saw something far different: an endless series of obstacles between them and the Red River. The volunteers' grumbling increased at every evening campfire. Wagons continued to break down, the oxen had slowed to a crawl, and the growing threat of hostile Indians raised the hackles on every man's back. The officers argued, the guides and spies disagreed at every turn, and at the helm McLeod fumed at the continuing breakdown of discipline.

The expedition, moving in a north-by-northwesterly direction by recommendation of Colonel Cooke and William Hunt, who had been in the area a year earlier, would create a diagonal route through the western Cross Timbers. This turned out to be the longest possible trail they could have cut into the tangled morass of underbrush and forest. Cooke remained confident that his so-called Military Road to the Red River outposts would be crossed in the timbers.[2] His forty-mile miscalculation cost the expedition critical days.

On the morning of July 22 the Pioneers set out through the Cross Timbers, making eight miles the first day and twelve the next, stopping in the dry bottom of the West Fork of the Trinity in the middle of dense woodlands. On the night of July 23 McLeod decided to pause for at least two days to repair wagons and await word from spies sent ahead into the under-

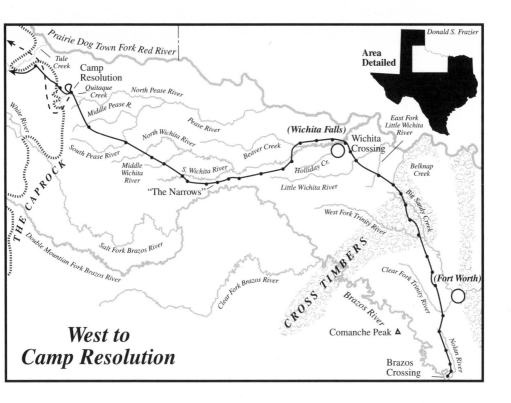

Donald S. Frazier

Area
Detailed

Prairie Dog Town Fork Red River

Tule Creek

Camp Resolution

Quitaque Creek

North Pease River

Middle Pease R.

White River

THE CAPROCK

South Pease River

North Wichita River

Pease River

Middle Wichita River

S. Wichita River

Beaver Creek

(Wichita Falls)

Wichita Crossing

East Fork Little Wichita River

"The Narrows"

Holliday Cr.

Little Wichita River

Belknap Creek

Big Sandy Creek

Salt Fork Brazos River

Double Mountain Fork Brazos River

West Fork Trinity River

Clear Fork Brazos River

CROSS TIMBERS

Brazos River

Clear Fork Trinity River

(Fort Worth)

Comanche Peak ▲

Nolan River

West to
Camp Resolution

Brazos Crossing

brush.[3] While the oxen and horses rested, the companies tended to the business at hand. Weary soldiers grumbled about being lost as they reshoed their mounts, and merchants worked on wagon wheels and reorganized merchandise in the creaking wagons. According to Falconer's calculations, they had traveled two hundred miles and had another four hundred to go.[4] After thirty-three days, still miles from the open prairie and the Red River, this news would hardly have been met with cheers.

On the evening of July 25 McLeod called a consultation that got out of hand; the officers argued about the predicament they were in and how to get out of it. Many placed the blame squarely on McLeod's shoulders, while others, like John Sutton and John Doran, came to McLeod's defense. The primary confrontation seemed to focus on McLeod and Howard, his aide-de-camp. McLeod believed Howard had tried to undermine his authority during his absence, while Howard thought little of McLeod's leadership.[5]

Everyone agreed that the expedition needed to make better time if they were to reach Santa Fe before the desultory days of August, but there was no consensus on how to accomplish this. McLeod believed that lightening the wagons and tightening the ranks would facilitate speed—spies and hunters were as useless as stragglers and wanderers for all the good they had accomplished. The idea of the spy company itself, ordered by Howard without McLeod's permission, was now on the agenda.

The growing distance between freshwater campsites caused frustration among the men, and any report of a water hole or spring tended to cause a chaotic break in the ranks as man and horse raced to quench their thirst. The lack of discipline had to be reined in, McLeod declared.[6] But Howard and others disagreed. The so-called "woodland environment" marching tactics McLeod suggested seemed frivolous at best. The Military Road could not be far away, Howard argued, and a system of double-rank marching orders would slow the expedition further.[7] Without the spy party, Howland and Caldwell insisted, the Pioneers would be blind. Marching into hostile country without proper warning could be fatal. McLeod agreed to the need for scouts but remained troubled by the idea of a company of soldiers out of sight, too far to give or receive help in an Indian attack.

At a secret meeting that evening, someone suggested that McLeod resign his command and turn over the march to Howard, and the demand met with a chorus of agreement.[8] McLeod, confined to his tent with a lingering fever, received a request for resignation in writing. He adamantly refused. By the end of the meeting Howard had offered his resignation as aide-de-camp. He was replaced by Captain Sutton.[9]

The next morning McLeod issued two directives before resuming the march. The first organized a "board of survey" to comb the supply and equipment wagons for items that could be cast off. Of special concern was a load of dried beef in the commissary wagon that Assistant Commissar John Holliday thought was rancid. McLeod's three advocates, William Lewis, Sutton, and W. D. Houghton, began the inspection tour just after dawn.[10]

General Order No. 12, issued the night before, spoke to the angry meeting and the discipline McLeod now announced:

> The attention of the Command is hereby called to the following regulations, which will be rigidly adhered to.
>
> The Quarter Master [Valentine Bennet] will prepare the transportation of the troops immediately after reveille, and report his readiness to march.
>
> No extra or useless baggage of any kind will be allowed in the Company wagons. The Company officers will inspect their wagons and enforce this order.

No firing without orders will be permitted on the march or in Camp. Those wishing to discharge their pieces, will apply to the officer of the day, who will inspect their arms, and give permission, if necessary, to discharge them at guard fire. The officer of the day, the company officers, will be responsible for the execution of this order.

Company officers will prevent all straggling from the ranks of their respective companies.

When water is required from a distance, parties will be sent by detail.

The tent poles, excepting the surgeons, and all useless baggage, will be destroyed to lighten the wagons.

The leading Captain will be particular in observing the proper distance between the wagons and the Companies in front of them, not allowing this distance to exceed one hundred yards. On arriving at Camp the Quarter Master will not discharge his teams until the post of the wagons has been assigned.

McLeod closed the order with as strong a statement as he could: "The foregoing regulations are essential to the security and facility of the march and encampment, and will be rigidly enforced."[11] He sought to establish his authority, perhaps for the first time on the journey.

Whether McLeod's orders could be enforced or would make any difference remained to be seen. Certainly the murmuring discussion that followed McLeod's announcement raised as many questions as answers. The Pioneers stood in the middle of a thick forest, unsure of their surroundings and what awaited them should they emerge. Howland had apparently given up as the expedition's guide,[12] and word of Howard's resignation stirred feelings on both sides. Companies A and B, along with Lewis's artillery unit, seemed willing to support their captains and McLeod, but the other three companies held back for the moment.

After the inspection was complete, the wagons lightened, and the tent poles burned, Caldwell and half his company headed west-northwest through what they judged to be an easier trail. The expedition made ten hard miles that day over brushy hills that disguised treacherous, loose-stoned soil, overturning two supply wagons in the first hours. Gullies appeared every few hundred yards, and steep embankments required laborious digging and cutting.[13] The temperature soared, and no breeze could make its way into the thick timber. The brass cannon got stuck in a dry gulch, and the work to extricate it left Lewis's company well behind the main party. Although Kendall had healed enough to ride his horse, Navarro continued to travel in the Jersey wagon, pulled by two mules and driven by Fitzgerald. For several hours, despite the excruciating pain, Navarro was forced to ride horseback to keep from being flung from the unwieldy wagon. The sighting of an abandoned Indian winter camp to the east did nothing to ease the discontent, nor did it evoke more than a casual glance or brief diary entry.[14] At dark the expedition was in no position to camp and continued well past midnight, having had practically no respite, and no water, since morning. The makeshift camp finally spread without order over several miles of the broken countryside. Most of the men simply stopped where they were and went to sleep on the hard, stony ground. Kendall crawled into the Jersey wagon and "slept hard."[15]

The next day was more of the same, and the lead companies carved only seven miles from the Cross Timbers. The merchant wagons and the artillery company lagged even farther behind. That evening Falconer and fellow Englishman Lt. G. H. Hull calculated the party's position by lunar observation at 97°44′ west longitude by 33°35′ north latitude. This was the first time a precise location had been recorded, and it must have fallen on deaf ears.[16]

The diaries chronicle a growing fear among many of the unproven Pioneers, no doubt exacerbated by the more experienced frontiersmen speaking around the campfire of "seeing the elephant," an old frontier tale that metaphorically signaled one's last hopes before melancholy and desperation set in.[17] Trapped in the interior of the unending woods, bedraggled and sullen and lost, the young men and most of the merchants surely wondered if their days had come to an end. Kendall wrote of these fears, concluding for the first time that the officers had made a mistake.[18]

Once more, and fast upon the heels of the vitriolic officers' meeting, McLeod faced a critical moment. Desertion or mutiny, or both, seemed plausible options during those night hours. On July 28, as the expedition struggled roughly in a forward, northwesterly direction, men disappeared from their companies in search of water or a trail out of the brush. Despite McLeod's sternest efforts, the Pioneers seemed to be disintegrating into a motley pack of individuals, forgetting all discipline and fending for themselves. His command was saved when the lead companies broke out of the Cross Timbers later that day and found themselves staring across a wide open plain, as welcome as a spring-fed pool. The trailing wagons did not emerge until the following day, catching up with the others settled six miles west along the fresh waters of Belknap Creek.[19]

The trek through the Cross Timbers cut less than sixty miles off the journey. One of the surgeons, Dr. Whitaker, turned up missing and did not return for six days, having wandered off at the edge of the wilderness. His survival was nothing short of miraculous.[20]

On July 31 the march resumed. Halfway across that day's more amenable eleven miles, two incidents brought mixed reactions from the Pioneers. The first was the crossing of what seemed to be a man-made trail cut east to west. The Chihuahua Trail had been marked years before by traders moving merchandise between Louisiana and Mexico, but it served no purpose for the Pioneers other than being the first sign of civilization in nearly two weeks. For a mile in every direction around the cut trail, a fire had scorched the prairie.[21]

That evening, as the lead companies camped along the banks of the East Fork of the Trinity, the wagon train still meandered more than a mile behind. The Jersey wagon, driven too hastily by Fitzgerald, with Navarro and Kendall gamely holding on, rumbled at the back of the caravan and just out of sight. Suddenly a bison cow ran alongside the wagon at breakneck speed, startling the three men. Hard upon the backside of the cow rode three Indians giving relentless chase. They were so focused on their prey that they completely ignored the wagon and Navarro's cry of "Los Indios! Los Indios!" Two of the Comanches sped on. As Navarro grabbed for his rifle, the third hunter turned his pony away and rode off toward the southwest. The three Pioneers stared in amazement as the hunt carried forward, over the rise, past the remaining wagon train that lumbered ahead, and straight into the main camp of the expedition. At the edge of the camp the two Indians pulled up, snorted their disgust at the inconvenience of a campsite in their way, and rode off. The bison cow upset men and kettles and coffeepots until Robert Scott fired a round at the charging beast, tumbling it into a dead slump that soon became supper for the disheveled camp.[22] The stories that night seemed more spirited and enjoyable than usual.

August 1 was McLeod's twenty-seventh birthday, a fact that went unannounced. The Pioneers marched northwest for ten miles across the rolling prairies to the Little Wichita River, where they decided to camp, believing they had reached the main branch of the Wichita itself. During the day's more relaxed journey, Howard, still chafing from the confrontation with McLeod in the Cross Timbers, mistook one of his own men, Jim Larrabee, for an Indian and chased him for more than a mile, firing rifle shots that fortunately missed the man, much to the amusement of several scouts who witnessed the scene.[23] That evening in camp the first of a series of courts-martial took place, as Spencer Moffitt of Company E was found guilty of mutinous conduct and gross disobedience and sentenced to two months of fatigue duty and one month without pay.[24] Later a pack of whining half-breed dogs appeared in camp, begging for meat scraps. They would accompany the expedition for many days.[25]

Mistaking the Little Wichita River on August 1 compounded the next two days of travel to the west-northwest, as the expedition believed they were fast approaching the Red River. Ten miles on August 2 and twelve on August 3 brought the Pioneers within view of a majestic belt of timber running east-west along the banks of a wide stream.[26] All assumed it was the valley of the Red River, and the recommendation was to turn west at this juncture rather than dealing with the hundreds of dry gulches and tributaries surely spread along the river's edge. Thus, on August 4, McLeod ordered the companies to veer on a more westerly course for the first time since they had left Austin, keeping the presumed Red River off to the right and a few miles from their new trail.[27] This deeper river valley turned out to be the Wichita and not the Red River, and the error soon proved disastrous.

Later that day the spy company encountered a group of Waco Indians ahead of the expedition. The Wacoes did not seem inclined to give directions, but neither did they pose any threat. Soon the company sighted the Waco village on the banks of the Wichita. Caldwell returned to report the news to McLeod, who ordered the lead companies to scout the village. By the time the soldiers arrived back at the site, the Wacoes had abandoned the area, leaving only the emptied poles of tepees, smoldering campfires, and an array of arrowheads and trinkets that soon became the Pioneers' souvenirs.[28]

That evening two young men, Franklin Coombs, the Kentucky governor's son, and Caldwell's twelve-year-old son Curtis, became lost in the dark. They wandered into the camp just as a heavy rainstorm deluged the expedition, soaking clothing and equipment so thoroughly that most of the men still complained of being wet the next day.[29] Robert Little of Sutton's company was court-martialed that evening for "general disobedience and refusal to observe silence" and lost two months' pay.[30]

McLeod decided to cross over to the north banks of the river on August 5 and work his way as far west as possible. At this moment what seemed to be a gift of providence but later proved one of the most catastrophic incidents of the expedition took place. Juan Carlos, a Mexican trader and a member of Company B, stepped forward to tell the officers that he recognized this area of the Red River, having trapped along this valley many times before. He offered to guide the Pioneers west to San Miguel, which he claimed was "only forty or fifty leagues away."[31] Carlos had worked as a mail carrier before joining the expedition. With little alternative without the original guides, the decision to send the Mexican with the advance scouts gave the party a false, and ultimately deadly, sense of security and optimism.

The Pioneers marched west along the Wichita's north banks for two days, ever in the belief that they looked out over the Red River. On August 7, as the gullies and streams became more numerous and treacherous, they crossed the river again and made eight miles nearly due west. They traveled another six miles the next day along Beaver Creek, leaving behind the rolling prairies for a difficult countryside that broke wagon wheels and scattered horses and cattle. On the western horizon was a mountain range that Carlos assured everyone was in New Mexico.[32] Meanwhile the going got tougher over rocky hills and myriad unnamed creekbeds and mud holes. One night the camp endured another stampede, spending the hours until dawn retrieving oxen and horses.[33]

On August 10 the expedition entered a particularly difficult area of long ridges and precipitous cliffs. Carlos identified these as the narrows of the Red River, the broken land between the Red and Wichita valleys. This meant Santa Fe could be no more than eighty miles away. An old traders' road, replete with broken wagon wheels at one junction just as Carlos had predicted, confirmed the Mexican guide's competence.[34] In fact, the narrows were the broken ridges between the Wichita and the Brazos to its south, and Santa Fe lay nearly four hundred miles to the west.

McLeod was losing control again but did not realize it. In camp that evening he made another attempt to restore discipline to the expedition by court-martialing three more men, including Pvt. Charles White for disobedience and H. B. Sutton for sleeping at his post.[35] Sutton was not even an original volunteer; he had caught up with the expedition at Brushy Creek on his way to Santa Fe from Mobile, Alabama.[36] The sentences were remitted in each case, much to the frustration of McLeod, who sought to make an example of the miscreants. Since he had the officers together for the courts-martial that night, he took the opportunity to discuss the journey's objectives and to map out the next phase of the plan: contact with the authorities in New Mexico. They were only eighty miles from Santa Fe, the commander argued, so an advance greeting party seemed in order. Howland, the original guide, was charged with riding forward to San Miguel to inform citizens of the commissioners' imminent arrival. He would be accompanied by two men from Lewis's artillery company, Alexander Baker and William Rosenberry. They were to take some of the pamphlets for distribution to Santa Feans, as well as formal greetings from Cooke, Brenham, Navarro, and McLeod. They departed camp the next morning.[37] Kendall received permission to accompany them and record the first encounter with Santa Fe, but his pack mule broke down and he was forced to remain in camp.[38] The expectation, of course, was that the journey would only last several days and that a return message could be expected in the next two weeks. The Pioneers would continue on apace along the so-called Red River.

With New Mexico literally around the bend, McLeod could also take care of one of the incidents that had rankled him since his return from Bryant's Station. Special Order No. 15, dated August 11 at Camp Carlos, abolished the spy company and declared that "hereafter no soldier will be allowed to go in advance of the command of the march, except by special permission."[39] There would be no need for a scout troop now that the route was clear and short.

The expedition remained in camp another day to repair the wagons and made twelve miles on August 12 and ten more on August 13. They saw cedar trees for the first time and motts of mesquite along the ridges and valleys. They made camp in midafternoon to search for fresh water. The springs in the area had gushed brackish, copperas water, and the Red River's water was unpalatable.[40] Several soldiers, including Kendall, made their way down a steep embankment to a nearby stream. The prairie grass was high, and the oxen and cattle soon wandered. At one of the merchant campsites, a spark from the dinner fire plunged the entire area into a windswept prairie conflagration, sending men and animals running for their lives. Falconer, attempting unsuccessfully to rescue one of the merchant wagons, was caught in the fire and severely burned. The wagon and an estimated $7,000 of merchandise was lost to the flames, which spread over thousands of acres in minutes. The men could still see the smoke behind them several evenings later.[41] This was the worst disaster to befall the expedition since its start. Although no lives were lost, and miraculously no animals either, the loss of the wagon of merchandise along with bedrolls, clothing, and other articles set the party back and dashed some of the optimism for the journey's end.

But the worst news of the day, and of the expedition, came in a report from Caldwell later in the night. He had ridden out of camp that morning and headed south to scout for Indian signs and fresh water. What he had found, only twelve miles away, was the Brazos River. Over the years traders had reported that two rivers ran red through this wilderness, but the Brazos ran brown like the Colorado and Trinity and the others filled with mineral salts. If the Brazos flowed just to the south of these narrows, then the river they skirted had to be the Wichita.[42]

The camp sat stunned in silence. No one could think of anything to say. Carlos stood off by himself as eyes glared in his direction. Caldwell waited for McLeod to respond, but after several questions about distance and location, the commander stood speechless with the others. If these were the narrows of the Red River, Santa Fe was just over the next mountain range; if not, the men had no idea where they were.

The next morning a shocked, disconsolate, mostly silent expedition marched west through the Brazos-Wichita narrows and camped at the edge of the rough-ridged country near a foul-tasting gypsum spring. The animals and men that yielded to their thirst fought diarrhea and cramps for the next twenty-four hours.[43] Rumors spread of conspiracies against Carlos, some of which might have been carried out were it not for the fact that at dawn on August 15, Carlos and one lone friend were discovered missing.[44] Whether it was worse to have an untrustworthy guide or no guide at all proved moot; the Pioneers were thirsty, exhausted, and completely lost.

McLeod needed a break or he would have his hands full of mutineers. He ordered Caldwell to muster an ad hoc spy company to head north in search of signs of the Red River valley. Caldwell led thirty men into the Wichita Mountains, a range none of these men had ever seen on a map.[45] The rest of the expedition would follow gingerly north. The Pioneers made eight miles that day and eight more on August 16, and then settled in for a five-day wait. Caldwell returned with no news that day and left the next day with fifty men. A scout returned to the main camp three days later with a discouraging report.[46]

In camp, McLeod ordered strict rationing of the available food and water and sent hunters out to shoot deer and antelope in the area. Although bison had been seen in the vicinity, only one was killed and butchered during the five-day camp.[47] On August 17 one of the surgeons, a Dr. Brashear, died of liver failure after several days of illness. He was buried with military honors.[48] McLeod would not give up on the strict operations he still sought to establish. On August 18 a court-martial found teamster J. T. Watkins guilty of disorderly conduct. The hearing was postponed when evidence showed that another man was also involved. That trial was held on August 25.[49]

Meanwhile Caldwell's scouts headed north to the Pease River. Mistaking it for the Red River, Caldwell sent word for the main expedition to meet them along the north-south route.[50] On August 21 McLeod broke camp and led the company ten miles due north to the South Fork of the Wichita, where they met up with Caldwell. Encouraged once more that they could get back on track, the Pioneers marched fifteen miles on August 22, pausing only long enough to shoot prairie dogs in one of the underground burroughs that spread for acres across the open country.[51]

That night six horses were stolen from the edge of one of the campsites, and signs the next morning pointed to Kiowas. Brenham's fine white steed, tied up in the middle of the commissioners' campsite, had been stolen without a single alarm to men who slept only a few feet away. An artillery mule, apparently too stubborn to be led off, was found shot through with a Kiowa arrow.[52] The danger that lurked in the shadows was more serious than an untrustworthy guide or rough, waterless country. The merchants and many volunteers became frightened at every night noise and at any prospect of Indian sightings—another obstacle for the expedition commander.

McLeod finally began to show his true colors as a leader. No longer vacillating or compromising, he seized control of the situation and became the leader the Pioneers desperately needed. He huddled with the officers and spat out orders with confidence and authority. Those who had been enemies fell into line without question. Sutton, Lewis, Doran, and Caldwell proved their value to the expedition every hour of the day. The expedition turned northwest for the mountains, which were actually the caprock of the Llano Estacado. They marched fifteen miles on August 24 and thirty-two more in the next three days.[53] The terrain was level and made for rapid progress. McLeod urged the lead companies on, riding back and forth between the merchants and soldiers, encouraging or shouting or both as the need arose. He sent scouts north and west in search of better trails or a sign of Howland's party. At night the Kiowas harassed the campsites, stealing horses and supplies, and McLeod reenforced the sentry duty to minimize the damage. Several men wandered off despite the commander's best efforts to keep everyone in order, and most of them never returned.

In the afternoon of August 28 McLeod ordered a halt at a creek whose waters flowed abundantly out of the caprock off to the west.[54] Men and animals quenched their thirst, and freshly killed meat provided what diarists later declared the best meal of the journey. Scouts went looking for a safe ascent onto the caprock; guards watched for Indians. McLeod led the wagon train twelve miles north the next day in search of a westward trail; finding none, they returned to the campsite on the Quintufue, known today as Los Lingos Creek, a tributary of the North Pease where it is in confluence with Quitaque Creek.[55] McLeod chose to call a council meeting with the officers. While soldiers rested and merchants repaired wagons for the last leg to the Llano Estacado and New Mexico, McLeod resolved to get the commissioners to Santa Fe. On August 30 he named the Quintufue site Camp Resolution.

CHAPTER 8

Camp Resolution to Santa Fe

The Pioneers marched for seventy days to the Quitaque, covered more than 350 miles of mostly unmapped territory, endured the harsh summer weather and unforgiving terrain, and fought among themselves more than against any Indians. Now they stared up from the eastern base of Coronado's Staked Plains, knowing that somewhere on the other side lay the objective they had volunteered for a lifetime ago. A dozen men had been lost, and others had died from various ailments along the route. Three had been sent ahead to greet the people of New Mexico but sent no word back. Admittedly lost since leaving the Waco village four weeks earlier, the officers resolved to salvage the expedition by any means necessary. McLeod had taken control of the deteriorating situation and seemed more determined than ever to lead the Pioneers to their destination.

To that end, McLeod sent scouting parties north and south to ascertain the territory as the party prepared for the last leg of the journey to the Rio Grande. Captain Caldwell continued to scout the north horizon, while Captain Strain and members of Company E looked for additional freshwater springs in the vicinity. Both parties left the main camp on August 28; two days later, both scouting companies remained away without report.[1]

At dawn on August 30, Lt. John Hand of the artillery company led ten men northeast in search of food, while George Hull, James Dunn, Francis Woodson, Sam Flenner, and William Mabee headed for a stand of trees less than half a mile from the main campfires. The groups had been gone for less than two hours when a volley of shots echoed across the prairie. McLeod shouted the alarm and mounted his horse, heading over the rise before many realized what was happening. Fifty men soon joined the race toward the foreboding sounds.

McLeod saw a large band of Kiowas riding away from the scene, yelling over their shoulders and firing off a last round from their rifles. When he rode to the edge of the mott of trees, he saw the results of the noise. Five Pioneers lay dead in a variety of grotesque positions. George Hull, the only son of the esteemed British soldier Maj. Gen. Trevor Hull, had been mu-

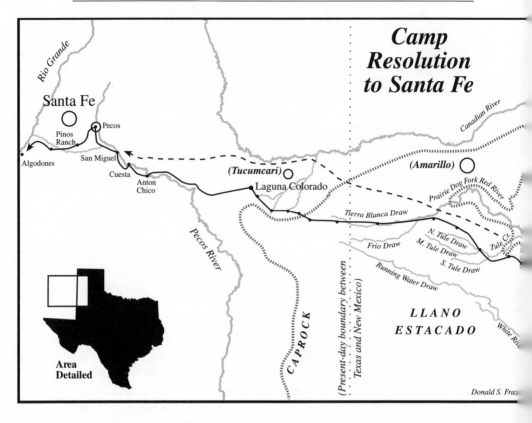

Camp Resolution to Santa Fe

Santa Fe

Pecos

Pinos Ranch

Algodones

San Miguel

Cuesta

Anton Chico

Rio Grande

(Tucumcari)

Laguna Colorado

(Amarillo)

Canadian River

Prairie Dog Fork Red River

Tierra Blanca Draw

Frio Draw

N. Tule Draw

M. Tule Draw

S. Tule Draw

Tule Cr.

Pecos River

Running Water Draw

LLANO ESTACADO

CAPROCK

(Present-day boundary between Texas and New Mexico)

White Riv

Area Detailed

Donald S. Fra

tilated with more than thirty lance wounds and arrows. Dunn, Flenner, and Woodson had been scalped and partially stripped, and Mabee's skull was crushed. Mabee's heart had been carved from his chest, and he still held the broken butt of his rifle.[2] The fight had been brief and torrid. Apparently the Kiowas had been waiting in the trees when the men walked into the early morning trap. Rifles and revolvers lay empty on the ground, along with the bodies of several Indians, including the great warrior Sloping Hair (Adhalabakia).[3]

McLeod barked orders to the men who arrived on the scene and led a pursuit of the Kiowa band. For the next two hours the soldiers rode over several rises, occasionally spotting the estimated one hundred Indians when the attackers paused and turned, as if preparing for battle. Each time, however, they raced away. Several Pioneers noticed that some of the Indian ponies carried the bodies of warriors killed in the dawn fight. As the chase wore on, the Indians' mounts seemed more resilient, and finally McLeod ordered an end to the pursuit.

The five dead soldiers were buried with military honors near their last stand. Strain and Hand returned without news. Tragically, three more soldiers went missing and were never heard from.[4] In late afternoon McLeod called a council of officers to assess the situation. The meeting lasted into the evening, until only two choices presented themselves: destroy the wagons and merchandise and return east, or divide the expedition and send a cavalry party quick-marching over the caprock for help from New Mexico.[5] Most of the merchants and many of the half-starved, thirsty volunteers would have voted to abandon the enterprise in favor of survival and retreat. In several days the expedition could reach the upper Brazos and follow its increasingly familiar course down to the Falls settlements, an estimated three-week trek. More importantly, the likelihood of continuing attacks by Kiowas would diminish as the Pioneers retreated eastward, although the territory was Comanche country—no easy obstacle to overcome.

On the other hand, dividing the expedition in half went against everyone's better judgment. Frontiersman and West Pointer could agree that the division would weaken the companies' ability to defend themselves. The party that went forward would have to include the healthiest men and horses, for the ride would be fast paced over unfriendly terrain. The weaker soldiers, merchants, and volunteers would have to sit tight in the Quitaque camp and fend off the summer heat and dry conditions, as well as probable Indian attacks. The estimate of five days' rations, even if all of it were left at Camp Resolution, was not enough to hold them until help arrived. Hunting and foraging parties would have to be more successful than they had, hardly an optimistic possibility.[6] Strain and Hand's report did not encourage anyone.

McLeod made the decision late that night. He would send an advance cavalry of one hundred men into New Mexico; there would be no retreat. The cavalry commanding officer, Captain Sutton, would be accompanied by artillery Captain Lewis, Lieutenants Lubbock, Munson, and Brown, and adjutant Theodore Sevey. Colonel Cooke would act as the spokesman when they reached the first settlements. Also going ahead would be Howard and Howland; civil commissioner Brenham and his secretary, George Van Ness; Archibald Fitzgerald; and young Franklin Coombs. Cooke's surveyor, William Hunt, would act as guide. Two of the expedition diarists, Kendall and Grover, went with the advance party, and Falconer and Gallagher remained at Camp Resolution. In addition to the officers and official expedition representatives, eighty-five of the best cavalrymen and healthiest merchants swelled the party to ninety-nine.[7] All of the wagons and merchandise, of course, and the meager livestock would be left in camp.

On the morning of August 31, McLeod issued the orders to the entire camp, gave a brief speech about bravery and confidence and the success of the mission against all odds, and sent the Sutton-Cooke party on. "Comrades," McLeod began,

> Our march through a wilderness hitherto unknown, except to the savages, has never been surpassed, and perhaps seldom equalled in military annals by the obstacles you have encountered, and the courage with which you have surmounted them. The rugged steeps and yawning chasms over which you have toiled, and constructed roads; and the fortitude and energy you have displayed, under the most adverse circumstances, extort the warmest thanks of your commanding officer, and merit the gratitude of your country.
>
> A period has arrived which calls for a higher sacrifice and bolder execution. Our situation is known to you all. We are hemmed in by mountains and ravines. Our subsistence is reduced to a few beeves, without coffee, bread, or scarcely salt. The teams employed in the transportation of the merchant goods . . . are jaded and worn down, and to increase our annoyance our hunting parties . . . are overwhelmed by hundreds of Comanches.
>
> To continue our march under such circumstances, would only prolong our difficulties for a few days. And to abandon the property of the merchants would be a violation of our faith and honor.

After delineating the separation into two parties, with Cooke accompanying the advance party, McLeod concluded, "If necessary, we [who remain behind] must subsist on our [oxen] teams, but I hope we will endure with cheerfulness privations which are unavoidable, realize the hopes of friends, and disappoint the malice of enemies, and redeem of our pledged honor, to surmount privations, toil and danger, by marching successfully to our claimed territory of Santa Fe."[8]

The cavalry made eight miles that day and camped at the Llano River in preparation to ascend the Llano Estacado. Still on the Quitaque with McLeod were Caldwell, Houghton, Hudson, Strain, Hand, and Bennet. Navarro also stayed behind with the remaining Pioneers, who numbered about one hundred eighty-five.

Sutton led the advance party onto the caprock on September 1 and struck out on a northwesterly course to intercept the Red River seventy miles away. They halted prematurely when they could not cross Quitaque Canyon and had detoured around it by midday. On September 3 they reached Tule Canyon, taking a full day to descend to the stream and up the other side; they made thirty miles on September 4 and again on September 5. They killed antelope and bison on the run, paused briefly at dry camps, and crossed the caprock west of Palo Duro Canyon, descending the high flat plains on September 7. Continuing northwest, the cavalry made the Canadian River on September 9, following a wagon-rutted trail west that soon gave out in the sands of New Mexico.[9] They had traveled more than two hundred miles in nine days and were wracked by hunger, thirst, and utter exhaustion. The weather had alternated between excessive heat and squalling thunderstorms. Two men wandered off and disappeared, and sleep deprivation brought on renewed grumbling against Sutton, who mustered his remaining energy to keep order.

The party spotted the mountains of San Miguel on September 9, and three days later they arrived at a Mexican campsite at the west end of the Angosturos, or narrows, of the Canadian River. Howard paid three of the traders to return with his servant, Matias, and act as guides for the men at Camp Resolution. On September 13 Howard, Lewis, Fitzgerald, Van Ness, and Kendall went ahead of the cavalry to arrange for reception of the expedition with the Mexican authorities.[10] In the village of Anton Chico it became clear that the reception would be less than cordial, as the villagers seemed terrified of the Texans. Conversation made it obvious that the Mexican authorities had warned the people that the Texas army would brutalize them. Unable to convince the villagers otherwise, the five men rode north toward San Miguel. On the outskirts of the hamlet of Cuesta a contingent of Mexican troops under the command of Capt. Dámaso Salazar forced them to surrender their arms and mounts.[11]

Two days later Sutton's party left the camp on the Gallinas River and rode toward Anton Chico, expecting to find preparations well in hand. Instead they faced Salazar and a force of four hundred soldiers. Sutton sent three men with a Mexican interpreter into the village to negotiate with Salazar. Salazar told the men that New Mexico's Gov. Manuel Armijo marched with four thousand soldiers only a day away and that it was useless for the Texans to resist. Then, to the messengers' surprise, Captain Lewis rode up with the Mexican troops, speaking in Spanish to Salazar and announcing his intentions to help with the negotiations.

Lewis rode out to report the conversation to Sutton and Cooke and told them he believed Salazar's intentions were honorable and precautionary only. But the officers became wary of the mixed invitation, and a heated debate ensued as they sat on horseback, staring at the Mexican troops beginning to flank them. Lewis insisted that Salazar had promised a trade negotiation once their arms were turned over; Lubbock, Munson, and Sutton considered making a break to the rear in hopes of returning to the main body in time to warn them of the impending danger. Sutton had spotted a flock of some seventeen thousand sheep near the lake: if some of those could be secured to feed the men, an escape seemed plausible and better than the alternative.

Strangely, Lewis turned his mount and rode back to Salazar, causing several to wonder aloud if other promises had been made to turn Lewis traitor. Cooke, a fellow Mason to Lewis, offered to speak privately with him and ascertain the truth according to the brotherhood. Cooke rode out from the main party and motioned for Lewis to meet him alone. The two spoke for several minutes, and, while Lewis maintained his position, Cooke rode back to Sutton, reporting that he believed Lewis and that their surrender of arms to Salazar would only be a sign of peace, nothing more. Sutton reluctantly agreed.

The Texans dropped their rifles and pistols to the ground, and Salazar rode up to Sutton. "You are our prisoners," he declared, loud enough for all to hear. As the Texans glared at him, Lewis without expression turned and rode behind the Mexican lines. Cooke filled the air with epithets of anger and embarrassment. Lewis did not reply.[12] The ninety-two Pioneers were prisoners of Mexico.

Two hundred miles to the southeast of Anton Chico, across the Llano Estacado and down into the Quitaque valley, the Pioneers at Camp Resolution watched as the advance unit rode away on August 31. McLeod ordered the camp moved less than a mile up the creek, closer to the caprock base, at a bend that seemed more defensible against Kiowa attacks. The merchants and teamsters arranged the wagons into a large square as a stockade around the outside of the camp, with the horses, oxen, mules, and cattle inside the enclosure. At night the men slept just outside the wagons; everyone had become a sentry.[13]

On September 1 McLeod organized a court-martial at 11 a.m. to try Pvt. C. C. Willis for stealing meat from a supply wagon the morning before. Caldwell and Lts. William Nelson Henry and Volney Ostrander served on the court and found Willis not guilty.[14] The trial may have been McLeod's attempt to reassert discipline and order. That night, during a torrential, cold rain, despite efforts to guard the camp, Indians stole Caldwell's horse. The next morning two men who had wandered off in search of water and had been presumed lost turned up no worse for the wear. They reported seeing signs of Kiowas but nothing more.[15] Nevertheless McLeod decided to move the camp still farther up the creek.

Striving to maintain some semblance of military order, McLeod ordered a drill exercise for the afternoon of September 3. This met with a rousing objection from the men, who hollered, "Beef! Not drills!" Caldwell, representing some of the men in a discussion with McLeod, argued the need to conserve energy, whereas McLeod saw the need for a well-defined response in the case of an emergency. McLeod relented but insisted his officers arrest any man who hollered in defiance of an order again.[16]

It rained heavily again that night and the next morning. McLeod ordered the livestock moved into the prairie grass just off the south banks of the river toward a gentle rise. About two hours after dawn, the alarm was sounded by a sentry who spotted Indians on the hillock. Shouting and firing rifles, the Kiowa warriors drove the livestock into a wild stampede at the center of camp. Breaking off just out of range of fire, the Indians circled around and across the creek as the stampede continued unchecked. The wagons on the south line of the square proved no match for the cattle and oxen bearing down. Men dove for cover or for horses, and others loaded rifles for the pending Indian assault. Many horses broke their tethers in the mad rush and joined the stampede as it cut through the camp, scattering bedrolls and crushing equipment, and drove across the creek and off to the north. The Kiowas raced to the edge of the roiling herd and began to steer them away from the camp. A Mexican servant named Ramón dashed across the creek to grab the reins of his horse and was killed and scalped in a matter of seconds.

Above the din, McLeod shouted orders and mounted his horse to give chase, riding ahead of the others in pursuit of livestock and Indians. Several dozen riders joined him, and all of the cattle and oxen were soon back in the fold. One of the pack mules had been lanced, and eighty-three horses stolen. The camp had been decimated, and six dozen men were left on foot.[17]

The next day McLeod ordered the camp moved another mile up the creek, onto a higher, level plain with a better view of oncoming enemies. The cattle could be set on a nearby prairie under better security. Seven oxen were butchered for camp meat, leaving few more than that alive for the journey over the caprock.[18] Merchandise in the wagons that continued would be carefully selected. The next few days passed uneventfully at the resettled Camp Resolution. A norther blew through, and it rained intermittently day and night as the temperature dropped. The half-breed dogs made good sentries, growling or barking in the night whenever the Indians crept too close. McLeod held two courts-martial on September 8; Pvt. E. C. Westgate was found guilty of leaving his post on September 5, and John Hamrich was found guilty of negligence.[19] This brought the court-martial hearings to seventeen.

On the night of September 10, Paymaster Benjamin Sturgess, a native

Georgian, died from a consumptive ailment. The camp buried him with military honors the next morning, and McLeod spoke of Sturgess as "an honorable man, faithful in his engagements, and high-minded even in his quarrels."[20] Two more Pioneers died on September 12 when Indians trapped them during a forage away from camp. One of the men managed to escape and ride into the camp to sound the alarm. He was followed by the bloodied and dying Thomas Glass, who had managed to mount his horse after being lanced and scalped. The third man's body was found on the prairie.[21]

The camp was being driven to despair, and McLeod knew it. That evening he told his officers that they would wait one more week, until September 20, for word from the Sutton-Cooke party. If they still had no word, Caldwell would return to Texas to gather a rescue party. McLeod remarked that most of the men would likely volunteer to accompany Caldwell.[22] For three days, the Pioneers waited. Indians harassed the sentries every night, wounding one man. Another man was pierced through the arm by a misdirected shot in camp, the bullet whistling past McLeod's ear. The temperature continued to drop.[23]

Finally, on September 15 Matias and the three Mexican traders rode into Camp Resolution, much to the Pioneers' relief and delight. One offered a letter to McLeod from Cooke, who explained the situation and advised McLeod to hurry to San Miguel, abandoning all but the sturdiest wagons and whatever supplies might be held therein: "Dear Mac, I send you guides—come on—all is going right—I shall be in the settlements in a few days and send you help."[24] The messengers' five-day trip across the Llano could be retraced in no more than an extra day or two under these conditions. The trader told McLeod that he thought the Pioneers had managed to take the longest route possible to Santa Fe—for no reason that he understood. The Pioneers spent the remaining hours consolidating and packing for the last leg of the trip.

After twenty days on Quitaque Creek, the Pioneers abandoned Camp Resolution on September 18. They made four miles north-northwest along the escarpment to their left that day and began to ascend the rugged 400-foot side of the caprock the next day. They reached the grand prairie after a great struggle with the wagons and traveled fifteen more miles on September 20.[25]

For the next eight days the party moved steadily over the high plateau making anywhere from fifteen to twenty miles a day despite the biting wind. McLeod sent Caldwell ahead to make contact with Sutton and Cooke. Fear of Indian attacks diminished with each passing day, although on September 23 three men left camp in search of water and were never heard from again. The next day Matias pointed to a spot where he had spoken with a band of Indians the week before. By September 26 some of the men began to wonder aloud if they were lost again, as the area was particularly desolate above the Tierra Blanca. The guides turned the party west at an abandoned Mexican campsite, and on September 28 they pointed out the western edge of the caprock ahead. The Pioneers managed the steep descent off the Llano without incident and camped at watering holes that night and the next. They made only five miles on September 30, for it seemed that the Mexican traders grew nervous as they approached the territory guarded by Salazar and Armijo. McLeod moved ahead with some of the company, leaving Houghton with the wagons and the others half a day behind.[26]

On October 2, with no word from Sutton or Cooke—or Caldwell for that matter—McLeod's party halted for a day and another night. The commander sent Lieutenant Burgess and four others, including Matias, ahead to scout the area but instructed them not to go into San Miguel. On October 3 McLeod left the Arroyo de Monte Revuelto area and rode ten miles west-northwest to the head of Tucumcari Creek near the Canadian River.[27] His Mexican guides were useless with nervousness, but McLeod refused to believe that the lead parties would not have warned him of a dire emergency. That evening, however, sentries reported mounted figures on the rise to the west—Mexican soldiers, perhaps.

On October 4 McLeod's party came within sight of the Laguna Colorada and made a midday camp in a dry lake bed filled with dead cedar limbs. Two Mexican soldiers rode into the camp soon after with letters of introduction from Col. Juan Andres Archuleta and requested that the Texans surrender their arms as a sign of peaceful intent. McLeod refused. He ordered the party to break camp and set up a protected position alongside the lake itself. He sent word to Archuleta that he would see him that evening. After establishing the camp and ordering everyone on full alert, McLeod, accompanied by Navarro, Whitaker, and a Mexican servant, rode to Archuleta's military tent around the edge of the Laguna Colorada. The conversation was brief and polite. McLeod assured the Mexican officer that he would deliver a decision to him by 9 a.m. the next day.[28]

The debate at the Texan camp lasted until midnight. McLeod wanted to make a stand, but he could count on no more than seventy men who were physically able to join him. If they could hold off the Mexican demands for a day or two, perhaps Caldwell or Sutton would arrive as reinforcements. Admittedly, a retreat was out of the question. The odds were formidable but not impossible. Most of the Pioneers lay exhausted or ill with scurvy and malnutrition, wearied from a journey in its 106th day.

Archuleta promised that the Texans would be treated fairly and would be well fed upon surrendering their arms and ammunition. They would be escorted to San Miguel to meet with representatives of Governor Armijo's government, and negotiations for the commencement of trading could begin soon after.

McLeod's response to a merchant's argument for surrender as a way not "to defeat the trading objects of the expedition" revealed both the alternative objectives of the expedition and McLeod's frustration over what he saw as the only realistic choice. "I did not come here," he said sharply, "with any such picayune objects." [29] To surrender to the Mexican army without a fight was unconscionable. But what alternative, other than the party's complete annihilation, did McLeod have?

At midmorning on October 5 McLeod signed an agreement with Archuleta to lay down his arms before the Mexican army, with clear provisions for the safety and security of the men under his command, especially Navarro.[30] The surrender was complete by noon, and the Santa Fe expedition was no more.

CHAPTER 9

Failure of the Expedition

In his later recollections of the Santa Fe expedition, Kendall outlined the principal factors he believed had led to the failed enterprise. First, he argued, "the expedition began its march too late in the season by at least six weeks. Had it left Austin on the 1st of May, the grass would have been much better, and we would have had little difficulty in finding good water both for ourselves and cattle."[1] Indeed, the delay from the very beginning made success unlikely. But a May 1 departure date was not a possibility because of the flooding rivers that coursed across central Texas in late spring. Without bridges or ferries, fording the spring-flooded Brazos or Trinity River could be a fatal mistake. Kendall correctly noted the opportunity to move across the wilderness after the rivers subsided and before midsummer heat destroyed the prairie grasses if the expedition left nearer its original date, June 1.

"In the second place," Kendall wrote, "we were disappointed in [not] obtaining a party of Lipan Indians as guides." He presumed that with Indian guides the expedition might have cut off up to three hundred miles of unnecessary travel and might have detoured past "many places extremely difficult to travel."[2] The Lipans were effective, largely trustworthy guides for large companies of traders traveling in unknown territory. They had proved their worth to men like McLeod, Howard, and Caldwell, tracking down the Comanches along the Colorado and San Sabá valleys in 1840.[3] The reason the Pioneers chose not to use Lipan guides, or why the Lipans may have refused, is not known.

Speculation, however, centers on these two factors. First, the route to the Red River would not be any easier with Lipans on point. Cooke's Military Road, blazed a year earlier out of Austin, required no more than a march due north from the capital to Coffee's Station, a journey of 250 miles and three weeks. At the Red River the party would simply follow its course west to the mountains of New Mexico and then from village to village to Santa Fe. The expedition assumed that a welcoming party of New Mexicans would meet them on the prairies, ensuring a smooth last leg. Indian

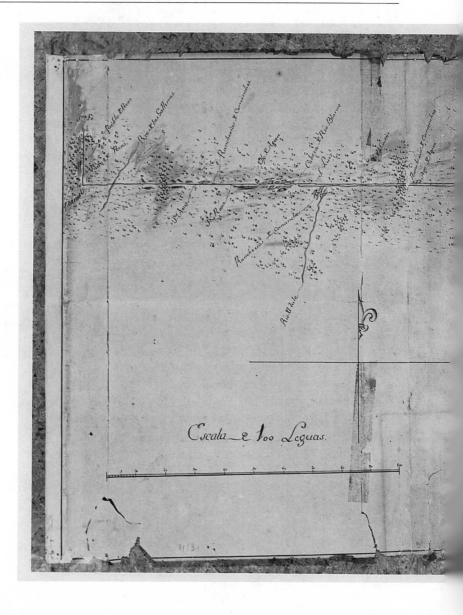

guides may have seemed an extravagance. Additionally, the Lipans may have refused to guide the expedition for any price. Chasing Comanches was a high risk for the tribe, and traveling into Kiowa country only increased the danger.[4] After the failed expedition, Navarro criticized the officers for failing to employ Indian guides, believing the end would have

94

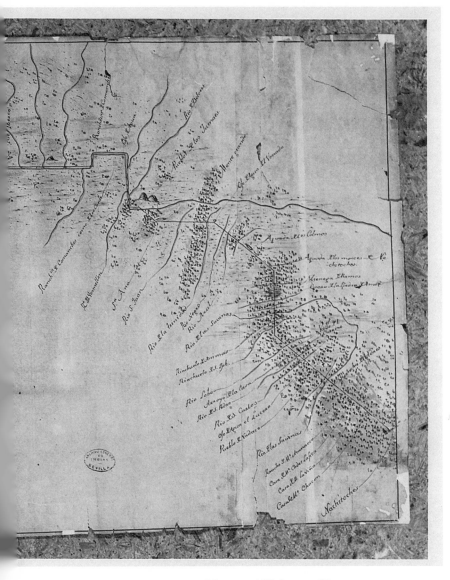

1788 Mares and Vial map of Texas.
COURTESY TEXAS STATE LIBRARY & ARCHIVES COMMISSION.

been different.[5] This appears unlikely, except for the possibility that the party would have recognized the Red River. Even so, the assurances of Carlos and the spy company probably would have carried the day.

Kendall blamed Lamar for not furnishing "wagons and oxen enough to transport the goods of the merchants . . . causing tedious delays."[6] There can be little argument that the wagon train's breakdowns slowed the Pioneers to a crawl. Adding more wagons and oxen to the caravan, however, would not have eased the situation. Even lightly loaded merchandise wagons broke down on six-hundred-mile trips across the uneven terrain of West Texas. Crossing the gullies beyond the Brazos, fending off the rocky soil of the Cross Timbers, and managing the Brazos-Wichita narrows and the caprock escarpment would have damaged the newest, sturdiest carts available. The slow-paced oxen, necessary for such an endurance test, fulfilled the highest expectations of the teamsters who drove them. At least two oxen continued on part of the prisoners' journey into Mexico.[7] More and lighter wagons, perhaps led by mule train, might have made better time across the prairies and flatlands, but the difficulties during the harder times would have negated that progress.

Kendall argues that the lack of sufficient beef cattle for the Pioneers' rations, including the supply Grush brought, was another factor in the failure. Lack of food left the men "weakened, dispirited, and unfit for duty" before the larger contingent of Mexican soldiers.[8] Butchering cattle during the initial delay appears to have been solved by adding to the herd later. But, as Kendall notes, the "improvident waste of provisions while in the buffalo range" kept the rations at a minimum for the remaining journey.[9]

Certainly the commanding officers' and the commissary's failure to place an early limit on the men's food intake led to later disaster. Again, the estimated six-week journey would be across land plentiful with deer, antelope, fish-clogged rivers, and even bison—Indian food that was not on a Texan's menu except in dire circumstance. Seventy head of beef should have been sufficient, and the thirty head added the second week appeared to be an abundance of meat.[10] The responsibility of herding a larger livestock supply, along with the horses, mules, and oxen teams, would have slowed the march further.

The food supply must be connected, in Kendall's evaluation, to the final awareness that "the distance [of the march] was vastly greater than we had anticipated in our widest and wildest calculations."[11] With the backtracking and wandering, the expedition had miscalculated the march to Santa Fe by nearly one-third. Original plans calculated a 250-mile journey to the Red River, which was fairly accurate. The 350 miles west to the upper Rio Grande turned out to be a fabrication of optimistic ignorance. Even the best route—north and then west—would have placed the distance from Austin to Santa Fe closer to seven hundred miles. Adding the one hundred miles between the Waco village and the Quitaque camp, plus minor wanderings in the Cross Timbers and along the escarpment, brought the mileage closer to eight hundred.

At twenty miles a day, an unreasonable prospect, the journey could have been accomplished in the original six-week objective. At fifteen miles a day, still an optimum expectation, the wanderings might have added another two weeks. In fact, the 107 days between Brushy Creek and the Laguna Colorada totaled exactly twice the projected time. There can be little argument that Kendall's assessment of this factor is correct.

Kendall's argument that the Indians' continued harassment "annoyed us much" is in keeping with the expedition's initial expectations.[12] McLeod had five companies of infantry and cavalry and an artillery company with a brass six-pounder—all of which alludes to the prospect of trouble. The significant challenge of unknown territory, surely inhabited by Indians, was not ignored. In fact, delays due to Indian attacks were relatively minimal. The August 30 massacre and the campsite stampede six days later proved the only critical confrontations. Certainly the deaths of at least two dozen men to Indian attacks at the march's perimeter cannot be taken lightly, although most of these men had wandered off in search of food or water, or as deserters. No significant delays can be blamed on Indian harassment.

"Finally," Kendall noted, "the character of the governor of New Mexico was far from being understood, and his power was underrated by all."[13] Governor Armijo had been apprised of the march as early as July and in fact had plotted the response to such a foray fully two years earlier.[14] He had no interest in allowing the province to fall under Texas' commercial, political, or military control and made plans accordingly. When he received reports of the Texas merchants' pending arrival, he called out his troops, including nearby military support, and spread the news of the approaching danger. News of an assault by the Texas army, along with deliberate rumors of the atrocities against the women and children of the Rio Grande villages, spread abject fear across New Mexico.[15] No wonder the people of Anton Chico and Cuesta had such a terrified response when the Pioneers tried to greet them—and no small matter the sight of these grizzled, half-starved, filthy figures.

Kendall says the division of the parties into smaller, less defensible groups, "broken down by long marches and want of food," and Lewis's betrayal made Armijo's "course plain and his conquest easy. Far different would have been the result had the expedition reached the confines of New Mexico a month earlier, and in a body. Then, with fresh horses, and a sufficiency of provisions for the men, the feelings of the inhabitants could have been ascertained; the proclamations of General Lamar would have been distributed among them; the people would have had an opportunity to come over to Texas without fear, and the feeble opposition Armijo could have made . . . could have been put down with ease. Fate decreed otherwise, and by a series of unforeseen and unfortunate circumstances the expedition was thrown into [Armijo's] hands."[16] Thus did Kendall summarize the factors leading to disaster, notably exonerating McLeod and the officers, with the exception of their decision to divide the parties on the journey's last leg.

Although contemporary accounts referred to the expedition as an "ill-starred and foolish enterprise"[17] and "a wild goose campaign,"[18] a later evaluation addressed other factors that may have led to failure. First and foremost, "the immensity of the task which had been undertaken largely explains its failure."[19] The high expectation of establishing trade and a trade route between Austin and Santa Fe, as well as the geographic challenges of such a task, proved insurmountable. The political ramifications of Texans marching into Mexico, against whom they had recently struggled for independence, was neglected by the Lamar administration but not by Santa Anna. Only five years after San Jacinto, and without Mexico's official recognition of Texas, any overt movement was at best ill advised and at worst an invasion by a revolutionary state.

Archrival Sam Houston later agreed that Lamar's vision was more practical than many gave him credit for. In a speech on the U.S. Senate floor, Houston declared that "had orders been given differently, and had the expedition been placed under sagacious and wise leaders [as opposed to McLeod], they would have possessed themselves of the country." A scholar of the next generation added a succinct evaluation: "Lack of success has often damned a great concept."[20] Taking these and later evaluations into account, then, along with the individual perspectives that surfaced afterward, three critical factors emerge.

First, the disingenuously mixed objectives of the Santa Fe Pioneers sabotaged the outcome from the beginning. On the surface, Lamar's objective of a commercial tie between Texas and New Mexico bespoke his expansionist ideals for an economic network to rival the United States and Mexico and span the continent to the Pacific Ocean. His announcement of the expedition for trade relations and the call for civil commissioners was more than just a front, but it did not constitute the whole objective. Information from men such as Dryden and Park, plus Lamar's desire to expand the Republic to the southwest territories, made it easy for him to believe what he wanted to. He could not be dissuaded by Congress or political allies from the idea that the people of the upper Rio Grande wanted to be a part of the Texas dream.

Too many times Lamar and others in his administration considered Santa Fe's conquest a realistic objective, with or without the commercial benefit. If Santa Feans lived in subjugation and fear of Armijo's reputed tyranny, all the more need to liberate them. The additional rationale—that the upper Rio Grande lay too far from the seat of Mexican government for any sense of continuity or profound allegiance—only underscored Lamar's wish to be Santa Fe's deliverer.[21]

The makeup of the expedition dashed Lamar's hopes of conquest under the banner of commercial alliance. If he sent a thousand soldiers to Mexico with a handful of merchants, his ulterior motive would be obvious. On the other hand, a small party of representative merchants might be swallowed in obscurity and ignored by the people hungry for release from Armijo's oppression. How could Lamar appropriate the moment and proclaim his economic intentions clearly, taking into consideration that a show of force would preclude the need for war in New Mexico? How could he gain Santa Feans' support without alarming Mexico City? The questions were compounded by the fact that Mexico would be anything but surprised by a Texas or U.S. invasion. Although one newspaper in northern Mexico had already decried "the insolent pretensions of our perverse neighbors, new Carthaginians, defenders of slavery and worshipers of silver," most of the Mexican press assumed some future, if not imminent, attack and remained silent about the expedition during and after its trek.

Lamar's solution to a cautious yet clarion approach was the Santa Fe Pioneers. One hundred merchants loading two dozen wagons with an estimated $200,000 of materials sent a firm message of commercial intent.[22] This was no small expression of Texas' hopes for an economic network across the West. Here marched a viable invitation for a Santa Fe Trail that would wind through Texas to the Gulf, not through the Midwest to St. Louis. This was a significant offering, in the name of cooperation and expansionism, for a transcontinental trade system.

Accompanying the merchants and commissioners were six companies of soldiers, more than two hundred Texans and frontiersmen well armed and dedicated to the operation's ideals. A military escort of this magnitude would be more than sufficient to ward off dangers along the way. Indian fighters of renown, such as Howard, Caldwell, Fitzgerald, and Lewis, complimented by professional soldiers such as Cooke and Sutton, would bring to the expedition integrity and courage, experience and order. No one anticipated a problem.

Any thought of defiance by Armijo was unjustifiably foolish. The people of Santa Fe would make the distinction between their liberators and their tyrannic governor. They would not be afraid to support a political transformation. Likewise, the Mexican army, ever underestimated by Lamar and most Texans, would put up little resistance. In the years before and after the revolution, putting Texans on the battlefield against odds of eight or ten to one never bothered these frontiersmen: two hundred volunteers would match up against however many soldiers Armijo thought he could muster. Lamar had been assured by reports from Santa Fe that only an army that marched up from Mexico City would require an alternate plan.[23] Reports of a merchant wagon train with escorts would not provoke such a reaction from the Mexican government, or so Lamar thought.

The choice of McLeod as commander met Lamar's expectations for success. A West Point graduate and Indian fighter, McLeod shared his cousin-in-law Lamar's expansionist dreams. The twenty-six-year-old's exploits at Nacogdoches in 1836, against the Kickapoos and Caddoes in 1838 and the Cherokee in 1839, and his bravery at the Council House Fight in 1840, earned him a reputation for courage unsurpassed on the Texas frontier. His relation by marriage to the president's cousin, later criticized by some, had no bearing in Austin when it was announced that he would lead the trade expedition.[24] McLeod would bring discipline and order to the march, command an armed response against Indians along the way, and meet any resistance in New Mexico. He understood and agreed with the broader goals of the journey. The conquest of the West for the greater good of the people there and in Texas made perfect sense to McLeod, and it would be carried out with military integrity, political efficacy, and personal conviction.

How tragically ironic, then, that the second critical factor leading to the expedition's failure centered on the grievous mismanagement of a plan set in motion nearly three years earlier. That the plan was so poorly orchestrated and implemented speaks not only to the operation's mixed objectives, but also to the inadequate information base from which the planners functioned. Lamar's insistence on carrying out the expedition upon his return to Texas, despite the fact that the legislature adjourned without acting on his request for appropriations, was a mistake. He missed the congressional debate and must have accepted bad counsel when he resumed office late in February.[25] He found loopholes that allowed him to finish what he had started three months earlier; that equipment and other preparations had already been assembled following initial support in the House proved a weak defense.[26] The desire to raise the Lone Star over the Santa Fe market square held sway over responsibility. Lamar's unswerving belief in the expedition ameliorated concerns that a returning, angry Congress would object. How could they resist the great victory for Texas that would await them that fall?

Not a single map, accurate or otherwise, was taken on the march. That such a map existed and lay within reach of recording journalists Kendall and Falconer during their San Antonio visit does not deflect the blame from expedition leaders. True, Cooke had made the first leg of the journey only the year before and others had roamed across the Brazos country to the edge of the Cross Timbers. Trader trails from the Red River valley led west to the mountains of New Mexico, and the Chihuahua Trail cut across some of that terrain. To the north and along the upper Canadian River, the well-known Santa Fe Trail, which connected to the middle Mississippi valley, had been traversed for nearly two decades. The plan was to hit that trail before reaching Santa Fe. But the actual distances west along the Red River, the terrain of the so-called narrows of the Red and Wichita Rivers, the cuts onto the caprock and the distance across its plateau, and the formidable canyons were a mystery. Landmarks, few and far between, were mistaken or missed entirely—the best example being the Comanche Peak sighting. Locating decent river crossings meant hours or days of delay and backtracking. Protected campsites with fresh water would be discovered accidentally by scouts, and this proved more difficult than the commanders had hoped.

The decision to go north and then west was made with the uncertain knowledge that this was the most expedient, safest, most amenable, and, in the long run, most direct route. Oddly, the belief that following the Brazos to its headwaters and thence across the Llano Estacado—the most direct route as the crow flies—would cross too much unknown territory led to this alternative and, if nothing else, even more unknown territory.[27] Juan Carlos, who claimed he knew the expedition's whereabouts at the Cross Timbers and could lead them up the Red River, exacerbated an already intolerable situation. The scouting parties should have found a better route through the edge of, or even around, the Cross Timbers instead of settling for the longer diagonal cut through its center. Cooke and Howland should have kept the expedition on the Military Road they had carved out in 1840. Surveyor Thomas Hunt had sketched that trail himself, but he seemed unable to direct the Pioneers along it at the crucial moment. The fact that any northerly trek would ultimately hit the Red River allayed everyone's fears but cost time and energy; adding or subtracting a few miles at that point seemed meaningless.

Finally, the misinformation that led to imprisonment for some, death for others, and anguish for everyone concerned Armijo's powerful influence and the estimation of his people's feelings for liberty from Mexico. Lamar, along with McLeod and others who planned the expedition, desperately wanted to believe that New Mexico's citizens eagerly awaited a liberating force. They ignored other warnings. Some blame goes to men such as Dryden, whose plea for trade negotiations with Santa Fe encouraged Lamar beyond reason, and George Park and Jefferson Jones, who portrayed Armijo as a leader without support and vulnerable to revolution. Still, Lamar could have sought opposing viewpoints in March, 1841, when a cautionary approach might have saved the expedition.[28]

The third critical factor can only be characterized as terrible misfortune—just plain bad luck. Notwithstanding the superstition surrounding the three premature deaths of expedition volunteers, the first days and delays of the massive operation presented the first in a series of disasters that nothing, or no one, could prevent. McLeod's tardy arrival and the subsequent delay in the march northward began the enterprise on a sour note. McLeod's illness, a fever likely related to an arrow wound from the year before, prevented his departure from Galveston to Austin. Lamar officially promoted McLeod to brevet brigadier general on June 17, more than two weeks after the expedition was scheduled to depart.[29] McLeod arrived at Brushy Creek on June 18, ordered the march to begin on June 20, and was forced to leave the troops only five days into the journey. A chilling rainstorm raised his fever once more, and his thirteen-day absence at Bryant's Station weakened his authority. Growing tension between McLeod and Howard after the Brazos crossing, which led to Howard's resignation amid angry debate, might have been prevented if McLeod had come to Austin on time and stayed with the expedition throughout the march.

Misfortune shadowed the Pioneers into the Cross Timbers late in July, when a more judicious detour to the west would have prevented a week of disastrous struggle through dense woodlands. Again, Carlos's mistake at the Red River cost the volunteers valuable time at the halfway point. Giving Carlos the benefit of the doubt, as some have done in retrospect, suggests only that his bad luck rubbed off on the expedition. If the scouting parties had found better campsites or more water holes, the privations that drained the Pioneers at the end might have been averted. As it was, the scouts missed freshwater springs and ponds all along the trek. The September 5 stampede could have been avoided, given the commanding officers' careful instructions for protecting camp and livestock; the loss of eighty-three horses seriously damaged the fortunes of Camp Resolution. Sentries were posted, the livestock carefully put out to pasture, and the wagons well placed along Quitaque Creek. The Kiowas still managed to stampede the horses away from the guards and outrace the company that gave chase.

Perhaps the most debilitating decision of the expedition's later stages was the separation of the Pioneers into several parties. Dispatching the three messengers in mid-August was a logical way to make early contact with nearby friendly citizens, but this turned out to be no more than a warning to Salazar and Armijo's forces that the Texans were approaching. When the Sutton-Cooke party went ahead on August 31, McLeod made a strategically sound decision based on the information he had: both parties remained large enough to fend off resistance, although no one anticipated any trouble. When he sent Caldwell and others ahead on September 23 to negotiate the Santa Fe reception, it seemed appropriate. The Pioneers arrived in New Mexico in four separate groups, each marching into the clutches of a waiting enemy. The four hundred soldiers under Salazar's command might have had second thoughts about dealing with a unified force of Texans, even a weakened and dispirited force. And McLeod, with Caldwell and Sutton to support him, would have been more willing to hold his position. When the groups of three, five, ninety, and ninety-two dragged into the area, Salazar simply picked them off. Lewis's betrayal must have exhausted any remaining spirit of defiance.[30] Trusting in Lewis's fluent Spanish and the persuasive ways for which he was known, the Pioneers slumped in shock and disillusionment at the sight of the soldier accepting the gratitude of Salazar and Armijo for his aid in the expedition's capture. No misfortune evokes anguish as much as the unexpected perfidy by a friend.

McLeod cannot escape blame. His uneven leadership over the first two months left him contentious and his soldiers distrusting. The confrontation with Howard may have been the first time McLeod asserted his authority as commanding officer, and his subsequent belief in the diagonal trek through the Cross Timbers and in Carlos's appointment as guide seriously undermined the march. When McLeod reasserted himself in mid-August against the Indian attacks, it was probably too late to save the expedition. His decision to split the Pioneers left the parties unable to defend themselves against the Mexican troops. He wanted to fight at the Laguna Colorada, but he remained mindful of Lamar's strict instructions not to engage Armijo's forces. The humiliation of being the first Texas army to surrender without a fight would haunt him for the rest of his life.

Although Cooke and Howard would later criticize McLeod's leadership, most soldiers who voiced an opinion in the months and years after supported their commanding officer. On February 5, 1842, four months to the day after McLeod's surrender to Archuleta, the fifty-nine Pioneers imprisoned at the Castle of San Christopher deep in Mexico wrote a resolution expressing their sentiments:

Resolved, 1st. That we regard General McLeod as a patriotic and chivalrous officer; as a gentleman and a friend.

Resolved, 2nd. That the constant and untiring solicitude of Genl.

McLeod for our welfare since our captivity merits our lasting gratitude.

Resolved, 3rd. That whatever may be the fortunes of Genl. McLeod, or of ourselves, in after life, we shall ever regard him as having been our friend; as an honorable and a high-minded man.

Resolved, 4th. That a copy of the foregoing resolutions be handed to General McLeod; and that a copy be handed to the editors of the New Orleans *Picayune,* for publication in their paper.

John Doran
Robert Bisset
William Johnson
J. T. Case
John Haines, Committee[31]

The Pioneers reached their destination without the results they had hoped for. Their journey over, many expected a temporary wait before being released back to Texas, especially with Salazar's assurances to Cooke and Archuleta's promises to McLeod. But their march had barely begun. A worse fate awaited the 190 men: La Jornada del Muerte.

CHAPTER 10

La Jornada del Muerte

On September 4, 1841, the three messengers McLeod had sent ahead to greet the citizens of Santa Fe found themselves surrounded by an advance force under Salazar on the outskirts of Anton Chico. They readily agreed to surrender their arms, believing they would be allowed to share their message and would be released soon after. Marched roughly toward Santa Fe, they arrived in San Miguel, aware now that their treatment would be far from cordial. They were prisoners of Mexico. That evening after sundown, Samuel Howland, Alexander Baker, and William Rosenberry tried to escape. Seized at the edge of the village, Rosenberry was shot and killed as he resisted, and Howland and Baker were imprisoned under tighter security.[1]

Ten days later the six-man party led by Van Ness, which included Howard, Fitzgerald, and Kendall, relaxed in a small Mexican hacienda in Anton Chico, where they had been warmly greeted and well fed. Ignorant of the looming danger, they planned a brief ride the next day, September 15, into San Miguel to contact authorities. Awakened in the middle of the night by a friendly citizen who warned them to leave, the Texans instead slept until dawn, ate a large breakfast, and headed northwest. At the tiny village of Cuesta they encountered Salazar and more than a hundred troops. Salazar seemed agreeable to negotiating as soon as the Pioneers disarmed, but after they did so his mood quickly changed. He had the six prisoners searched and their personal possessions seized. When Mexican troops surrounded the small party and raised their weapons, Fitzgerald shouted an alarm and prepared to put up a final struggle before the apparent execution squad. A local Mexican rancher, Don Gregorio Vigil, miraculously intervened on behalf of the unarmed Texans, and Salazar ordered the prisoners marched to San Miguel. They walked through the villita of Puertocito, where they were given food by several women—a scenario that would be repeated often over the next few months—and into San Miguel, where they spent a cold night without supper or blankets.[2]

On September 16 the prisoners began a forced march toward Santa Fe.

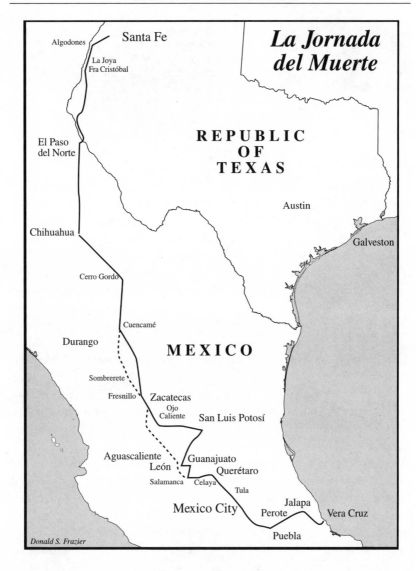

Twenty miles down the road they encountered more than a thousand Mexican troops led by Armijo; they were headed the other way, presumably in search of the remaining Pioneers. Armijo ordered the prisoners sent back to San Miguel, where they would be interrogated the next morning. A driving rainstorm halted the march that evening, and the Texans slept on the muddy ground, bound to one another by coarse ropes. By mid-morning the prisoners had crowded into a tiny room in a building off the square of San Miguel.[3]

A noise outside brought the men to the window, where they watched in horror as Baker was shoved into the open marketplace by a squad of soldiers and shot in the back. As he lay dying, an officer walked up and shot him through the heart; the powder ignited Baker's bloody shirt and smoldered for several minutes. Soldiers arrived to take the other Texans to the square, and they assumed a similar fate awaited them. Instead they were forced to witness the execution of Howland, who was marched from his cell, blindfolded, and shot in the back next to his slain comrade.[4]

That same day, in nearby Anton Chico, the Sutton-Cooke party surrendered to Salazar's forces. Two days later they arrived in San Miguel. Separated from the Van Ness party, the Pioneers did not realize for three weeks that the others were there. By that time most of the Cooke-Sutton soldiers had begun their march south toward Mexico. In the meantime Caldwell's advance party, which had left McLeod on September 23, surrendered to Armijo's forces on September 29.[5] After ten days under house arrest at Vigil's ranch, Caldwell's party marched through Sarita. They reached San Miguel on October 9, two days after McLeod and his officers arrived, and at that point the Pioneers' plight became painfully clear. Caldwell later wrote from a hospital cot in Guanajuato, Mexico: "Never did eyes behold a more miserable sight than to see the poor men [of the McLeod party] stripped naked, starved, and their feet bleeding as they were driven before the lances of their cruel enemies. . . . These villains of New Mexico whom we were encouraged to believe were our friends are all of them, none excepted, a gang of villains of the darkest, deepest dye."[6]

Armijo arrived in San Miguel on October 12 to interrogate the prisoners, and McLeod seized the opportunity to communicate with him. Borrowing stationery from a Mexican officer, McLeod addressed "His Excellency" for the purpose of providing a list of "officers, that they may be treated according to their rank." He mentioned the several merchants and subjects of other governments who had accompanied him, insisting that the expedition was "calculated by its objects to introduce a peaceful intercourse between countries which, from their relative positions, must, some day, be of great reciprocal value."

Denying any aggressive purpose to the march, McLeod continued: "Do me the justice to believe that I should not have been Quixotic enough to have undertaken the conquest of your country with a handful of men, exhausted by the most unparalleled marches and sufferings. Nor can it be supposed that I expected to force a commerce with a hostile people. All my operations were based upon the presumed good will of the people with whom we had no cause for war, and with whom a peaceful and regulated traffic would conduce to the happiness of both. . . . Our age is too enlightened to tolerate the barbarous idea of eternal hostility and hatred between

Christian nations." He defended his decision to lay down arms, perhaps in preparation for a later debate: "Your troops found me divided in force, and exhausted beyond the means of advance or retreat, with a detachment in your hands. To fight would have been mere bloodshed without any object, and would have involved the fate of others already in your power. I was compelled to submit to the necessity of my position, and will, I have no doubt, be honorably redeemed."

The letter concluded with an echo of Caldwell's later assessment: "We have been furnished with bread but twice, [and] are also deprived of our clothing and of some articles of comfort which were taken from us." McLeod requested the return of his personal trunk, which contained the expedition's official papers, including the complete rolls of those accompanying the Pioneers. "For myself individually, I ask nothing, but what I may enjoy in common with my comrades," he wrote. His trunk and papers were never returned, and Falconer reported that Armijo never formally responded to McLeod's letter.[7]

For the next four months, the Pioneers marched south across the Paseo del Norte, through Chihuahua and Zacatecas, and into the area around Mexico City, where they awaited their fate. The Sutton-Cooke party left San Miguel on September 17 and generally kept about a three-week lead on the others. McLeod and thirteen officers left on October 16, one day ahead of the rest of the party. The McLeod group, which included Whitaker, Houghton, Hudson, and for the first half of the journey Navarro, received remarkably good treatment throughout most of their march. McLeod, however, suffered the indignity of being stripped of his uniform regimentals in San Miguel square. Years later Armijo bragged to visiting dignitaries of his "trophy that no other Mexican official was able to display."[8]

The Van Ness and Caldwell parties reunited with the rest of the men from Camp Resolution on the square before beginning the march to Mexico City, which covered more than 1,600 miles—twice as far as the expedition to Santa Fe. Although parts of the journey proved relatively mild in terrain and climate, most of the winter march pushed the men to the edge of survival. The dry desert, frigid mountain crossings, lack of adequate food and shelter, an often punishing pace, and beatings tested the men to the limits of human endurance. Because they had arrived at San Miguel already haggard and ill, the forced march created a dire situation in which even healthy men might have fallen.[9]

Although the first day, October 17, was warm and showery, the trek into the mountains turned bitterly cold, especially at night. Salazar seemed to enjoy the cruelties extended to the weakening, hungry prisoners, tossing small barley cakes in their midst and watching them scramble for a morsel. At the Piño ranch close to Santa Fe, McLeod's party spent a night in comfortable quarters, but the main party was forced into a crowded cow pen. In the village of Algodnes on the Rio Grande, Kendall reported that two small rooms "hardly large enough for twenty men were provided, and into these over one hundred eighty of us were driven like so many sheep. Half suffocated, and with sensations of sickness and giddiness, thoughts of the Black Hole of Calcutta, with its attendant train of horrors, now came over us; and I am confident that an order for instant execution would have been preferred, by many, to passing the night in that dismal, dark, and horrible place."[10]

The most dreaded, and deadliest, leg of the journey came early: a ninety-mile stretch of open desert between the village of Fray Cristobal and the Paseo del Norte, known as La Jornada del Muerte, or the Journey of Death.[11] The prisoners were pushed at a pace of thirty miles a day, with only the bare ground as bedding on sleepless nights. Salazar distributed meager rations once a day and allowed his men to brutalize the prisoners as they wished.

Before dawn on October 24, with the trailing prisoners of the Caldwell-Kendall party crowded together for warmth, it was discovered that Tennessean Felix Ernest of Company D had died of exhaustion. His body was left, still curled in a sleeping position. Later that day another Tennessean, artilleryman John McAllister, was forced off a supply cart he had been allowed to sit on to rest his badly swollen ankles. Refusing to walk and defiantly challenging Salazar, McAllister was shot; his ears were cut off as souvenirs, and his body was left beside the road.[12]

A week later a similar fate met three more Caldwell-Kendall party prisoners along the desert stretch. On November 1 Salazar executed merchant Amos Golpin as the sick man was pulling his shirt over his head to trade for a ride in the sick-wagon. The next day Edward Griffith could not keep up with the others, and a Mexican soldier beat him to death with a rifle butt. Both bodies were left unburied, their ears sliced off as trophies. At the Paseo del Norte a third sick prisoner named Gates died of heart failure even as soldiers threatened to shoot him.[13]

By November 9 all of the Texans had crossed the north pass of the Rio Grande and were on their way to the large city of Chihuahua, where once again citizens greeted them warmly and passersby fed them. In Zacatecas, the next major stop, conditions deteriorated for the Sutton-Cooke party, which arrived in late November, and the Caldwell-Kendall party, which spent three days there and largely ignored the fact that New Year's Day had passed. The party crossed the mountain passes around San Luis Potosí in the worst part of winter, and dozens of the prisoners stayed behind in makeshift hospitals at San Cristobal.[14]

By February 1 most of the Pioneers had reached their destinations for the next three months. Bouts of malaria and smallpox had attacked both of the larger parties along the way. Valentine Bennet wrote optimistically to his children from quarters at San Cristobal on February 3: "I expect to leave in a few days. . . . Do not feel any anxiety about me, as I am in good health and doing as well as I could expect." A few days later he entered Mexico City, and one popular, apocryphal tale has it that as he rode into the capital, he shouted to the women who gathered around to stare: "Weep not, ye daughters of Mexico! Your rulers are coming seated on asses!"[15] The prisoners' resilience took many forms.

Meanwhile McLeod and his small entourage followed a similar route under less stringent conditions. The fourteen prisoners departed San Miguel, fuming as they watched the traitor Lewis standing with Armijo and gathering boxes of supplies and prisoners' belongings for himself.[16] Lt. Teodoro Quintana escorted McLeod through the rigorous desert stretch to Paseo del Norte.[17] Along the route the prisoners saw but were not allowed to speak to a caravan of American trade wagons. At the head of the wagon train rode its owner, former U.S. consul James Wiley Magoffin, Kentucky born and bred and married into the wealthy Valdez family of Mexico. In Chihuahua, Mrs. Magoffin acted as hostess to this group and some of the trailing Caldwell-Kendall men, making sure they were well fed and reclothed for the next part of the march.[18]

McLeod was turned over to Col. José Maria Elias at the Paseo del Norte and cared for during the brief stay by local priest Father Ramón Ortiz and an Anglo woman identified only as Mrs. Stevenson. Kendall recalled spotting McLeod and other officers on a bridge in El Paso, "clean shaved and neatly enough dressed, and bore every appearance of having fallen into kinder hands." At a fandango and dinner hosted by Elias, McLeod castigated Salazar for his abusive treatment of the prisoners. Later it would be Elias who turned evidence of Salazar's butchery against him in a court-martial hearing.[19]

The next stage of the journey passed without incident, and the November weather began to set in cold and wet. In Chihuahua, despite the efforts of Mrs. Magoffin and a host of servants, William Larrabee died of fatigue shortly after the prisoners resumed their march south. The others left the city with money, more warm clothes, and new pairs of shoes donated by a Dr. Jennison.[20] New Mexican officers took turns leading the captives toward Mexico City, with changes made at Cerro Gordo, Zacatecas, San Luis Potosí, and Queretaro. At Cerro Gordo McLeod found the names of the Sutton-Cooke party carved on a wall, indicating that the prisoners had passed through about a month before.[21] At Ojo Caliente the men bathed in warm springs at the edge of town accompanied by some of the women from the area—no doubt a relief and a distraction from their plight.[22]

The McLeod party rode donkeys through the Sierra Madre mountain passes and received a cash gift of $500 from Mexican Gov. José Heredia in Durango.[23] After passing through Cuencame on December 20, the party followed a slightly different route from the others over the next four weeks, resuming the main trail at Salamanca. Those who marched through Guanajuato seemed struck hardest by the smallpox that infested the prisoners in January and February. The Caldwell-Kendall party, joined by McLeod at the friendly village of Celaya on January 22, marched into Tula on February 1 and learned of the imminent release of Falconer and Van Ness.[24]

For months the expedition's fate had remained a disturbing mystery in Texas and the United States. The first formal acknowledgment of the Pioneers' surrender and their march into Mexico came in a December 16, 1841, letter from U.S. envoy Powhatan Ellis to U.S. Secretary of State Daniel Webster. Webster wrote Ellis on January 3 with strict instructions to aggressively pursue the release of all U.S. citizens. Letters rapidly followed. Texas envoy Joseph Eve wrote Webster on January 22 when he learned of the forced march. Webster responded on March 30, replaced a still unsuccessful Ellis with the more assertive J. Waddy Thompson, and fired off letters to Mexico City and Texas throughout April and May.[25]

Thompson's first report from Mexico City came on April 29, with a follow-up letter to President John Tyler on May 9. Conversations with Mexico's foreign minister José Maria de Bocanegra in May succeeded in gaining the government's attention. The U.S. consulate reached an agreement for the release of Coombs, the Kentucky governor's son, and Fitzgerald soon after. During the negotiations and through Thompson's diplomatic efforts, McLeod raised objections about Navarro's separation from the group and his particularly harsh treatment, but his protests were ignored.[26]

Word of the Pioneer's fate also reached public ears in the United States. A young Guy M. Bryan, attending Kenyon College in Ohio, wrote his stepfather James F. Perry on January 8: "For some weeks past I have been kept in one continued state of excitement and anxiety relative to the fate of those forming the Santa Fe Expedition. There is now no doubt in regard to the fate of that hapless expedition. O! how my heart bleeds for those unfortunate men . . . who have fallen into the merciless hands of the savage and treacherous Mexican. When shall there be a day of retribution? How long will these men be suffered to drag out a miserable existence unavenged and unfreed from the nauseous damp of the mines of Mexico?" He added: "Are there no Deaf Smiths or Karnes left to lead the daring and the brave into the enemies' country to seize the wealthy and influential, and hold them hostage for the safety and well treatment of our captured fellow countrymen? Then up and be doing, awake the fire of liberty and manhood in those who can go. Let the press send forth its thunders, and Lamar and Burnet ply their pens and unfurl to the breeze the broad folds of the tri-colored flag, whose star shall cast its rays of hope into the inmost recesses of the mind and the darkest corner of the dungeon."[27]

On February 9, with the Sutton-Cooke party already at hard labor on the Santiago road gangs, the Caldwell-Kendall and McLeod parties met at San Cristobal to wait for their next marching orders. Most went on to Puebla, a crowded prison of hard-core criminals. Navarro later wrote of his abject fear of being sodomized by the inmates.[28] The eighty or so men who remained there worked long, hard hours under intense scrutiny. McLeod and fifty-one others ended up at Castle Perote, a notorious dungeon where other Texas prisoners from Mier and Salado would end their days two years later. The dead were unceremoniously dumped into the alligator-infested moat.[29]

Escape attempts were mostly unsuccessful. Four men slipped away one night along the Jornada del Muerte but were recaptured, and three more tried to run near the Paseo del Norte. Manuel Alvarez, the U.S. consul to Santa Fe, pulled off one of the more dramatic escapes. Attacked in his home by Armijo partisans, Alvarez stole away during the night, eventually making his way to Independence, Missouri, where he reported the incident to Washington.[30] Only six of the original Pioneers succeeded in eluding the Mexican army and returning to Texas. Tom Lubbock and Louis Mazur were the first to get away, out of the prisoner camp at Santiago. Four others escaped from Puebla in two attempts in the spring of 1842, including Radcliffe Hudson and George Howard. Hudson, dark-complected and fluent in Spanish, stole into Mexico City, spent two weeks entertaining himself, and carved his name into a cathedral tower wall before departing for Texas.[31] Lubbock commented in his memoirs that prisoners might have made more attempts had there not been "another traitor among us," but he does not say who the man was.[32]

By March 1 the survivors were ensconced in their final prison or hospital residences. Cooke and McLeod worked to make connections with local consuls, including ambassadors from France, Prussia, Switzerland, and the Vatican, in addition to Sir Richard Pakenham of England and L. S. Hargous of the United States.[33] Thompson's arrival in April signaled a significant change for the prisoners and an increased pace in negotiations for release. He brought letters and vouchers from Webster and several U.S. congressmen and state governors, including a letter for Santa Anna from former U.S. President Andrew Jackson. This last may have spurred the release of McLeod.[34] Hargous loaned a total of more than $6,100 to Cooke and McLeod in March and April, allowing the two to replenish rations and medical necessities to their men in Santiago and Puebla.[35]

On April 21 McLeod requested and received permission for additional rations so that his men might celebrate an unidentified holiday. Mexican guards and townspeople watched in amusement as the Texans sang and toasted one another well into the night. If members of the crowd remembered that this was the sixth anniversary of the Battle of San Jacinto and the final victory of the Texas Revolution, they said nothing. Certainly the Mexican president would have remembered, but he was distracted in Mexico City.[36] Unfortunately McLeod wrote a letter thanking the government for agreeing to the festivities and remarking that the officers were being treated well. This presented an unwelcome obstacle to Thompson's efforts.[37]

That same week the efforts of Pakenham, Webster, and especially Thompson began to pay off. Thompson's assertive character shows in his confrontation with Santa Anna in May. Following a dramatic visit with Kendall at the San Lazaro hospital, where "Kendall was quietly seated among the lepers," and thence to the convent at St. Jago "on the great square of Tlatilalco to see the remainder of the prisoners," Thompson sat in Santa Anna's office and "expressed the hope that all the privileges of prisoners of war would be extended to the Texans, and that no act of undue severity would be committed." Santa Anna replied that the prisoners were not American citizens and that Thompson had no right to intercede on their behalf, to which Thompson retorted, "They are human beings . . . and it is the duty of all nations to see that Mexico does not violate the principles and usages of civilized war." When Santa Anna huffed at such a notion, Thompson reported, "I rose from my seat, and said, 'Then, Sir, shoot them as you choose, but you will at once involve in this war a much more powerful enemy than Texas!'"[38]

Twenty-six prisoners in Santiago and Puebla, including Kendall, were soon informed of their release, and by May 12 the U.S. cutter *Woodbury* sailed out of Vera Cruz for New Orleans with fourteen Texans aboard. On March 9 Falconer had sailed on the *Atalantique* and Van Ness had sailed on the schooner *William Bryan*.[39] On June 13 Santa Anna personally declared the release of 231 prisoners from Perote, Puebla, and Santiago. He had sent a stern message to Texas in Vazquez's March invasion of San Antonio and a second intrusion on the Nueces River that week, and this allowed him to portray himself as both the final authority in his nation and a benevolent despot. In front of ten thousand troops he marched into Puebla on June 16, the anniversary of his patron saint, to the cheering throngs of more than forty thousand citizens. Santa Anna sat astride his white horse in full military regalia as sixty-five haggard Pioneers stumbled onto the square. His apparent magnanimity was not lost on the crowds, although the prisoners, still suspicious of their captors' motives, appeared less than overjoyed. At the urging of officials in the crowd the people greeted the prisoners warmly, offering food, clothing, and other articles as the men wandered across the square. The troops cheered their general, and U.S. representatives soon rounded up the liberated men to inform them that they were indeed free.[40]

McLeod and the prisoners at Castle Perote, who were not present at the ceremony, learned of the troops' release in the days that followed. By mid-July arrangements had been made for the escort of 185 Pioneers east along the road through Jalapa to Vera Cruz, leaving 75 men in hospitals recovering from exhaustion, smallpox, and other ailments. Navarro remained in the disreputable Acordada prison in the western section of Mexico City. Tried and convicted of various crimes against Mexico, the Tejano spent the next fourteen months alone in prison. During that time a mostly apocryphal story circulated that Santa Anna had visited Navarro, hoping the prisoner would beg for mercy. But Navarro refused the Mexican president his moment, preferring to suffer than recant his so-called crimes. In December, 1843, Navarro was transferred to Vera Cruz, where a sympathetic jailer allowed him freedom to walk along the coastal jetties. When an American merchant vessel happened by, Navarro seized the opportunity to escape and eventually made his way back to the United States.[41]

An outbreak of yellow fever struck Vera Cruz only days after the released Pioneers' arrival, necessitating a long delay until the quarantine was lifted. Their ship of passage, the *Rosa Alvina,* remained docked from July 27 to August 12. When it prepared to sail, forty men remained ill in Vera Cruz and could not depart Mexico for another month.[42] But 145 joined McLeod for the trip home. Although many would take passage to New Orleans, McLeod and others would disembark at Galveston, his home, on August 21. An eyewitness described the pitiable scene: "A Brig with a white flag at her fore and Mexican at her Pique came in—bringing the Santa Fe prisoners under Colonel McLeod, from Vera Cruz 10 days. 14 men had died in Vera Cruz of black vomit [yellow fever]. . . . There were some 160 or more huddled together—it was dusk—thus little else than a sluggishly moving mass of sun-burnt visages and ill-clothed men could be observed. The effluvia on board was unpleasant. . . . A Captain [John J.] Holliday had died on the passage. They appeared well generally—some observed that 'they had had enough of such expeditions,' some 'that they were ready for another.'" The observer gave his own perspective on the failed expedition: "The Santa Fe Expedition, if it were a judicious one—was too long preparing—thus Santana [sic] had time to give his orders and prepare for defense against them—their object being to revolutionize against Mexico and trade . . . and here are some 160 of them in a most deplorable state of poverty and wretchedness."[43]

An eyewitness from La Grange wrote of seeing two expedition leaders shortly after their arrival: "General McLeod and Dr. Brenham came late in the Summer of that year, and spent a few days with us. Such way worn, dusty, sad looking men, could hardly be imagined, with worn boots—I remember distinctly that General McLeod was out at the toes—threadbare clothes, and faces that showed the suffering they had gone through, eyes that had looked upon Howland, when he was shot, a tied prisoner! by order of Armijo, of McAllister who was shot on the march from San Miguel to Paso, by order of Salazar! Griffith's brains scattered on the ground, by order of Salazar!" The La Grange observer concluded, "These were the sights that dimmed the sparkle of [an] eye and fixed in it instead, a firm resolve, 'to be even with them yet.'"[44]

War-weary and ill though he was, McLeod did not pause in the weeks that followed his release. Arriving in Galveston on August 21, the disheveled commander set out almost immediately for Austin to report to his government. One hundred miles into the journey, accompanied by Dr. Richard F. Brenham, McLeod stopped at the La Grange home of John Winfield Scott Dancy for what turned out to be two nights. McLeod and Dancy knew each other from their work in Congress, where Dancy was a state senator. The men shared political and economic ideology, had invested in the burgeoning cotton industry together, and would later work to bring the first railroads to Texas.[1]

Dancy, a thirty-two-year-old widower born and raised in Virginia, hosted another roomful of guests that summer. Samuel Maverick's wife and three children lived in La Grange for most of the summer and fall of 1842, having fled their San Antonio home twice since the 1840 Council House Fight because of threats of Mexican invasions. Mary Adams "Ma" Maverick watched over five-year-old Samuel, his brother Lewis, and baby Agatha. She was due the following spring with a fourth child. Mary's sister, Lizzie, and their uncle, John Bradley, also lived with them. Griffin, a slave whose size and strength belied a fond relationship with the Maverick family, stayed in quarters away from the house.

Samuel Maverick rode the trail to San Antonio the same week McLeod and Brenham arrived in La Grange hoping to visit him. The restless Maverick had made the round-trip at least three times since March, when the Vazquez raid emptied Bexar of most of its citizens for several weeks. The family resided for much of April on the Colorado River, boarding with the Brookfields and now John Dancy. Maverick purchased twenty-six acres of land from Dancy on August 21 with the intention of building a homestead in case San Antonio became too dangerous for his family. Less than two weeks before the next elections, he pressed toward San Antonio to assess the situation amid rumors of yet another Mexican invasion.[2]

McLeod and Brenham rested at Dancy's into a third day, recounting their experiences to a rapt audience of neighbors. Not fully recuperated but anxious to continue west, the two rode along the Colorado Trail for an afternoon, stopping at Woods' Prairie and Zadock Woods's inn and fort, where they were graciously hosted a night. The Woods family had come to Texas from New England with Austin's Old Three Hundred by way of Missouri. First settled in Brazoria, Zadock and Minerva (Cottle) had come up the Colorado in 1828 to build the fort at the behest of Austin's colony. They brought four grown sons to Texas, and their eldest daughter came later with her husband and children. The Woods's middle son, Leander, died at the Velasco fort battle in June, 1832, but Norman, Montraville, and Henry Gonzalvo carried on the family's efforts and added wives and children to the population along the river valley. Minerva died in 1839 at the age of sixty-three. Zadock, a renowned and respected Indian fighter and stonemason, became a stalwart leader of the western territory just weeks from his sixty-ninth birthday.[3]

A stopover at Woods' Fort meant an excellent repast, a good bed, and a great evening of storytelling by the host. Zadock's long, white, ruffled hair waved as he recounted his exploits in the War of 1812 and the battle for San Antonio in December, 1835. On this late August night, the tales may have distracted McLeod from haunting memories of Castle Perote.

By September 1 the travelers had moved closer to Austin, past Mina, and finally into the capital. Activity swirled through the streets; threats of Comanche raids and Mexican army invasions had everyone on edge. President Houston continued to argue for moving the administration back to the village named for him on Buffalo Bayou. The political tensions of east and west continued unabated, and with the Lamar administration out of office pressure to haul the archives and official records from Austin increased. Another political crisis stemmed from the angry debates over the future of the Texas navy, a sore subject for Houston, whose personality conflicts with Commodore Edwin Moore exacerbated an already deteriorating situation. Finally, cries for assaults against Mexico and shouts for annexation by the United States created a cacophony of confusion that was typical of the Republic's middle years.

McLeod hardly had a moment to breathe in the flurry surrounding his return. On September 13 news from San Antonio sent yet another alarm. Two days earlier the Fifth District Court meeting in San Antonio with presiding judge Anderson Hutchinson was interrupted by the arrival of more than a thousand Mexican troops under the command of Gen. Adrian Woll. Woll rounded up members of the court and city council along with other dignitaries, including Samuel Maverick, and held them under house arrest for a week.[4] Texans raced for San Antonio from Gonzales, Seguin, and as far away as La Grange and Austin. McLeod decided that his continued poor health precluded a contribution to the counterattack, but nearly two hundred riders made it to the banks of the Salado Creek east of Bexar in time for a September 18 confrontation with Woll's forces. John Hays's Rangers arrived about the same time as fifty others led by Caldwell and set up a camp on the creek. Caldwell, just back from Mexico and aiming for revenge, became the informal commander of the growing Texas force. On the morning of September 18, Hays, Ben McCulloch, and the Taylor brothers drew five hundred of Woll's troops into a devastating trap at Salado Creek, and a daylong battle commenced.

Arriving late in the afternoon, fifty-three Texans under the command of Nicholas Mosby Dawson of La Grange attempted to break enemy lines for the creek, but they were decimated on the open prairie a mile away. The Mexican troops killed thirty-six men, captured fifteen, and allowed two to flee. Henry Woods escaped the massacre by donning a Mexican's sombrero and disappearing, wounded, into the high grass. Captives included Norman Woods, badly injured in the fight, and John Bradley. Left dead on the high ground were Dawson, Zadock Woods, and Griffin, the Mavericks' slave. Bradley and Griffin had joined the makeshift company to make contact with Samuel Maverick once they arrived in San Antonio. Fearing her husband's capture, Ma had sent Griffin with a full money belt of ransom. Eyewitnesses recounted that Griffin died in a volley of Mexican gunfire as he swung a massive tree branch into the attacking enemy, taking several with him in death, the money strewn across the battlefield.[5]

Meanwhile, on the Salado, Woll's troops took a savage beating from Caldwell and Hays and retired into the city as a rain squall ended the pitched battle. Only one other Texan died that day, while Woll lost more than one hundred to death or injury. Woll chose to claim victory for his army in the name of Santa Anna and snuck from the city during the night with more than fifty prisoners. He managed to elude his pursuers and cross the Rio Grande into Mexico without further damage.[6]

Texas' response to the Woll invasion, the Somervell expedition, came in November after Houston's attempts for conciliation collapsed. Presidential orders for a counteroffensive came as early as September 16, when the militia was called to defend the western boundaries of the Republic against the invaders.[7] Marching along the Rio Grande just behind the evacuating Mexican troops at Laredo and Guerrero, Alexander Somervell finally ordered the militia to return to Gonzales; the imminent threat of invasion had passed. But three hundred soldiers adamantly refused to leave without a fight. Against all orders, this unauthorized force crossed into Mexico under the command of Col. William S. Fisher. On the day after Christmas in the square of the small village of Mier, Fisher's outnumbered troops surrendered and became prisoners of Mexico, adding another two hundred to an eerily familiar march to Puebla, Acordada, and Castle Perote.

Still in Austin in late September, McLeod was ironically saved from a return to Mexico in chains. But he did not stay in Austin. Recuperated, he traveled north along the mail route toward the Red River, accompanying fellow Mason and expansionist George Knight Teulon, editor of the *Austin City Gazette*.[8] Why they went north and where they ended up is unknown, but by November Teulon was back in Austin and McLeod was in Washington-on-the-Brazos. Teulon may have enticed his friend to retrace the first part of the Santa Fe expedition, at least as far as Coffee's Station on the Red River, where the Pioneers believed they had skirted their mark fifteen months earlier. It may be that McLeod needed to retrace his steps for consolation, if not vindication, although there is no evidence that he ever spoke of such a need. It is possible that he had planned a second attempt on Santa Fe, or at least had agreed to participate in such a plan. The forts of the original Cooke plan were being constructed along this route, and the two men may have taken the trail to gather information for future newspaper articles.[9]

A September 28 letter from Teulon to Cooke before their departure hints broadly at growing animosity between Cooke and McLeod over blame for the failed expedition. As a fellow Mason and high priest of the Austin's chapter, Teulon wrote to Cooke entreating harmony between the two.[10] A week later the Austin lodge sent a public letter reiterating the call for the dispute between Cooke and McLeod to "be handled with civility."[11] Where Cooke resided is unknown, but if he was supervising the fort construction, the journey may have been aimed at reconciliation. But reconciliation did not occur, and in early November McLeod embarked on another phase of his public career. Samuel Maverick had been elected in September to the Seventh Congress of the Texas Republic, representing the Bexar District and San Antonio. On September 11, however, Maverick was a prisoner of the invading Mexican army and found himself marched southward. When Congress convened for its first session on November 14, McLeod was to sit as Maverick's replacement. A compromise by the Houston and Lamar-Burnet political forces had planted the legislative session in neither Austin nor Houston, but up the Brazos at Washington. After a brief, symbolic holdout by the western partisans, McLeod and the others arrived to create a quorum on December 1.[12] The comedic attempt to secretly remove the official records from Austin while Congress sat distracted hundreds of miles away—the so-called Archives War—ended more or less peacefully as 1842 came to a close.[13]

The session itself, from Houston's feeble speech on December 1 to its adjournment on January 16, 1843, made little or no impact on the Republic. Aside from a handful of resolutions, the partisan Congress accomplished practically nothing, as one wag wrote, "for they are continually sparring at they know not what themselves."[14] Houston, panned by the western newspapers, signed a treaty with the Netherlands, continued to plot the end of the navy, and vetoed a frontier protection bill. McLeod supported the frontier bill against Houston, defended the navy against Houston's attempts to sell it off, and helped with legislation that chartered and funded the Galveston Orphan's Friend Society.[15] Adjournment came none too soon for everyone involved with or affected by the legislative session.

McLeod now faced a personal dilemma. Although he had lived in Texas for nearly seven years, he had no permanent homestead. He owned land on Galveston Island and in Van Zandt County.[16] He had spent time in Nacogdoches, Houston, and Austin, mostly in temporary quarters as he served the Republic. His travels had taken him to nearly every corner of Texas, from the Nueces to the Red River—almost—and across to the Sabine River, along the Gulf, and to the bayous. He had a law practice to open and business interests that included the lucrative cotton industry, which stretched across the southern United States. He had worked with cotton merchants since he was fourteen, and connections with the Lamars in Georgia would facilitate many opportunities for success. A political career still appealed to him, but a homestead was the starting point.

More pressing than a dwelling was a family, and that translated into one person: Rebecca Johnson Lamar. The two had known each other since childhood and had corresponded, directly or through their families, for two decades. Rebecca, the tenth of twelve children and a first cousin to Mirabeau Lamar, was raised in Richmond County, Georgia. Her father, Basil Lamar, died when she was sixteen; her mother, Rebecca Kelly, died two years later. Two years her junior, McLeod had last seen Rebecca when he visited Georgia in 1837, and they continued to correspond. Fear struck his heart in the summer of 1838 when he heard of the sinking of the *Pulaski* with Rebecca on board. But she had survived as a heroine.[17] It was time for McLeod to visit his Georgia kin.

In the spring of 1843, Charles A. Warfield organized a secret expeditionary force to take control of the lucrative trade out of Mexico along the Chihuahua and Santa Fe Trails. When William Christy convinced Houston that the venture would be more successful than the Pioneers' fiasco, the secret mission commenced. Houston instructed Secretary of War George W. Hockley to issue the necessary authorization, which included Warfield's raising of five hundred Texas volunteers.[18] On May 9, 1843, the Houston *Morning Star* unveiled the mission with excerpts from Warfield's plan, including his expectation that "McLeod with 150 men will meet me on the False Washita" up the Red River from Coffee's Station. McLeod never arrived, and neither did anyone else.[19] The venture collapsed.

McLeod had gone to Georgia. In Savannah he celebrated an extended reunion with his family, including his brother, Daniel, who had just been promoted to chief surgeon in the U.S. Navy.[20] He courted Rebecca in Augusta, and she accepted his proposal to marry. McLeod would not bring a bride back to Texas until a homestead awaited them, so the decision was made to wed the following year. This would give McLeod time to establish himself, build a house, and return to Georgia for Rebecca. Back in Texas by the summer of 1843, McLeod had decided Galveston was the most promising location for their future. He spent the next fourteen months working on the island, setting up his law practice, selecting a site for a house, making investments, and calling on friends and business associates. He did not ignore politics; rather, he continued to immerse himself in the issues of the day—mostly anything that opposed Houston's stance, whatever the topic. He campaigned for several candidates running for seats in the Eighth Congress and responded to several who suggested that he run in 1844.

McLeod began plans to construct a horse-driven cotton press near the Galveston docks. Enoch John and his son, Noah, had put up a small steam hydraulic press in 1842 that compressed 250 bales of cotton a day. Later that same year Thomas Lewis and Lawrence Dennison erected similar presses. Even with all three presses operating simultaneously, however, not even a thousand bales could be processed, and this was insufficient for the volume that arrived on the Galveston docks. McLeod's larger press would nearly double the capacity and turn a healthy profit. He planned to have it operating by 1845.[21]

In January, 1843, the Texas Congress passed a secret act that would ultimately bring the Republic's navy to an end. Over the next six months, the feud between Houston and Moore distracted citizens and politicians from more critical issues: international recognition, annexation, the frontier, and the economy. Finally, on July 14 the navy sailed into Galveston Bay and dropped anchor for the last time. Moore's supporters, including McLeod, met the tiny force with a parade of appreciation and honors, and a testimonial dinner on July 28 included several vitriolic speeches against the Texas president.[22] When news came that Congress intended to put the navy up for sale, an uproar ensued. The October 14 sale date was postponed as a result of the outcry, and on November 18 Galvestonians crowded into Shaw's Hotel for a public meeting. A committee was authorized to contact Congress and to work for indefinite postponement of the sale date. The meeting's highlight was McLeod's typically dramatic speech condemning Houston and his partisans and lauding the efforts of Moore's navy. At McLeod's urging, resolutions were adopted indicating the makings of a fight should anyone arrive at the harbor with intentions to "meddle with the property . . . that these persons may be liable to be stayed and dealt with accordingly." Ultimately, no fight occurred. Two of the three ships, the *Archer* and the *Wharton*, were sold for $935, and in 1846 the *Austin* was towed to the U.S. Navy Yard in Pensacola and later dismantled.[23]

In November, 1843, McLeod dealt with more aftershocks of the Santa Fe expedition, responding to British Chargé D'Affaires Charles Elliot, who asked if the Pioneers had surrendered a British flag to the Mexican government. On September 28 Percy Doyle, England's envoy to Mexico, had attended a gala in Mexico City where a Union Jack was displayed with other articles "taken from Texas prisoners of war." When his demand that it be removed was refused, Doyle stormed from the palace and initiated a series of diplomatic letters that flew back and forth until late November. Rumors circulated that a Union Jack had been taken on the Santa Fe expedition, "used as a sleeping cover . . . and found by the Mexicans." If this was true, the Mexican government might assume British support for the Texan misadventure. Assuring Elliot otherwise, McLeod wrote, "No such flag could have been officially used, and if any individual carried one it was without my knowledge. Indeed I am quite sure it was not done." When Elliot wrote Doyle that the flag had apparently come from a soldier on the Mier expedition the next year, and that it was not displayed by the soldier but used "as a wrapper to his kit," the matter was resolved.[24]

Mcleod, still upset that Navarro remained in a Mexican dungeon, took the opportunity to address the situation once more. "Would it be improper," he wrote Elliot on November 26, "to solicit your kind offices, unofficially, for my unfortunate companion, Mr. Antonio Navarro. His release would be but an act of justice to himself, and would confer happiness on a large family and numerous friends." Navarro's escape only weeks later would have overjoyed McLeod and most of Texas.

In May, 1844, word came that a U.S. steamer out of Vera Cruz would dock at Galveston in a few days. Continued concern for the Mier prisoners, many of whom languished at Puebla and Castle Perote, caused citizens to seek news of possible releases and to watch for loved ones arriving on such a ship. The United States continued its efforts, through Thompson and others, to get the men home. Good news came on April 22, when Samuel Maverick stepped off the USS *Vincennes* at Galveston after a journey through Pensacola and Mobile. Gaunt but undaunted, he was home by May 5 to see the house that had been built while he was away and his newest child, Augusta, born while he was in prison.[25]

A special welcoming committee was organized to greet dignitaries aboard the steamer, including none other than Thompson himself. Two American envoys joined the editor of the Galveston *Texas Times* and H. M. Smythe and McLeod at the harbor. As sailors wandered onto the city's docks, McLeod led the committee on board, where Thompson responded to their warm greetings. After an hour or so Thompson accompanied the committee into town for continued festivities. The ship would soon head to New Orleans, and Thompson would return to the ship then. Thompson and McLeod renewed their acquaintance, reminisced about the difficult days of 1842, and concluded their visit the next day.

Forty-eight hours after Thompson's ship sailed from Galveston, the two American envoys became ill with soaring temperatures and nausea. Yellow fever struck Smythe the next day, and then McLeod. Richard Drake Sebring, the newspaper editor, fell ill soon after, and reports of the terrible disease spread through town. Two sailors had brought it ashore, and the committee had been infected on board. The envoys and Sebring died by the end of the week. Smythe and McLeod recovered after a long convalescence.[26] The plague ran rampant through Galveston and into the Houston area. For eight weeks the city suffered the horrors of the black vomit. By the end of July, as it gradually subsided, four hundred people had died, nearly one-third of the island's population. Dozens more succumbed on the mainland as the malady spread westward across the frontier. This was the second major yellow fever crisis in Galveston in five years, but not the last.

As McLeod recovered and the September elections appeared on the political horizon, he received a request from the citizens of San Antonio. With Maverick still disabled from his time in Mexico and living in La Grange, they asked McLeod to run for the Bexar District seat in the Republic House. Residing within one's district was not a strict rule, and this type of request was not unusual. McLeod accepted.[27] The prospect of a campaign was exciting, and serving in the Republic's legislature would provide a political forum for McLeod, an avid, and recognized, opponent of the Houston faction.

The political arena was especially exciting in August, 1844. Presidential elections were being held in Texas and the United States, and chief among the issues was Texas' annexation. In America James Knox Polk won the Democratic nomination over Martin Van Buren and faced off against the Whigs' venerable Kentuckian, Henry Clay. Manifest Destiny charged American citizens and their leaders with the prospect of westward expansion to the Pacific, including Oregon, Texas, and California. In Texas Dr. Anson Jones took on Gen. Edward Burleson for the presidency of the Republic. Jones ostensibly held the support of the Houston annexation group, while Burleson, a former Houston partisan, drew the support of former President Lamar and the western faction. Most agreed that these candidates did not represent the best choices; the real duel was between Houston and Lamar. This election would go a long way toward determining whether Texas remained independent. The debates between the Jones and Burleson factions were often volatile, as was expected in Texas politics. James Reily wrote James Harper Starr, "I dread to see the men in power that Burleson will have around him if elected: Cazneau, McLeod, Jeff Green, Archer, Chalmers, et al." And McLeod wrote Thomas Rusk: "I write amidst a crowd of talking politicians. Burleson leaves for Washington and the East [to see you]. . . . I shall rejoice in the meeting of two men who have the real interest of the country at heart."[28]

The combination of elections, from local to Republic to United States, presented a perfect stage for the long-winded, dramatic, elocutionary talents of McLeod. Perhaps his most memorable speech came at an August dinner gathering of ardent Burleson men. Burleson, a hero at San Jacinto, was credited with one of the majestic quotes of the Texas Revolution. Advised of the tragedy at the Alamo, he said poignantly to his soldiers, "Thermopylae had its messenger of defeat; the Alamo had none." Stirred to anger and action, the Texans under his command would be among the first to cry out "Remember the Alamo!" in their charge across the battlefield. In the interim years, controversy had stirred over who said this, or to whom credit should be given. Burleson, a native North Carolinian, possessed no particular bent for great speech making, a fact to which he would have readily agreed. Some had already assigned the heroic remark to Col. Guy M. Bryan, and others to Gen. Thomas Jefferson Green.

In his keynote speech at the dinner party, McLeod praised the simple, dignified leadership Burleson had shown over the years and then explained his understanding of the quotation's source. At the critical moment, when the soldiers under Burleson looked to him for inspiration, his adjutant, Thomas Green, had penned the speech his general would give, including its most famous line. Burleson, said McLeod, had even objected to saying the line, as it was not his style. But say it he did, declared McLeod, poking good-natured fun at his candidate when he remarked, "General Burleson looked at Green and said, 'Well, don't let me make any mistake in pronouncing it.'" This brought a round of laughter, and McLeod once more proved himself one of the better public speakers in Texas political circles. Burleson followed McLeod to the podium and enjoyed the opportunity to laugh at himself, saying, "I had almost as much difficulty at Thermopylae as the Persians."[29]

In the Texas elections that September, Jones defeated Burleson by more than 1,500 votes of 13,000 cast; McLeod won the congressional seat unopposed. In November Manifest Destiny outdistanced caution as the Democrats' dark horse, "Young Hickory" Polk, defeated Clay. Texas was on the verge of annexation.

Before September's end McLeod left Texas for Georgia and his beloved fiancée. They were married on October 24, 1844, in the large sanctuary of the First Presbyterian Church of Augusta by Rev. Charles S. Dod, an affable, well-spoken minister who had come to Augusta in 1842 to fill the pulpit.[30] People turned out from as far as Savannah, including members of the Lamar family, to help the newlyweds celebrate; both were prominent figures for the respective exploits and contributions to their states. McLeod, sporting a noticeable paunch, and his slender, dark-haired bride spent six weeks in Georgia, bidding farewell to family and packing Rebecca's belongings for the journey to Texas, the couple's new and permanent home.

When Texas' Ninth Congress met on December 2, 1844, Representative McLeod missed the roll call. Still on his way from Georgia with his bride, he did not hear outgoing President Houston's farewell address on December 4 nor his valedictory on December 9 at Jones's inauguration. Not that missing these speeches by his sworn political enemy would have perturbed the general. Still smarting from Burleson's defeat in September, McLeod and other pro-Republic politicians were at least glad to be rid of Houston. Jones's mixed loyalties to the previous administration on the annexation issue gave hope to some that the Republic might survive the latest attempt at statehood.

McLeod departed Galveston around December 15 bound for Washington-on-the-Brazos.[31] Stops along the way delayed him until Christmas, but he was there when the session resumed on December 26. Except for the speech-making at the opening ceremonies, McLeod missed only one bill of local interest to him. The Galveston City Guards, a volunteer militia that had formed six years earlier and answered the call in 1842 to defend against possible coastal attacks by Mexico, were incorporated as the Galveston Guards with the passage of a December 18 bill. Galveston merchant A. C. Crawford remained captain of the company, and the protectors of the island city, in their Garibaldi shirts, continued to drill and lead ceremonial parades for the next fifteen years.[32]

For the next five weeks McLeod was recognized as a leading voice in Congress, along with his close friend William Cazneau of Travis County,

Tod Robinson, James W. Henderson, George B. Erath, and others.[33] McLeod sponsored a bill on December 30 that for the first time included Galveston on a mail route and followed that with another bill providing funds for the delivery of ice to the island from Houston. He stood with the rest of Congress in support of a memorial to C. B. Snow on January 20 and voted that day to abolish the Department of Indian Affairs.[34] On January 30, with the session nearing its last days, McLeod cosponsored a joint resolution out of the House to establish a Galveston hospital. The tax that would support the building, staffing, and maintenance of the hospital would be collected at the port of Galveston from the captains of arriving passenger ships. The duty included "fifty cents for every foreign white male cabin passenger over sixteen years of age, and twenty-five cents for every foreign white male steerage passenger over sixteen years of age." McLeod made a speech on the House floor before the bill passed.[35]

For three weeks McLeod chaired a special House Committee on Tariffs, an issue particularly sensitive on Galveston Island, where tariffs were significantly higher than along the Red River or the Sabine borders. In a three-page report sent to the House floor on January 22, McLeod noted, for example, that in 1844 Galveston paid a tariff of $182,902 on imports totaling $501,734—a staggering 36 percent. The committee called for a 10 percent reduction in Galveston tariffs—more in line with those reported at San Augustine. Congress accepted a compromise tariff.[36]

On the last day of the Ninth Congress, February 3, 1845, McLeod and others helped pass a bill creating a Galveston Chamber of Commerce. A committee of Galveston merchants had petitioned Congress for the organization and a for list of city leaders to be nominated as members of the island's first mercantile body. The chamber was voted into existence with a twenty-year charter. Members included Samuel May Williams as president and twenty-two leading merchants whose influence would be felt for decades to come. Among them were John S. Sydnor, M. B. Menard, Albert Ball, Capt. Lent M. Hitchcock, Charles Power, Col. Thomas F. McKinney, and McLeod.[37]

One of the most controversial issues, the location of the Republic's seat of government, drew editorial comments and fiery speeches throughout the session. Pitched debates between eastern and western factions over whether to establish the capital in Austin, Houston, or elsewhere had kept the political arena lively—and even deadly with the so-called Archives War during the Seventh Congress's session. In the House the eastern faction, led by W. R. Scurry, James "Smoky" Henderson, M. T. Johnson, and John S. "Rip" Ford, proposed a temporary move of "the Executive, together with the Heads of Departments, and the Archives now at this place," back to Austin until a referendum could be established for a permanent seat of government, "so that when the people have pronounced their fiat, they can be removed to the point which may then be chosen, without difficulty or delay."[38]

McLeod and Cazneau spoke for the western faction, which insisted that Austin already stood by law as the permanent capital of Texas. After Jones vetoed a bill on January 8 that would have settled the issue, the debate flared up again, and on February 3 McLeod argued against the veto as unconstitutional and "the most crying injustice—the grossest fraud." Although Jones seemed willing to support a temporary move back to Austin, complete with a $5,000 appropriation for expenses and government building repairs, McLeod insisted that he supported such a move only as it would be considered permanent, "a fact which his predecessor [Houston] was compelled to deny—and which outrage it is the purpose of the veto message to excuse." Condemning Jones and Houston for their "prostitution of the veto power to the lowest purposes of faction," McLeod assaulted the executives as "artful demagogues, arraying our once united Republic into bitter sectional parties."[39] It is unlikely that such rhetoric eased the stormy situation, but McLeod never hesitated to attack Houston and the easterners.

The larger issue of annexation likewise never abated, even after adjournment. Jones appointed a special resolutions committee to consider both sides of the issue. The nine-member panel met beyond the session's adjournment and did not reveal their report until early March. The March 15 issue of the *Texas National Register* carried the opposing viewpoints. James Armstrong and Scurry spoke for the Houston faction, which leaned toward statehood, acknowledging that although "from the citizens of the United States we have received encouragement and been met with sympathy, the Government has never by a single indication manifested a disposition to aid us in our struggle."[40] Those opposed to annexation met this vacillation, typical of the eastern faction and indicative of the same from its unpredictable leader, with scorn.

The opposing opinion was voiced by McLeod, who argued that vacillation on the part of the U.S. Congress and the Houston clique was hurting the people of Texas: "[They] are now suffering from the attitude in which the discussion of this matter is now standing; they are incurring odium in all their foreign relations; they are now in a state, as it were, of national suspension. The question before us is, shall we allow our foreign relations to be interrupted, our interest throughout all time to be jeopardized and perhaps sacrificed by a servile submission on our part?" Next McLeod broached slavery, the subject that was tearing the United States apart:

"There is a proposition publicly discussed in the United States not only to curtail our territory, but actually to deprive us the constitutional guarantee for our institutions which other portions of the confederacy possess. It proposes to erect a portion of our country into a nonslaveholding state." The general left no doubt about his position on the matter, that "we not only know our rights, but that whenever the proper period shall arrive, we will act upon and secure them. That we will accept no condition which will place us in an attitude of craven servility towards the United States or any other government." After a brief diatribe on submission and "the sisterhood of states," McLeod concluded with a defiant objection to the resolutions for annexation: "I consider them perfectly unexceptionable and manifestly expedient."[41]

The *Texas National Register* carried McLeod's speeches for four weeks after the adjournment of the Ninth Congress, including the incendiary February 3 speech attacking Houston and Jones and the resolutions committee's March report on the annexation problem. Many Texans believed statehood had become a moot issue—"a dead cock in a pit," declared one wag.[42] American expansionists placed much of the blame on Houston, whose covert efforts to achieve annexation for Texas had backfired. Others credited men like McLeod and Cazneau for their efforts to keep Texas independent.

Nevertheless, lame-duck President Tyler's administration continued the process toward Texas statehood, urging A. J. Donelson to return to Texas to secure the necessary support. After March 4, newly elected President Polk pushed harder. With Mexico's assent to Texas independence paramount to the process, annexation supporters worked furiously through the spring days. Jones and Secretary of State Ashbel Smith prepared a memorandum on March 29 intended to lead to a treaty with Mexico. By May 19 the Mexican government seemed willing to agree to the conditions, and by the end of the month Jones had called for a special session of Congress on June 16. Sam Houston's support was achieved by Donelson, who met with the retired Texas president in Galveston on May 4, assisted by Archibald Yell of Arkansas. A May 16 banquet on the Methodist Church grounds in Houston gave Sam Houston an opportunity to reiterate his support for Texas statehood, and newspapers carried the announcement even as Houston headed for Tennessee to be at the bedside of his dying friend Andrew Jackson. Houston learned that his mentor had died before he could reach him.[43]

McLeod, along with the others, began the work of the special session on June 16, 1845. For thirteen days the volatile debate continued. A decided majority of the session opposed Jones's plans for working toward annexation; many, however, believed that statehood under the proper conditions could be achieved. On June 25 McLeod voted against Jones's bill to set apart a portion of the public domain of Texas for the payment of the public debt. The bill passed by a vote of 26−10, and the last of the obstacles leading Texas to statehood had been swept away.[44] With sentiment running almost unanimously in favor of annexation and the conditions of the process not entirely unfavorable to Texas, McLeod presented a resolution on the House floor on the last day of the special session. Attacking Jones as "unpatriotic and unwise," the resolution (which failed 23−14) called for a "certain, effectual, and economical mode of securing our annexation" without the obstacles that had been "thrown in the way" by a cautious administration "attempting to thwart the people in their well-known wish to reunite themselves to the great political family of the United States."[45]

McLeod had ridden the wave of popular sentiment both ways, managing to attack his enemies and keep his own political future afloat. He had also walked a fine line by supporting annexation while not being associated with either the Jones or Houston factions, a delicate high-wire act of political creativity. It seemed in July that he had succeeded.

Jones called another special convention, chaired by Rusk, in Austin on July 4. An ordinance endorsing the annexation process was passed without debate and with only one dissenting vote. By August 28 the convention had drafted a state constitution, which was ratified by popular vote that fall and approved by the U.S. Congress on December 29. The Union's twenty-eighth state celebrated the raising of the American flag in Austin on February 19, 1846. The drama of the Republic of Texas was no more.

McLeod returned to Galveston on July 1, 1845, already active in state and national politics. Before leaving for the special session, the general immersed himself in the local organization of the Democratic Party of Texas. He would enjoy various positions of responsibility for the next two years, including corresponding secretary of the state party in 1846. He prepared for the presidential elections in the fall campaign of 1848 and contemplated a run for U.S. Congress as representative of Texas' Western District. Mirabeau Lamar recommended McLeod to Polk "for command of a [U.S. Army] regiment should one become available" and later shared a letter from J. M. Storms of New York City indicating support for a McLeod congressional candidacy, should he desire it: "Heaven send that General McLeod comes to the House though I think him too brave, honorable and gifted to be the choice of a large portion of Texas. . . . No honest man could be chosen."[1]

For now the Galvestonian had business at home to attend to, and he spent the remainder of the year taking care of his finances and family. As a charter member of the Galveston Chamber of Commerce, McLeod met with the city's merchants on several occasions to discuss the needs of the young but growing city of more than five thousand. Of special importance was the burgeoning cotton business along the docks. McLeod's horse-driven cotton press began operations in 1845, outproducing his nearest competitors, who, unable to compress more than five hundred bales a day, soon gave up. McLeod prospered for more than a year as the first and, for a time, only press at the busy harbor. Not until Charles Emerson and A. P. Lufkin introduced the steam-powered Marine press late in 1846 did McLeod's business begin to suffer. By 1848 he had abandoned the business in favor of a more successful law practice and political career.[2]

After a decade of struggle, Galveston finally began to boom in 1846. The market house and the hospital opened, thanks in part to government subsidies by the Ninth Congress and McLeod's efforts on behalf of his adopted hometown. An auditorium above the market house hosted the citywide entertainment that came to the island: plays, orations, banquets, and balls. The first bank in Texas was chartered in Galveston and housed in McKinney and Williams's two-story brick building on the downtown square. The Commercial Agricultural Bank subscribed $300,000 at the outset and elected Colonel Williams as its first president. Several original wood structures in the business district came down in 1846 and were replaced by more modern brick buildings.[3]

The harbor came alive in 1846 and 1847, and ships moved in and out from the ever busier docks. Emigrants, especially from Germany, poured into Texas through Galveston and made their way inland to New Braunfels and Fredericksburg. Some stayed, including Ferdinand Flake, a future Galveston newspaperman and Unionist who married there in 1847. A tragic shipwreck on the west end of the island on New Year's Eve, 1846, left dozens of German families injured and destitute of clothes and supplies, but citizens quickly contributed hundreds of dollars for emergency relief and housing.[4]

Churches came to Galveston during these prospering times, including the Presbyterians, Episcopalians, and Methodists. The McLeods attended the Presbyterian Church at Nineteenth Street and Avenue F, and Rebecca taught Sabbath School there for years.[5] The Planter's Hotel stood at Twenty-second Street and the Strand, and Baker's and Smythe's Hotels hosted dignitaries and visitors. The Menards' William Tell Hotel adjoined the Galveston *News* building on Market Street, and mercantile establishments filled blocks in every direction.

On July 27, 1846, the McLeods received head rights to land on Galveston Island and a homestead on the wide Avenue J (later Broadway). The general's astute business dealings eventually turned the acreage into ownership of parts of fourteen blocks within city limits. With land grants in Henderson and Van Zandt Counties, his property totaled more than 2,700 acres by 1847.[6] The homestead at Twenty-sixth and Avenue J, half a city block, soon sported a two-story main house, a carriage house, servants' quarters, and wooded acreage on the west side. The main house faced south toward the Gulf. McLeod opened his law office downtown on the Strand.

The McLeods actively supported Galveston's cultural growth in those early years, especially Mayor John S. Sydnor's efforts to establish a school system on the island. Efforts had failed in 1838 and again in 1844, although small private academies were organized by E. Walbridge in 1842, Baptist preacher James Hutchins and his wife in 1843, and the Episcopalian rector Rev. Benjamin Eaton in 1844. The city owned a lot and a building for a school purchased in 1838 by the Galveston City Company, but it had been unable to pay for good teachers and supplies. McLeod successfully lobbied the state legislature to confer authority upon a board of aldermen for the purpose of collecting a special tax for the maintenance of a school system in Galveston, and on April 2, 1846, the legislation went into effect. The tax, a one-half of 1 percent levy against city property, enabled trustees to purchase a ten-year lease on a building, buy sufficient supplies for students, and pay reasonable salaries to faculty. The school opened in 1846 to the cheers of hundreds and operated without serious problems for two years. Unfortunately a series of poorly prepared aldermen on the board, along with an increasingly unsupportable budget, closed the school in 1848. Two more feeble attempts, in 1850 and 1851, met a similar fate. But public education would soon come to Galveston to stay, as Sydnor and McLeod continued their exhaustive, acclaimed efforts over the next decade.[7]

Another of the McLeods' primary interests was the growing, politically influential Temperance League. First organized in 1839 as the Galveston Temperance Society, the movement grew quickly across the Southwest through mainstream Protestant churches. On April 1, 1846, McLeod gave the keynote address to a large public gathering at the Presbyterian Church, hosted by the society. His bombastic, hour-long speech met with great applause as his voice rose, and with hushed silence in the dramatic quiet moments. He spoke of the morals of America's society and of the political overtones of the sale of liquor in the United States. He listed the physical and spiritual evils of drink and contrasted America with an already besotted Great Britain: "[The] gay and giddy Queen who annually squanders in her royal whims, will mourn in studied phrase of woe. Her titled flatterers will rehearse her character, not as it was, but as it ought to have been." The orator rose to the occasion, according to later informal reviews, waxing eloquent on the disastrous effects of drink: "For soon it becomes the desperate remedy of the drunkard, who flies to the bottle as the only solace he knows for his unstrung nerves, and gorges an appetite as insatiate as the grave. Thus cause and effect—the destroyer and the victim—go hand in hand, till death closes a scene at which nature long had blushed." McLeod accused his own city of "21 or more retail drinking houses," whose rent, taxes, wages, supplies of liquor, and profits "we may reasonably state the whole amount at $75,000: enough to establish the public schools, build the bridge from the island to Virginia Point, and erect a lighthouse independent to the government."

"In closing, ladies"—McLeod's voice descended to empathetic tones—"because you are always its unoffending victims, and it leaves you only the alternative of silent endurance, may it never be your fate, as it has been of thousands—nay millions—to watch till midnight, for the return of an erring husband—to listen in anguish, that only a wife can know, and the last faint hope crushed by the sound of the tottering footfall that proves him a drunkard. . . . If I shall have been the means of withdrawing only one of my fellow men from the chances of a drunkard's grave, I shall feel that I have not lived in vain."[8]

The popular speaker had little time to enjoy the plaudits of the Galveston audience. Within a month he was on his way to Point Isabel, where the United States was preparing for war with Mexico. "I am ready to enlist and fight," McLeod wrote his wife on May 4.[9] Although he did not enlist and did not fight, the enterprising West Pointer made his mark in the early days of confrontation.

The election of Polk proved a victory not only for the Democrats but for the national expansionists, whose philosophy of Manifest Destiny carried the day over the more conservative warnings of Whig Henry Clay. Campaign promises for the acquisition of Oregon, Texas, and California led many to believe that only war with Mexico would obtain the latter. As Texas worked through its annexation process and British and American diplomats dissected the Oregon Territory at the forty-ninth parallel, Polk sent Gen. Zachary Taylor and more than four thousand troops into Texas to secure a military posture at the Nueces River. In August, 1845, Taylor's troops began to arrive at the still struggling hamlet of Corpus Christi. As the military forces grew, Corpus Christi grew as well, with supply trains making their way from as far away as St. Louis and ships arriving after short jaunts from New Orleans and Galveston. By the end of the year, what had been a sleepy village of no more than fifty families had become a prospering, bustling military outpost. The U.S. mail ran regularly along the coast, and retail merchants crowded along the bluff to sell their wares.

Galvestonian Samuel Bangs, newspaperman and entrepreneur, left his island paper, the *Chronicle,* in the able hands of B. F. Neal and made a cursory visit to Corpus Christi in September. He became a permanent resident by December, sold land rights in exchange for a new printing press and supplies, secured a partnership with George W. Fletcher, a Corpus Christi physician, and engaged José de Alba, a leader in the area's Spanish-speaking community. By the end of December Bangs had set up a printing office adjacent to Taylor's army camp, and on January 1, 1846, he published the first pages of his *Corpus Christi Gazette.* The experienced printer and newsman proclaimed the slogan, "Be sure you are right, then go ahead," and then went ahead, printing a biweekly, four-page issue that included local advertisements, news from the United States, and information of interest to soldiers stationed in the area. Portions of most issues were printed in Spanish for the locals.[10]

For two months the *Gazette* made a hearty profit for Bangs and Fletcher. But on March 8, Taylor used Bangs's paper to issue a series of orders for the camp's removal from the Nueces south to the Rio Grande. The extra edition warned citizens and merchants not to accompany or follow troops into what appeared an increasingly dangerous situation. The dissolution of the military camp signaled doom for the prospering newspaper, and by the end of March Bangs had left Corpus Christi headed for Fronton, or Point Isabel. There he partnered with the young, dashing Gideon "Legs" Lewis of the Galveston *News* and announced his intention to publish the *Rio Grande Herald*. Lewis, ever the adventurer, had followed Taylor to the Mexico border that spring with the hope of joining the fight as well as reporting it.[11] Bangs and Lewis made their separate ways down the coast as others in Galveston organized that spring for battle.

Weeks before the shots beginning the Mexican War were fired along the Rio Grande, men in the Galveston Guards enlisted for an immediate rendezvous with Taylor at Point Isabel. The April meetings included the most prominent citizen-soldiers on the island, including McLeod, Albert Sidney Johnston, and William P. Ballinger. Out of these meetings grew the Galveston Riflemen. Johnston and McLeod were elected as ex-officio commanders of the company, with Capts. Ephraim McLean and Robert Howard, 1st Lt. Ballinger, and 2nd Lt. Oliver C. Hartley. Dozens of Galvestonians volunteered for a three-month hitch, awaiting only the United States' declaration of war and Taylor's call for volunteers.[12]

Sixteen volunteers decided not to wait, and by May 3 they had made their way to Point Isabel under the command of Charles Seefeld, with Edward Connor and John Lynch as officers. Seefeld returned to gather the others, but the Riflemen had already embarked down the coast and few volunteers had not already been swept up by brigades marching through from Arkansas and East Texas. Meanwhile, near Point Isabel, Company A found itself under attack by Mexican Gen. Mariano Arista's artillery while Taylor prepared a defense for the strategic coastal town. The main company of Galveston volunteers did not arrive until after the American victory at Palo Alto on May 8.[13]

McLeod faced an uncomfortable dilemma. Having resigned from the U.S. Army on December 31, 1835, to join the Texas Revolution, his status on rejoining was uncertain. Military procedure would probably prohibit reenlisting; the best-case scenario would probably mean a reappointment as second lieutenant, the rank McLeod had held when he resigned eleven years earlier. Anxious to join the fight but reluctant to accept the lower rank, McLeod decided to withdraw from the volunteer army.

By the middle of May Taylor had marched away from Fort Brown and

Resaca de Palmas, leaving Matamoros in the hands of American troops as he prepared for an assault against Monterrey. McLeod found himself about to be left behind. Most of the Riflemen marched forward with Taylor, although at the end of three months many came home. Johnston was elected colonel of the First Regiment of the Texas Infantry, McLean was lieutenant colonel, and William Smith was major. Menard remained with Company A, as did Ballinger, Howard, and more than sixty Galvestonians. Seventeen-year-old Henry Seeligson joined the Texas Rangers after Monterrey and distinguished himself in battle at Buena Vista, gaining Taylor's attention.[14]

In Matamoros McLeod found Bangs and Lewis setting up their press for the first editions of the *Rio Grande Herald*. Before they could get under way, however, Lewis abandoned the enterprise to join Taylor's army, serving with distinction for two years. The newspaper never materialized, although Bangs continued without Lewis. McLeod also ran into W. G. Dryden, the Santa Fe merchant who had encouraged Lamar to annex the New Mexico territory in 1840. McLeod and Dryden spoke at length regarding the establishment of a pro-Republican newspaper.[15]

Revolution was brewing along the Rio Grande border, as it had been for years, under the resistant forces of Antonio Canales and José Maria Jesus Carbajal. Now Carbajal had seized the opportune moment to again proclaim an independent Republic of the Rio Grande, enveloping the towns and territories of Tamaulipas, Nuevo León, Coahuila, and Chihuahua. In February Carbajal came to Fronton from the Canales camp to meet privately with Taylor, offering assistance in return for support of his revolutionary intentions. A division of the northern Mexico states from Mexico City would aid the American army in its quest for victory.[16] McLeod was well aware of the Canales-Carbajal movement and had been actively supportive since as early as 1839. Apprised of the revolutionary leader's presence in the vicinity just weeks before, he believed that Texas' public support for a Rio Grande republic would make a difference in the unfolding war's outcome.

In the second half of May a volunteer company of mostly Louisiana printers and newspapermen arrived in Matamoros, having been discharged after six months of service. The company, which included J. N. Fleeson, John H. Peoples, Joseph R. Palmer, and R. A. DeVilliers, broke up, and many prepared to return to New Orleans. Fleeson became interested in an old abandoned Mexican press—from the Matamoros *Boletin*—and contemplated starting his own paper. McLeod and Dryden overhead a conversation about it and asked to join him.[17] Thus was born a partnership of printing expertise and political savvy. While DeVilliers replaced Lewis and went to work with Bangs, McLeod and Fleeson made preparations to publish a biweekly paper whose mission was printed on the masthead of the first issue: "To persuade the people of the states of Tamaulipas, Nuevo Leon, Coahuila, and Chihuahua to an appreciation of the merits of a separate Northern Mexico federation."[18]

The Republic of the Rio Grande and The People's Friend (subtitled in Spanish as *Republica de Rio Grande y Amigo del Pueblo*) produced its first issue on June 2, 1846, preceding Bangs's new *Matamoros Reveille* by three weeks. The issue included advertisements from several local American merchants, a section of Spanish vocabulary intended for volunteer soldiers on their way to the front, and an inference on the editorial page that Taylor had given his blessing for the enterprise. Also on the editorial page was McLeod's scathing attack of the Mexican government. To the citizens of the Rio Grande valley he wrote, "Abandon the Mexican vulture, that preys upon your vitals—the fitting symbol of a government, that has no deeper commiseration for your sufferings, than the voracious bird upon her crest feels for the serpent that writhes in its beak; assemble your delegates within the American lines, organize your provisional government at once, and declare your independence to the Sierra Madre. . . . *Rise then and Shout for the Republic of the Rio Grande!*"[19]

McLeod and Fleeson published four more issues of what turned out to be a weekly paper: June 9, 16, 23, and 30. It caught the attention of reporters from the New Orleans *Picayune* and its competitor the *Weekly Delta,* the *Telegraph & Texas Register,* and the Clarksville (Texas) *Northern Standard* and even made a column in the New York *Sun* lauding any efforts that "denounced Mexican abuses—especially tariffs—and 'British insolence,'" and urging that the northern Mexico inhabitants "proclaim an independent republic and free trade with the United States" even as the *Republic of the Rio Grande* had. "A new Star," the *Sun* editorial continued, in praise of McLeod's efforts, "is shining out amid the ragged clouds of war."[20]

McLeod continued his editorial diatribes in support of an independent republic, with references to the ongoing war effort near Monterrey and the Carbajal cause. In the June 23 issue he included a humorous anecdote that spoke to the occasionally mixed feelings of soldiers marching through Matamoros: "The volunteers wade into the rivers of Mexico on their way to victory, but some might consider returning to their homeland as soon as possible. As one soldier declared, 'I'll obey orders, but I'll not wade into the river if they only ask me to, for that will be volunteering, and I've had enough of that!'"[21] In another issue McLeod criticized the Mexican government for not maintaining schools in northern Mexico states and for governmental mismanagement that resulted in a mineral production decrease from $28 million to $800,000. He compared the drafting of its soldiers as "Mexicans driven to battle like felons to their punishment."[22] The editorial assault against the Mexican government escalated weekly.

On June 24 the Matamoros *Reveille* hit the streets with its Monroesque slogan: "The people of this continent alone have the right to decide their own destiny." Bangs and DeVilliers concentrated on news from Mexico, weather reports, and lighter fare than their competition and seemed to get off to a good start. But trouble came to both presses at the end of June. A Mexican printer, leasing Bangs's press to publish *El Liberal* in support of the Mexican viewpoint, caught the attention of American officers on Taylor's staff. Both the Mexican paper and Bangs's were shut down by orders of the U.S. Army, and Bangs was jailed briefly. Reading over McLeod's paper, the officers decided that outright support for Carbajal's filibustering efforts was too inflammatory and ordered it shut down as well.

One week later the special Fourth of July issue of *The American Flag*, under the auspices of new editors John H. Peoples and Joseph R. Palmer, replaced the *Republic*.[23] McLeod, furious with Taylor's staff and deeply discouraged at the sudden sour turn of events, packed his belongings and returned to Galveston on the next steam packet headed up the coast.[24] His involvement in the Mexican War came to an abrupt end, although his support for Carbajal did not. The future of an independent republic in northern Mexico remained paramount in his thoughts and activities in the years that followed. McLeod arrived home the second week of July and immersed himself in his business ventures: the lagging law practice and the failing cotton press. In September Rebecca announced that she was pregnant. The prospect of a family spurred McLeod through an energetic several months, and the year 1847, with the war no more than a distant memory, looked prosperous and full of good fortune. The McLeods established themselves as community leaders while others of their socioeconomic class marched toward Mexico City. Galveston continued to grow and prosper into the winter months, with a healthy increase in German emigrants and military supplies passing through.

McLeod intervened on behalf of his cousin-in-law, Mirabeau Lamar, to subscribe a loan request from Gazaway Bugg Lamar, Rebecca's brother and an influential bank president in Brooklyn, New York. He wrote Lamar later that year to assure him that the monies could be secured and explained why he had decided not to run for U.S. Congress in the upcoming campaign, adding that he might in 1849. Lamar received the newsy letter in Laredo, where he was stationed as commander of Taylor's First Texas Mounted Volunteers.[25]

In March, 1847, George Cazneau, Hugh and Rebecca's first child, was born nearly four weeks early, a frightening proposition that would cause their son a lifetime of frailty. But young Caz survived his infant days—including a devastating yellow fever epidemic that raced across the island that year—and reflected his mother's slender, fragile physique for the rest of his life. The remainder of 1847 brought an eerie calm to Galveston and to the McLeod family, as hundreds of the island citizens marched across Mexico to bring the war to a victorious end. A citywide banquet on November 25 honored a number of the returning war veterans, and a memorable toast by McLeod accented the evening festivities.[26]

The deaths of three friends—Samuel Walker, the famous Texas Ranger, killed in battle; George Knight Teulon in Asia; and William G. Cooke, of yellow fever—caused McLeod to reflect upon his life as he turned thirty-three.[27] It was also time to consider the causes that awaited his fervent support. Two enterprises fascinated the Galveston lawyer: a run for the congressional seat in Washington, D.C., and the prospects of a new future on the island city—the railroad.

CHAPTER 13

The Railroad

Encouragement from close friends and political allies, including Lamar, Cazneau, Ford, Rusk, and Williams, may have been the final push for McLeod to consider a run for the Western District seat in the U.S. House of Representatives in 1849. In the fall of 1848, McLeod traveled to Georgia with his wife and one-year-old Caz, a three-month journey that included family visits and political business. They showed off the newest McLeod in Macon and Savannah, where Rebecca remained with Caz while the general went north.

McLeod made his way to New York City, his first visit to his birthplace in thirteen years, to see his brother-in-law, Gazaway Bugg Lamar. The context of the conversations may have included funds for Carbajal's continuing revolutionary movement in northern Mexico, as well as the possibility of securing another personal loan for Mirabeau Lamar. McLeod returned to Georgia via Philadelphia and Washington, D.C. In Philadelphia he met briefly with Maj. George H. Crosman, political ally and a friend of Albert Sidney Johnston. Crosman sent McLeod with a letter to Johnston regarding the sale of some real estate, but the letter was lost en route. Fall politics along the East Coast heated up in the last days of the presidential election, with Taylor headed for victory in November despite what McLeod called his "incapacity and ignorance of affairs."[1] Hugh, Rebecca, and Caz returned home in mid-November. The general had missed election day in Galveston and did not vote, but he remarked to Johnston that Taylor's victory had "the dry bones of Houstonians shaking here awfully."[2]

If the trip east had any influence on McLeod, additional encouragement from friends persuaded him to toss his hat into the 1849 race for Congress.[3] He continued his law practice for the first several months of the new year and served on the Chamber of Commerce Trade Committee through spring.[4] Elections would be held on August 6, and in the summer months McLeod's campaign began in earnest. He traveled to San Antonio and Austin and back across Bastrop, Fayette, and Milam Counties. On June 20 he spoke to a crowd in Cincinnati, about fifteen miles north of Huntsville, and was warmly received.[5] In July he made speeches in Houston and in Brazoria County.

Four candidates fought for votes in the Western District. Robert Mc-Alpin "Three-Legged Willie" Williamson, a longtime Texas newspaper-man and public figure, ran well enough to finish a strong second in the race. Timothy Pilsbury finished a disappointing third, with 1,500 of the 8,500 votes cast. Pilsbury, of Brazoria County, had served in the 29th and 30th Congresses as Texas Representative. His age, sixty-eight, may have been his downfall. The fourth candidate, Volney E. Howard, had lived in Texas less than two years but had a reputation of political influence in New Orleans. Born and raised in Maine, Howard made his way down the East Coast states in his early years and then headed to Mississippi before arriving in Louisiana. A charismatic speaker, Colonel Howard also proved an able campaigner.

Howard won the congressional election, carrying thirteen counties and totaling 3,766 votes. He won big in Bexar (his county), Gillespie, Nueces, and Walker Counties and even took islander votes from McLeod, 225–101. McLeod ran reasonably well in Austin but finished dead last in the election with only 544 votes. The pro-Houston R. W. Scurry won the Eastern District seat and accompanied Howard to Washington to serve in the 31st congressional session.[6]

There is no indication that the results discouraged McLeod from future political involvement. He received support from several newspapers across Texas, including the influential *Texas State Gazette* in Austin. His political allies did not give up on him. News of Howard's voting record, supported in San Antonio editorials but scathingly attacked in Austin, Galveston, and Houston, spurred many to urge McLeod to consider a return to the campaign trail.[7]

The year 1850 began with celebration in the McLeod family, which had grown by one more. In January Rebecca gave birth to a daughter, christened Isabella after Hugh's late mother. Although a small recompense, the general also learned in February that the Texas Congress had passed a long-overdue relief bill for the Santa Fe survivors. At a monthly rate of $22.50, the pension would help many of the men who had served under him.

On April 21 the national census taker arrived at "Dwelling 534" on Avenue J in Galveston. He recorded four members of the McLeod family living there and a property value of $5,000.[8] Joy turned to sorrow only weeks later, however, when the frail infant Isabella died. Services were held in the same Presbyterian sanctuary where Isabella had been baptized, and she was buried in the city cemetery.[9]

Three years earlier, in the spring of 1847, Gen. Sidney Sherman teamed with Andrew Briscoe to purchase nearly five thousand acres of the defunct Harrisburg Town Company in a renewed effort to build the first railroad line in Texas. Briscoe had failed in his earlier attempt to establish the Harrisburg Railroad and Trading Company, but the influential Sherman believed the time was ripe for another try.[10] Sherman, born and raised in the Boston area, came to Texas from Kentucky with fifty-two volunteers in time to join the Texas Revolution and carry a flag across the San Jacinto prairie. He built a home on San Jacinto Bay three years later, and served Texas in the Seventh Congress and then as major general of the Texas militia. He presided over the controversial trial of Capt. E. W. Moore. Sherman's fame across Texas, and his connections back east, revived the foundering railroad plans Briscoe had envisioned.[11]

Briscoe and Sherman purchased the Harrisburg lots for $13,736.49, with a down payment of $1,005.50, and Sherman headed for Massachusetts to enlist investors.[12] On October 2 he wrote Briscoe from Boston: "The parties I am interesting own large railroad properties and they take hold of it with an eye to building the railroad to the Brazos. I shall be compelled to let these Boston people have a much larger interest than I had intended, but I suppose it will be the true policy as their aid and influence will be all important to us." Sherman raised more than $10,000 in Boston; the remainder would be covered by Texas investments. A written agreement dated October 31, 1847, laid out the details of the original investment in "a joint stock company for purpose of improving said lands and real estate and promoting growth of said town." Sherman was listed as first agent, and McLeod, William L. Cazneau, and John G. Tod were first directors.[13]

Primary investors from the northeast included Elisha Allen, John Angier, and Jonathan Fay Barrett. Barrett became president of the reorganized Harrisburg City Company, whose charter provided for building up the town, removing obstacles to navigation between Harrisburg and the coast, and "taking stock in any railroad having one of its termini in said town." Sherman's plan included a rail line that extended from the coast through Harrisburg and Houston, crossing the Brazos and someday the Colorado River.[14] Sherman took his railroad plans to the state legislature for additional assistance. A bill cosponsored by Rep. John Shea of Harris County and Sen. John W. Dancy of the La Grange District worked its way through committees and floor debates, passing on February 10, 1850. Although two other charters had been gained for Texas rail companies by this time, neither would materialize.[15]

On February 11 the Buffalo Bayou–Brazos & Colorado Railroad Company (BBB&C) was incorporated. Eleven names appeared on the charter as incorporators, including Sherman. Second on the list was McLeod. Barrett, Allen, and Angier represented the eastern capital interests. The others were from Galveston, Houston, and Harrisburg: Tod, William Marsh Rice, William Van Alstyne, John H. Stevens, B. A. Shepherd, and W. J. Hutchins. The charter stipulated that the railroad would start along Buffalo Bayou and make its way to the Brazos between Richmond and Washington, and then on to the Colorado. The BBB&C was given free right-of-way through state lands and would be fifty yards wide along the route. Capital stock was fixed at $500,000, and the company was to construct a minimum of twenty miles of track in its first two years of operation to avoid forfeiture of its charter.[16] The charter was revised on February 25 and September 4 to correct minor problems in the original legislation.[17]

McLeod and Tod raised money on the island, lining up dozens of investors at $100 each. Although Harrisburg and Houston citizens vied for control of the rail line, Galvestonians knew that wherever this line went, they would benefit. Transporting cotton by rail and connecting to the Galveston docks meant a prosperous future for those smart enough to invest in the BBB&C. McLeod bought additional stocks over the years, and the monies would see his family through hard times well into the 1870s.[18]

John A. Williams of Boston came to Texas in 1851 as the chief engineer and superintendent of the BBB&C and selected Harrisburg as the starting point and Richmond as the Brazos crossing. Since no standardized gauge existed in the United States until 1875, each rail company chose its own. Williams decided on the standard British gauge of four feet, eight and one-half inches. Although the first five miles of track were laid out in good order, delays in materials and land acquisition prevented final construction until 1852.[19] The depot in Harrisburg was built on the site of Benjamin Theron's property. Theron, a Frenchman and Galveston restaurateur, had his land confiscated in a bankruptcy dispute, and the BBB&C bought it at a greatly reduced price.[20] The depot building contract went to W. J. Kyle and B. F. Terry of Fort Bend.[21]

McLeod served on the board of directors and remained active in the railroad business for years. A well-attended Rail Road Convention was held in August, 1852, to help advertise the BBB&C and enlist more investors.[22] The first annual report to the directors, dated October 1, 1852, expected to raise some $700,000 from the sale of unused Harrisburg town lots, plus annual receipts of over $13,000 from passenger and mail income and $80,750 in freight earnings. Williams, who presented the report, indicated that the land's uniform level where the rails would be built would make for straightforward progress, and that a proposed side connection to Houston (later the Houston Tap, completed in 1856) could be expected. Other plans included extensions of the BBB&C across Texas and even perhaps in conjunction with a transcontinental southern rail.[23]

In November the first locomotive arrived by ship at the Galveston docks. Christened the *General Sherman*, its operation was delayed when it was damaged in a storm that struck the island in December. F. A. Stearns of Boston was its first conductor. The BBB&C purchased two more locomotives and twenty-four freight cars in its first four years of operation. On April 21, 1853, a huge barbecue was held at Thomas Point to celebrate the road's progress. McLeod and Francis R. Lubbock were the featured speakers, and the festivities were capped off by firing one of the famous San Jacinto cannons, the Twin Sisters, brought to the party on a flatbed car.[24]

The Galveston *News* carried a notice on September 2 announcing the opening of a new route from Galveston to Fort Bend, Wharton, and Colorado Counties via steamer, railway, or stage, to begin operations the following Wednesday, leaving Harrisburg and Stafford's Point twice weekly, a distance of twenty miles. "Every facility will be given for transporting horses and carriage by Railway," promised the announcement, written by Williams. The caption above the advertisement included a stagecoach and steamer, with two rail cars in between.[25]

The BBB&C enjoyed prosperity for the next seven years, until the Civil War interrupted its advancement and dried up its funding. By then the rail line had been extended thirty-two miles past Richmond, fifty miles to the San Bernard River, sixty-five miles to Eagle Lake, and then eighty miles to Alleyton in the fall of 1860. McLeod benefited from his investments many times over and worked exhaustively to extend the railroad east to the Mississippi River and on to the East Coast, taking a leading role in the politics surrounding bridge bonds. Ferrying trains across the major rivers as well as from Galveston to Houston was inefficient and often dangerous to passenger and freight, as evidenced by train accidents in 1855 and 1856. The Galveston-Virginia Point causeway issue would prove volatile in 1857.

In 1851, with the railroad operations progressing and his law practice faring as well as ever, McLeod looked once more to the political arena. Disturbed by the reports of Howard's voting habits, many Texans sought change. When Howard announced his intention to run for reelection and received the San Antonio newspapers' endorsements in the spring, opposing candidates lined up for the campaign. William Menefee of Fayette County argued his case in the influential *Intelligencer,* former Texas congressman Asa M. Lewis joined in the political contest, and Galvestonians Henry N. Potter and McLeod threw their hats into the ring. Four men would try to unseat Howard, but early indications were that McLeod would be his primary opponent.[26]

McLeod again traveled across the two dozen Western District counties, this time taking a jaunt down into the Rio Grande valley and as far as Eagle Pass, where his close friend William Cazneau lived with his new bride, Jane McManus. This was Howard territory, but McLeod said later that he had trouble "finding more than seven people who knew Howard, other than his partner at law, Rice Garland. I found them intelligent, respectable, industrious, and only suffering from some neglects of his, in letting their trade be hampered with restrictions by our own government."[27]

On the evening of May 7 in San Antonio, Howard and McLeod engaged in a lively, often bitter debate that lasted more than three and a half hours. McLeod spoke for the first hour, criticizing Howard's voting record and questioning his allegiance to the Democratic Party and his loyalties to Texas, where he had lived intermittently only since 1847. McLeod also hinted that Howard had committed "unjustifiable acts during the last canvass for that office," an issue the speaker considered "a proper topic of discussion."[28] The speech's primary focus was on Howard's poor representation of Texas in Congress. McLeod claimed that Howard vacillated on the critical omnibus bill that became the basis for the Compromise of 1850, supporting it only after it promised to pass anyway. He also chastised the congressman for backing both the low tariff and a major internal improvements bill. The 1850 Rivers and Harbors Bill authorized $200,000 in federal monies for Texas, but, railed McLeod, "for this year only, and by accepting it, [we] commit ourselves to a system that will take from our pockets $200,000 *annually* to be paid out for dry docks, canals, harbors, rivers, creeks, and ponds at Boston, New York, Buffalo, and Chicago." Referring to a San Antonio editorial about a "whig in disguise," McLeod queried with biting sarcasm: "Surely, Colonel, you are not going over, are you? Shades of Gen. Jackson and the Maysville Road forbid it."[29]

With Howard's response, the debate turned ugly and personal. Howard went on the attack, accusing McLeod of poor leadership during the 1841 Santa Fe expedition and citing cowardice as a factor in its failure. Observers remarked on the hush that fell over the audience. McLeod withstood the barrage as he sat on the podium, but his anger rose with every accusation. When Howard finished his diatribe, the debate concluded without an opportunity for McLeod to respond, and neither spoke to the other as they left the auditorium.

Ten days later in Austin, McLeod delivered a speech before hundreds of supporters, venting ten years of frustration and perhaps guilt in a retort to Howard's attack. In a lengthy defense of his decisions as commanding officer of the Pioneers, McLeod stated that the troops had been sent to escort the merchants and civil commissioners, and, although "we expected to fight the troops, not the additional forces which a population of seventy-five thousand souls could turn out—nor would that conquest have been worth the cost if we could have made it—for Texas was unable to maintain the expense of a forcible jurisdiction over a hostile and distant province. We expected that the population would at least stand neutral 'til the blow was struck, and not array themselves in the opposing rank." [30]

McLeod continued, describing the decision to divide the forces and send Cooke and Sutton forward: "We must either make a detachment strong enough to defend itself to hunt the settlements and get provisions, or destroy the wagons and march together in a body, eating the teams, or, lastly, return home." Citing the gallant efforts of Captain Sutton, who went ahead, and the returning message that called for McLeod, the general directed blame for the ensuing surrender partially on Col. George Howard and partly on Cooke. In a well-orchestrated moment McLeod called on Lawrence Beardsley. Beardsley, a Pioneer and Travis County resident, made an emotional speech seconding McLeod and castigating Howard for daring to call McLeod a coward. "At Vera Cruz," Beardsley said, "the General came to the hospital twice a day, to see the sick of yellow fever; and we all passed resolutions of thanks, and doing him justice, when we got back."

It was a poignant moment, and the crowd responded. After applause for Beardsley's remarks, McLeod continued, focusing again on Howard's voting record. "A northern paper says he undertook the difficult and apparently impossible equestrian feat of riding two horses at the same time," McLeod quipped, "going in opposite directions. He asks, with a sneer, which did best—I in conquering, or he in selling the country. Well, I'll bear that jibe—I had rather be unfortunate than dishonest. Let him enjoy the money value of his promises, if his conscience will permit."

Speaking to the Compromise of 1850, McLeod continued his retort to the May 7 debate. Criticized for changing his opinion on the issue, he admitted that "when the proposition was put to the people, I voted against it; it was accepted by a large majority, and there my opposition ended." McLeod's ardent proslavery stand seeped into his argument: "It is now a law of the land, and though it has reduced us on the line of slavery from 36 degrees, 30 minutes to 32 degrees, and deprived us by his own showing, of two million dollars, it has been acceptable to the people, and I am content. Further, I will be the last to disturb it, because unanimity is essential to the South for success in such a struggle. If the North respects it, the difficulty is at an end; if she does not, those who voted for the bill will see that all hope is gone, and will take the lead themselves. On this platform I abide." Responding to Howard's contention that McLeod was Sam Houston's enemy, the general admitted that the two had differences of opinion on the politics of their day but added, "I will do him the justice to say, that all our hard things about one another were said face to face; and he has repeatedly acknowledged the high courtesy I always observed in our intercourse."

After two more caustic anecdotes in barely veiled reference to his campaign opponent, McLeod concluded his defensive speech to the extended applause of the partisan audience: "If you elect me as your representative to Congress, you may not find the astute intellect and deep chicanery of my opponent, but you will at least get an honest man. You will get one who has lived too long in Texas to feel superior attachment to another home, or a former allegiance. You will get one whose children, born on this soil, will be reared here—one who, if you send him as your representative, will at least never betray you." One week later in Bastrop, McLeod wrote to Rusk, noting Howard's unjust attacks and demanding that Rusk endorse his candidacy through the Huntsville *Item* as soon as possible.[31] A month later McLeod, accompanied on the campaign trail by influential Galveston merchant E. B. Nichols, entreated Rusk a second time from Cincinnati.[32] Even as the second letter was mailed, McLeod received Rusk's response, written June 17, declining to endorse him on the grounds that "it would interfere in the election."[33] McLeod was stunned.

The election was held on August 4, with early returns first posted on August 15. The vote was close, and it would be another week before the *Houston Telegraph & Texas Register* would publish the nearly complete results. It had been a two-man race after all, with Lewis (1,100 votes), Potter (900), and Menefee (150) accounting for less than one-third of the polling. McLeod carried eight counties, with significant victories in Nueces (216–8) and Brazoria (114–42) and a total of nearly 1,700 votes. But Howard carried nineteen counties, amassing 2,900 votes and taking 47 percent to McLeod's 28 percent. Howard returned triumphantly for another two years in Congress.[34]

McLeod, though dispirited, refused to let the defeat affect his sense of humor. In an interview that fall he jokingly told of a stop on the campaign trail in Milam County, where he asked a citizen for directions to the local grocery. The man pointed to a sign over a nearby shanty, consisting of a dog's picture with the letters R and Y beside it. "Doggery," it read, for doggerel, a wry comment on his opponent's tongue.[35] In Galveston McLeod looked ahead once more, taking the defeat in stride and resuming his law practice and railroad business with renewed vigor. He and Rebecca added on to their homestead property and continued to make real estate deals, including the purchase of 1,200 acres from Henry L. Kinney in Nueces County. McLeod redoubled his efforts with the Freemasonry movement in Texas, visiting his own lodge in Austin frequently and supporting the recently established lodges in Galveston and Houston. The efforts of Carbajal's rebellion continued to interest the general, and his fund-raising in response caught the attention of the Mexican revolutionary. In December McLeod mourned the loss of Edward Burleson. In May, 1852, he heard exceptionally good news from Pensacola; his brother, Daniel, now in his twentieth year of U.S. Navy service, had been promoted to chief surgeon and assigned to the Navy Yard on the Florida panhandle.[36] A steamer's sail from Galveston to Pensacola would take no more than two days, affording plenty of opportunities for the two to renew their kinship after so many years' absence.

The Carbajal movement was just one of several causes on McLeod's mind: any enterprise that smacked of liberty for the oppressed interested him. Able to aid such causes financially, McLeod was on the lookout for those who wished to fight for independence in Texas, the United States, Mexico, or anywhere else. If his interests stemmed from a continuing need to vindicate himself after Santa Fe, so be it. He had brought such feelings with him to Texas in 1835, and he never looked back.

On January 14, 1852, former U.S. envoy Waddy Thompson wrote to Mc-
Leod from New Orleans, indicating receipt of a $1,000 loan in gold for
Capt. Forbes Britton. Britton, a forty-year-old Virginian and one of Mc-
Leod's West Point classmates, needed money to invest in Henry Lawrence
Kinney's latest enterprise. Britton and Kinney were neighbors in Corpus
Christi, and Kinney's grand idea of a state fair intrigued McLeod's former
army pal. With the help of McLeod and Thompson, Britton's investment
along with money from men such as Ashbel Smith and U.S. consul John P.
Schatzell underwrote the enterprising Kinney's spring festivities.[1]

This was no ordinary county fair. McLeod had already read in the November papers of Kinney's grand scheme. "The Lone Star State Fair," proclaimed the headlines, "including the sale of the largest stock of improved
cattle, horses &c at a fair to be held in Corpus Christi on May 1, 1852." A
week later, the *Texas State Gazette* predicted a crowd of between 20,000
and 30,000.[2] McLeod knew Kinney had something going on behind the
pomp and ceremony. Having dealt with Kinney on land sales and railroad
subscriptions in 1850, he suspected that Kinney needed money. With a reputation for great ideas and poor investments, Kinney nevertheless seemed
able to persuade Texans to support him after every financial disaster he
incurred. McLeod realized he, too, had been dragged into one of Kinney's ventures. Britton could be trusted with McLeod's money, but Kinney
could not.

McLeod probably decided to keep a close eye on the proceedings of
the state fair that spring after he received a personal invitation from Kinney to be one of the keynote speakers. To generate excitement and interest, Kinney asked McLeod to give the formal introduction for the main
attraction—Mexican filibuster José Maria Carbajal. Six years after Mc-
Leod's newspaper *The Republic of the Rio Grande* had folded, the revolutionary movement continued to spark interest on both sides of the border.
In the interim, Carbajal had been in and out of jail and was now involved
in the hotly reported Merchants' War out of Matamoros; he seemed intent

on raising support in the United States for yet another attempt to carve an independent republic from northern Mexico. Kinney invited Carbajal to Corpus Christi in the hopes that he would bring more crowds and reporters, enliven the political debates, and raise even more money.[3]

McLeod readily accepted the invitation and arrived in Corpus Christi during the first full week of the festival. Jeremiah Mabie's Grand Olympic Arena and United States Circus had pitched its big-top tent along Water Street, and wagons and cages were strewn in all directions. Booths and vegetable carts lined several blocks along the beach, and people crowded around the side shows. McLeod spent the first nights at Britton's home on the edge of town. Britton, the first state legislator from the Nueces area, caught his visitor up on the fair's success thus far, including a very low estimate of attendance, no more than two thousand. William and Jane McManus Cazneau had already passed through town on their way back to Eagle Pass. Schatzell was present, keeping an eye on his investment. McLeod visited with Edmund J. Davis, Britton's new son-in-law and a future Texas governor, who was deputy collector of duties in Laredo. Davis asked McLeod to support his anticipated run for district attorney in Brownsville.

Texas Gov. Peter Hansborough Bell opened the fair on May 1. Included in the sparse crowds were U.S. soldiers under the command of Gen. William S. Harney of the Texas Military District; they were expected to keep order when Carbajal arrived. His staff included several of McLeod's acquaintances: B. F. Terry from Fort Bend, James Durst from Nacogdoches, Col. Walter Mann, and fellow Pioneer Tom Lubbock.[4] A local reporter noted that on most evenings he could see these officers, along with McLeod, enjoying lengthy conversations on the porch of Kinney's home up on the bluff "as a small brass brand played nearby."[5]

Carbajal arrived in Corpus Christi on May 12 with an escort of two hundred mercenaries. A later news article reported that dozens of families packed their belongings and left the fairgrounds, fearing a violent confrontation with American troops.[6] No such engagement occurred. On May 13 Carbajal joined Kinney and McLeod on the podium near the circus tent before the largest crowd of the two-week fair. With typical grandiloquence McLeod opened with gentle humor and an acknowledgment of the dignitaries gathered before him. After kind words for Kinney's enterprise McLeod launched into a dramatic speech recounting the story of those who struggled for liberty. He criticized President Tyler's vacillation in support of a Mexican republic a decade earlier and wondered about the current administration's policy. This led to a resounding acclamation for Carbajal.

Carbajal spoke for thirty minutes, waving his good right arm for emphasis while his limp left arm, a red badge of courage from earlier wars, hung at his side. His impassioned pleas for support from U.S. citizens raised shouts from the crowd, as did his reiteration of the Plan de La Loba, his plan for a republic along the Rio Grande. McLeod led the applause at the end of the speech, which, wrote the *Gazette,* "stirred the crowds at the Fair." At the same time the newspapers blamed Carbajal's presence for the low attendance and disappointing returns of the first state fair.[7] Kinney's event, intended to spotlight the Gulf coast as an alternate route for gold diggers making their way toward California and to revive his fortunes, had failed on both counts. John Ford, who missed the proceedings while in command of some of Carbajal's mercenary army miles away, believed Corpus Christi lay too far south to interest gold seekers and later criticized Kinney for clouding issues that should have focused on Carbajal. But Ashbel Smith argued at the Baltimore Democratic Convention in June that "the Fair made a highly respectable showing."[8]

Upon return to Galveston McLeod had a more pressing problem. Kinney's exorbitant expenses had resulted in the loss of thousands of dollars, including McLeod's investments. Kinney was destitute—not for the first time—and the serious nature of his financial situation necessitated court action for investors to recover any losses. Yet McLeod also felt compelled to assist Kinney if he could. The only possession left of Kinney's estate was a ranch on Mustang Island in Refugio County. The 2,000-acre ranch supported six hundred head of Mexican-brand cattle, twenty-six Spanish mares, a stallion, and one mule.[9] McLeod reasoned that the foreclosure on the ranch's mortgage might put Kinney even, and the sale of the livestock might repay the debts to the fair investors.

In the summer of 1852 McLeod sued Kinney in an attempt to foreclose on the ranch. But Kinney resisted the attempt and countersued McLeod on the grounds that the suit was brought in Refugio County against a Nueces County resident and was therefore inadmissible in the Texas courts. Kinney's case against McLeod made its way to the Texas Supreme Court and was heard by Judge John Hemphill on November 2. James Webb argued for Kinney, while McLeod, in his only appearance before the high court, retained the firm of Oldham and Marshall to assist him. *Kinney v. McCleod* [*sic*] rested on the following condition: "As a general rule the defendant is entitled to be sued in the county of his domicile, but to this rule there are exceptions, among which are suits for the foreclosure of mortgages, in which cases suit may be brought either in the county where the mortgaged property is situated or in the county of the defendant's domicile."

Judge Hemphill wrote in his decision for McLeod that "the general rule that the defendant must be sued in the forum of his domicile is for the benefit of the plaintiff and not the defendant, and the latter cannot complain if suit be brought at his residence." In his decision Hemphill ordered the Refugio County sheriff to sell Mustang Ranch in order to satisfy the mortgage, but if the sale was still insufficient for said judgments and costs, "execution shall issue against said Kinney as in other cases, directed to the sheriff of Nueces County, commanding him to levy on the goods and effects of the said Kinney . . . to satisfy the judgment and costs." Hemphill concluded that if the sale exceeded the amount of said judgment, "then and in that case the sheriff shall return the overplus to the said Kinney." [10]

McLeod had won in court, enabling him and other investors to break even when the Mustang Island ranch and the livestock were sold that winter. It was Kinney's last great scheme in Corpus Christi. He left the Texas coast and fled a pending divorce the following spring, wandered through several more failed political campaigns, and died a violent death in 1862.

Nothing could have prepared McLeod for the tragic news he received the first week of September, 1852. His brother was dead. Only forty-four years old and at the peak of his naval career, Daniel McLeod had just returned to Pensacola after several years aboard the *Porpoise* and the *Albany*. In March he had been recommended by Commander Josiah Tattnall to replace retiring Chief Surgeon William L. Van Horn at the Navy Yard "for his knowledge of the topography of the lands in the vicinity of the hospital," essential for the proposed repairs and expansion of the facilities then "in a wretched condition." [11] Daniel accepted his appointment in May and was on duty soon after.

Hugh McLeod was not aware of the chest pains that had begun to concern his brother that summer. Tattnall ordered Daniel to undergo extensive tests in July and August, and he was placed under the constant care of Assistant Surgeon R. W. Jeffrey and Yard Surgeon Isaac Hulse. The medication prescribed for the chest pains proved inadequate, and around August 20 Daniel suffered a severe angina attack. He was placed in a private room adjacent to Jeffrey's hospital office and watched around the clock. Hulse was reassigned a week later when Daniel seemed to be responding to the medicine and resting more comfortably.

But just after midnight on September 1, Jeffrey was awakened by what he reported as "what I supposed to be the Doctor vomiting." The official report continued: "I went immediately to his room, and heard him say, 'Oh! that I should bleed to death.' I found him lying on the floor, moved my hand about the floor near him, and found clotted blood. The lights which had been burning, in the Doctor's bedroom, and one in the parlor, were both out. I called the servant, who, after a short time, got a light, and I, thinking that the blood proceeded from the Doctor's stomach, ran out and awoke the steward, and sent him to the Dispensary for medicine. . . . In a short time after, life was extinct." What McLeod learned that day by telegram, however, exacerbated the tragedy beyond comprehension. Jeffrey's official report read that Daniel had committed suicide by severing the carotid artery of the left side.[12]

Conversations with personnel at Pensacola turned up no additional information nor anything that would have explained Daniel's act. Jeffrey wrote that he "had no suspicions of the intention of the Doctor to commit this act, and from his conversations, which were sometimes sad and sometimes cheerful, very similar to those which we held together whilst he was in health, nor from any act could I perceive any basis upon which to found a suspicion."[13] If Daniel McLeod had a melancholy personality in his last days or months, as Jeffrey hints in his report, that still left unanswered questions for his family, as well as his fiancée, the widow of Commodore Alexander Dallas. Considered a hero to the people of Pensacola for his efforts during the deadly yellow fever epidemic of 1834, McLeod served the U.S. Navy during the Florida Seminole Wars, in the West Indies, and for several years under the command of Commodore Matthew Perry. No explanation was ever forthcoming about McLeod's last moments of life.[14]

Hugh McLeod learned of his brother's death by telegram. The body was sent to Macon for burial in a family plot at the Old Cemetery. Funeral arrangements were carried out by his sisters, Isabella Brower and Christianna Melrose, and their half-sister, Catherina Clark. Hugh and Rebecca sent money to Savannah to cover burial costs. They would pay their respects at his grave four years later.

The next three years, 1853–55, proved somewhat calmer. McLeod managed a successful law practice by the Strand, became widely recognized as a civic leader, and continued to monitor the efforts of his fledgling railroad company. The hurricane that struck the Gulf coast in 1854 badly damaged Galveston, and the yellow fever outbreak that followed took even more lives than the rising waters a few weeks earlier. But the city learned that it could cooperate and rebuild itself in the face of these natural catastrophes. Ironically, the hurricane's total destruction of Indianola down the coast left Galveston as the major port of call in Texas. Community leaders went back to work on the major issues of the day. In 1855 McLeod and Mayor John Sydnor tried a second time, again unsuccessfully, to institute a public school system in Galveston.[15] When he was not immersed in island affairs, McLeod made frequent trips to Austin, visiting Lamar and observing the Texas Congress—and its politics—as often as he could manage.

The ex-commander of the Santa Fe Pioneers worked for several weeks in 1853 to clarify the pension grants of Mrs. Frederic Plasman, widowed by the failed expedition in 1841. His letters to Austin enabled her to receive the monies due in her last years.[16] Oliver Hunter, another Pioneer and a lawyer for the Sturges estate in Henderson County, inquired of McLeod in 1854 about "the enhancement of the value of said estate" should the proposed Pacific Railroad come through East Texas. McLeod assured Hunter that plans for railways across the South would ultimately increase the real estate for anyone who stayed the course.[17]

Memories of the Cherokee Wars fifteen years past haunted McLeod in 1854. The state legislature was receiving petitions on behalf of claims made from the Republic era, reminding McLeod of an 1839 incident. He had loaned his horse to Lt. McNeely in the heat of battle along the Neches; the soldier was wounded, and his mount had died in the fray. McLeod rarely thought of those days, except when the shard of arrowhead embedded in his thigh acted up. But he filed a petition for a $200 claim on the horse. In October Congress validated the claim and sent the money to Galveston.[18]

In 1855 McLeod accepted civic leaders' invitation to represent Galveston at a commercial convention in New Orleans.[19] This was a forum for much of the political talk of the day, including the cotton industry's frustration with the growing influence of abolitionism in Congress. Vital economic issues surrounding the custom duties along the Gulf coast and trade with Mexico interested the businessman and the politician in McLeod. The two-week convention gave him time to visit extensively with old friends Waddy Thompson and Judge John Baldwin. At the meetings in January McLeod represented Galveston merchants and railroad interests. On the pressing issue of public health and the spread of disease through merchant shipping, he voted with the majority, declaring that states along the South Atlantic coast and on the Gulf of Mexico were "bound by commercial interests and their future prosperity" to establish rigid quarantines in all of their seaports during the summer months. He supported the southern cotton growers who complained of the labor shortage and high price of African slaves and advocated reopening the slave trade. With additional slaves, argued speakers like A. L. Scott of Virginia, the cotton culture could expand to "various naval stores, timber, and manufacturing enterprises," and the South would in time "assume a position of very great and permanent strength." The convention-goers agreed that, with British cotton at an ebb, higher prices for southern cotton were the prospect for the 1855 crop.[20]

The other major issues addressed the railroads' movement west and party politics of the 1850s. In Illinois Sen. Stephen Douglas pushed for the major rail routes to be extended from Chicago through the Kansas Territory. But the proposal for a vote of popular sovereignty in the Midwest to determine whether the territory would be slave or free caused such consternation and violence that editorials referred to the area as Bleeding Kansas. Reverberations from the Pierce Bill and the Compromise of 1850, along with the reports of a new Republican Party organized out of Wisconsin to contest the spread of slavery into the territories, made for fascinating debate in New Orleans. A reenergized McLeod returned home to report to the merchants and to engage in conversation regarding yet another political party—southern-based and proslavery—as an alternative to the Democratic Party.

McLeod still harbored hope that the heroic Carbajal would succeed in his revolutionary movement across northern Mexico. Rip Ford wrote McLeod before the New Orleans trip, expressing excitement to be involved again in what he considered a great enterprise.[21] When McLeod returned home, a January 24 letter awaited him from John Sidney Thrasher, whom he had met at the convention. Thrasher, a newspaperman originally from Maine, edited the filibuster paper *Beacon of Cuba*, promoting Carbajal's efforts along with interests working toward a Caribbean slavery empire based in Havana. Thrasher also mentioned a great enterprise about to get under way, as Ford had in his letter.[22] George Howard wrote McLeod from Zurich, Switzerland, in March, inquiring about the revolutionary movement of Cordova and his army.[23] McLeod traveled to Austin in early February and spoke to the Masonic lodge, again discussing the importance of defending the "rights of the South and of the sacred institution of slavery." Discussions with Cazneau, who had joined McLeod on the lodge podium for the annual conference, spurred both men's imagination of the southern states' future.[24]

McLeod continued to immerse himself in railroad business in 1855 and 1856 as the BBB&C expanded across the Brazos River and headed for the Colorado. He corresponded with Jonathan Fay Barrett in Boston on several occasions, as director to railroad president. In May, 1855, Barrett asked for an update on the Harrisburg Road extension and what would become of the Houston Tap. In October and November he wrote lengthy missives to Galveston, asking about the latest subscriptions to the railway, a possible hike in fees and rates, and other business. Another long correspondence in August, 1856, from Barrett to McLeod indicated both men's optimism for the railroad company's future and the possibilities of a connection with what would become the Southern Pacific Railway.[25]

That month McLeod again spoke in Austin at a gathering of Masons. His speech addressed efforts to establish slavery in Central America as well as the organizing of a "slave empire extended across the American South and the Gulf Coast." Hamilton Bee and William Beck Ochiltree expressed personal thanks to McLeod for the speech.[26] Also in August, a dispute arose among tenants on McLeod's East Texas Miller League near Union Hill. A Mr. Bryan had been selling liquor to the slaves and causing problems for the families. A subsequent letter from friends of Bryan spelled out the apparent misunderstanding, and the issue evaporated without McLeod having to take further action.[27]

For city investors such as the McLeod—and for the city itself—1856 was a boom year. The value of foreign imports coming through customs and to the docks surpassed $200,000 for the first time in the city's history—more than the eight previous years combined. Likewise the value of foreign exports doubled between 1855 and 1856, to $1,492,000. This included a record 117,500 bales of cotton, and 21,000 bales of hides and deer skins, shipped from Galveston. Receipts were at an all-time high for sugar and molasses manufacturing and shipment, and the total tonnage of foreign trade was the highest since 1846. In 1856, 350 vessels sailed or steamed into Galveston Bay, including 149 steamships. Commercial interests on the island soared, the railroad prospered, and men like McLeod reaped the benefits of years of effort to build up the offshore port.[28]

In the autumn of 1856 McLeod corresponded with political acquaintances in Georgia about both old business and new. A dispute had arisen over back payments between Georgia and the soldiers of the Texas Revolution, including loans for firearms used by Colonel Ward's company in 1835. The Georgia legislature demanded payment of those twenty-year-old debts, but former Georgian McLeod assured Herschel Johnson of Milledgeville, who wrote on behalf of Georgia's interests, that the debts had been settled.[29] Amid the correspondence, McLeod learned of the upcoming commercial convention in Savannah that December. Here was a golden opportunity to dive back into national politics, renew political and commercial contacts, and take the family home for a brief reunion. Hugh, Rebecca, and six-year-old Caz traveled to Georgia in early November and stayed with the Lamar family for two months.

While his wife and son visited with extended family, McLeod attended the convention, which met December 13–19. More than a thousand delegates gathered for the meeting, according to a count by the *Charleston Mercury,* and the atmosphere was charged with talk of slavery and secession.[30] The issue of reopening the African slave trade was introduced by a Georgia delegate, and a South Carolinian called for a vote that "the South alone might legislate her own affairs" and not feel compelled any longer "to recognize the right of Congress, the organ of the North, to impose restrictions on the slave trade." Three Virginia delegates, led by Andrew Hunter, argued for the postponement of such an inflammatory vote, for "it was a great moral question upon which the South should ponder long before it placed itself in a defiant attitude against the whole Christian world." Hunter warned, "It involved tremendous consequences, and time for reflection was necessary. The institution of slavery was an ordinance of God to bring the African to America, to educate him to be returned in good time to christianize and civilize the country from which he came." However, "the present discussion of the question would not be productive of good . . . was a direct attack upon the Union; and the South would lose many of the friends she now had." Hunter's colleagues agreed.[31]

Then McLeod took the podium, pledging the state of Texas to the views of the proslavery South without hesitation and stating that he saw no need to postpone a vote nor fear of the North's reaction. Furthermore, McLeod continued, Mexico was "falling to pieces and needed negro labor to develop its resources." It was the South's duty to remain strong on this issue, to introduce the institution of slavery to Mexico ("the peculiar institution," the *Richmond Enquirer* called it), and to counteract northern influences and "European intrigue." After a raft of other speeches the assembly voted to appoint a committee "charged to investigate the facts as to the condition of slavery, the international laws on slave trade, and the propriety of reopening slave traffic with Africa." The committee would report at the next meeting. One member, New Orleans editor James D. B. De Bow, called for increasing the South's agricultural productivity and for "the elimination of Northern participation in the trade between the South and Europe."[32] The fire-eaters had made their imprint on the convention, and McLeod had set his own unalterable course toward secession.

CHAPTER 15

Know-Nothings and Nicaragua

The American Party provided a significant alternative to some Democratic Party candidates and the last of the Whigs in the 1854 national elections. Cast in the role of a third party appealing to nationalists, anti-Democrats, and nativists, the Know-Nothings grew from a semisecret organization into a viable replacement, at least in their own estimation, of the dying National Republicans. Know-Nothingism had special appeal across a disgruntled South eager for political change in Washington and the maintenance of a way of life that included slavery. Anti-Catholicism reached into Texas with racist overtones directed at German and Mexican immigrants. Editorials railed against "indiscriminant immigration and all of the hyferlutin odds and ends of the world" coming to Texas in an assault against "our citadel of liberty." Not all Texans supported the Know-Nothing Party, however. Editorials against the party appeared in Texas newspapers as early as June, 1854.[1]

McLeod relinquished his Democratic Party membership in 1854 to join the Know-Nothings. Their ardent proslavery stance enticed him away from what he perceived as vacillation within his party, and he believed that Texas would fare better with this fresh political stance. In 1855, David Burnet wrote McLeod from his San Jacinto farm inquiring about the relative strength of the American Party in Texas.[2] James Harper Starr also corresponded with McLeod, proposing that "the public debt in Texas and across the country must be the number one issue of the day." He asked where the Know-Nothings stood on this.[3]

As early as December, 1854, the most surprising rumor in connection with the Know-Nothing movement suggested that Sam Houston would join them. The *Texas State Gazette* reported Houston's affiliation on February 10, 1855, and in Washington, D.C., Thomas Jefferson Green spread the word of Houston's duplicity and betrayal of the Democrats.[4] Houston was traveling for much of this time and did not respond directly, although he did attend the Democratic state convention in Huntsville in late April. In June he spoke at the San Jacinto memorial without commenting on the party, but a month later he had visited with Dr. W. G. W. Jowers, the Know-Nothing candidate for lieutenant governor. Houston's so-called Independence Letter of July 24 was his first outright expression on the subject. He concluded, "I believe the salvation of my country is only to be secured by adherence to the principles of the American Order."[5]

Hard as it was to believe, Houston and McLeod had both left the Democrats and joined the Know-Nothings, although their ancient personal rivalry never waned. The August 2 state elections instigated another venomous campaign across Texas, with old and new political enemies squaring off. W. S. Oldham, Louis T. Wigfall, and Anson Jones joined forces with Burnet and Lamar in a pamphleteering and editorial war against Houston. McLeod, however, warned the overeager pols to be careful: "Don't think of any personal attack upon Houston— he will make capital out of it. Wait til you have published the pamphlet, & then if you think there is anything left of him, I will stand by you, while you thrash him."[6]

Texas Know-Nothing candidates lost badly in August, with the exception of Lemuel Evans, elected to the U.S. Congress, and Stephen Crosby, elected Texas land commissioner. The Galveston Know-Nothings gained strength with the election of James Cronican as the mayor of the city. But the anti-Houston faction kept up its attack on the old warhorse. "Houston yet goes unwhipped of political justice . . . from a State whose interest he has twice betrayed," declared the Corsicana *Prairie Blade*.[7] On October 20 Houston gave a speech in Brenham in which he claimed to have always been a supporter of "the Democratic Party of Jefferson and Jackson," but even longtime allies like Ashbel Smith still wondered about his affiliation, and McLeod looked forward to any opportunity to criticize his political adversary for waffling the previous year.

The opportunity came in November at a statewide barbecue and rally for the Texas Know-Nothing Party. McLeod wrote John Grant Tod from Austin, where he was lobbying for a railroad bill in Congress: "They have posted me up here to speak alongside of Houston on 22nd—but I refuse unless it is understood that I am to speak of him as I please—This don't [*sic*] suit the programme and I reckon they will have to hunt other help. . . . The old thief has been, and always will be, the bane and disgrace of Texas—I'll give him 'the butt end of my mind' if I speak."[8] Despite an incessant, cold drizzle, thousands gathered to hear some of the leading political voices of the era. Julien Sidney Devereux wrote his wife at their Monte Verde plantation that "the great men of the country are congregating about Austin. Sam Houston, Commodore Moore, Genl. McLoud [*sic*] and many other prominent men are here." Houston arrived from Washington-on-the-Brazos accompanied by an entourage that once more included Smith; the two had worked out their disagreements during the campaign. McLeod traveled from Galveston with J. W. Waddell, a prominent businessman, editor of the Galveston *Confederate*, and Know-Nothing Party member. With Congress in session, a significant coterie of state leaders would be present at the political rally. A large group of citizens from the San Antonio area came to the festivities, many of them young women who orchestrated a parade complete with tricolor flags atop horse-drawn wagons.[9] But the real entertainment would come from the speech makers. Houston was first. He reiterated his stance as a Jackson Democrat but pointedly expressed his admiration for "the principles of the American Party, principles that will maintain the perpetuity of our free institutions." "I am," he concluded dramatically, "for Americans ruling America." The *Texas Republican* made it clear that Houston had thus "come out clearly and unequivocally in favor of the Know-Nothing Party."[10]

That same afternoon Rep. Isaac Parker of Tarrant County introduced a resolution that the speaker of the house invite Houston to sit in on the congressional session. A three-hour debate ensued and included a sardonic suggestion that Moore be allowed to sit next to Houston. The 48–32 vote indicated the continuing division of Houston and anti-Houston factions. The pro-Democrat *Texas State Gazette* enjoyed the fact that the long-winded controversy "had kept the great shanghai of Know-Nothingism waiting on the porch of the capital."[11]

McLeod took his turn on the political stage on the second day of the rally. Barbecue pits had been set up on University Hill within sight of the capitol, with the podium under a stand of live oaks and elms. Thousands of eager listeners and dozens of reporters awaited one general's attack of the other. McLeod did not disappoint. In his opening remarks he glanced at the dark skies and said: "I hope it [the inclement weather] is not an omen of the failure of our cause; but if it is, propitiate it by a timely sacrifice: throw Jonah overboard. The prophet has failed to deliver the true message to the people—his excuses are ingenious, but deceptive, and the ship will labor as the storm increases. The sacrifice is due to Nineveh, and the ship to Democracy and America. Jonah should be thrown overboard."[12] After a lengthy speech in support of the causes and principles of Know-Nothingism, McLeod retired to hearty applause. Editorials credited the Galvestonian with a resounding blow of one-upmanship against his perennial foe.

While McLeod worked his way deeper into the Know-Nothing Party, Houston's troubles continued. The senator began a trip back to Washington, D.C., where he still had four years left. But Texas had abandoned him, and he would face great political obstacles in the remaining sessions. The

Democratic state convention in January, 1856, endorsed the voting records of Rusk, Smyth, and Bell on the Kansas-Nebraska Act but overwhelmingly disapproved the vote of Houston "as not in accordance with the sentiments of the Democracy in Texas."[13]

The Texas American Party met in Austin to elect officials and endorse candidates state- and nationwide. Fifty-three counties were represented. McLeod and Waddell came from Galveston. Other principles included John Ford, E. Sterling Robertson, John Caldwell, and John Wilcox. William E. Jones of Comal was elected president pro tem, and Bastrop's Caldwell later served as permanent president. Waddell and five others were chosen to attend the national Know-Nothing convention as Texas delegates. McLeod served on the Resolutions Committee with Ford and eight others. They wrote the "cardinal principles of this organization," which began with these four: "(1) the elevation to public office . . . of those only who are native Americans or citizens of the Republic of Texas; (2) the preservation and perpetuation of the Constitution and the Federal Union as the bulwark of our liberties . . . and a prime source of national greatness and individual happiness; (3) a strict construction of the Constitution of the United States; (4) the extension of the current waiting period for naturalization."[14]

McLeod spent much of 1856 on the campaign trail for the Know-Nothing Party, often accompanied by J. W. Flanagan of Rusk and Thomas Blake of Leon County. They crisscrossed Texas from Eagle Pass to Jefferson and traveled along the coast. McLeod spoke on campaign stops in Huntsville, Cincinnati, and Nacogdoches and gave guest appearances in Austin, Houston, and Galveston. Although Houston kept a low profile, the American Party was nicknamed "Sam," much to the consternation of McLeod and other anti-Houstonites. Late in the campaign Houston spoke in Huntsville, Brenham, and Anderson, but the newspapers castigated him at every turn, describing his speeches as weak and flat, or as complete failures.[15]

On August 30, 1856, McLeod was in Austin availing himself of yet another opportune moment to shine. The Sixth Congress had set aside $40,000 for a bid to construct a permanent building for the General Land Office, and the contract had been given to architect Conrad J. Stremke and builders Baker & Nichols. Hundreds of citizens swarmed over the site where the foundation had been laid that summer. McLeod was invited to give the keynote speech for the laying of the building's cornerstone. Episcopal rector Rev. Edward Fontaine opened and closed the ceremony with prayer, and McLeod rallied the audience with a glowing oration that often strayed into the politics of the day.[16]

In the November national elections the Know-Nothing Party fared poorly. Their presidential candidate, Millard Fillmore, could not shake the two mediocre years he had served in that office. The newborn Republican Party came in second with John Fremont and their first try at presidential campaigning. The Democrats continued to hold the White House as James Buchanan succeeded Franklin Pierce. The short-lived American Party evaporated. For many ex-Democrats in Texas, including Houston and Mc-Leod, it was time to go home. Houston claimed never to have left the party, but his loss to Hardin Runnels in the 1857 gubernatorial race may have signaled his party's frustration with him as much as it did his political foes' strength.

At the 1857 Democratic state convention, party leaders glibly advertised a special evening session, claiming "that the doors of the great temple of Democracy be now thrown open and that all repentant sinners be invited to come back, confessing their sins, and be readmitted into the fold of the faithful." The first to volunteer for the political confessional was McLeod. Escorted by his friends Louis Wigfall and Texas Gov. Andrew Hamilton, McLeod ambled sheepishly through the shouting, laughing crowd that jammed into the convention hall for the good-natured fun. Several chandeliers threw shadows over the main participants, and people crowded closer to see who had come into the hall. They began to chant "McLeod! McLeod!" as he appeared near the stage. The general climbed onto the platform and tried in vain to quiet the noisy mob. When someone shouted that they could not see him, McLeod obliged by stepping onto a wobbly chair. Encouraged by the spotlight, he played to his audience by unbuttoning his coat and rubbing his rotund belly as if warming himself to the situation. The crowd broke into laughter.

When people quieted down, McLeod spoke in mock seriousness: "I do not like the way that resolution of yours reads. That the doors should be thrown open is all right, but I object to the part that calls all of us repentant sinners, and requires us to confess our sins. Fellow Democrats"—the audience roared its approval—"there are many honest-minded independent gentlemen who want to be with you, but will not bow the knee and come in under this resolution." A voice from the audience called, "Oh, yes, they will," and McLeod continued: "As for myself, I do not take back anything that I have done, nor do I intend to. I am not a repentant sinner; your principles are mine, and I never had any other." Sustained applause greeted the nonconfession, and McLeod turned serious: "The North is now arrayed against the South. The President of the United States needs help now, and every Southern gentleman should be invited in. Come up to the help of the Lord against the mighty. I have read a section of your platform, and if that means Democracy, then I have always been a Democrat!" Someone shouted, "But a damned long time finding it out!" McLeod ignored him and continued: "Gentlemen of the Democratic convention who will swear by this platform, everyone who will be true to the South, come in; then your convention can rely upon a united Texas and a united South!" With that, the general bowed to his audience, touching off applause and cheers as he was helped down from the chair. The evening belonged to him.[17]

Hugh and Rebecca McLeod lost three good friends in the mid-1850s. Judge John MacPherson Berrien passed away in Savannah at the age of seventy-five. Georgia's U.S. senator beginning in 1825, Berrien also served in President Jackson's cabinet as attorney general. A falling-out between the two leaders sent the judge back to Georgia in retirement, although his political influence would be felt until the day he died. Berrien had recommended young Hugh for admission to West Point and had followed the cadet through his rough-and-tumble years to graduation.

Polly Rusk died on April 23, 1856, in Nacogdoches after a lengthy illness. Her death left her husband despondent and unable to cope with the loss. No amount of consolation from his sons or friends seemed to help, nor did the distraction of the myriad political controversies he was involved in. When Thomas Jefferson Rusk took his own life on July 29, 1857, the McLeods grieved the loss and were reminded of the death of Hugh's brother, Daniel, five years earlier.

McLeod dug into the work at hand in Galveston, leaving his home only occasionally to travel to Austin. The two-month trip to Georgia to attend the commercial convention brought a much needed respite for the family, and the railroad industry's efforts to span the continent continued to attract McLeod's attention. Closer to home the need for a railway bridge between Galveston and the mainland became a primary issue in the winter of 1856 – 57. Fund-raising and political support from the eastern coalition of the BBB&C proved inadequate. McLeod, Sydnor, and Sidney Sherman, who had retired and was proprietor of the Island City Hotel, proposed that the citizens of Galveston raise bridge bonds. Judge Leslie A. Thompson supported the idea, but maverick newspaperman Lorenzo Sherwood, nicknamed "the Agitator," roused a contingent opposing the expenditures.[18] The debate escalated in the spring. In May, 1857, a huge railroad rally was held at Virginia Point, the bridge's proposed location. Friends of the Bridge hosted a barbecue and parade, and an estimated one thousand people turned out for the festivities. McLeod, the keynote speaker of the daylong event, spoke at length on the future of Galveston and its connection to mainland commerce. Reporters noted that his speech was well received and often interrupted by applause and cheers. On May 20 Galveston voted 741–11 in favor of the bridge bonds, a major political victory for McLeod and the railroad and perhaps a reward for more than a decade of service and leadership to the city.[19]

May, 1857, also brought a pitiful end to the filibustering misadventures of William Walker's Galveston Texas Rangers and their dismal participation in "the grey-eyed man of destiny's" last efforts to conquer and hold Nicaragua. As the stragglers arrived by ship, McLeod consoled himself that others had also been fooled by Walker and searched each arrival for several men who had been carried off in the excitement two years earlier. The McLeods were relieved to welcome back many close friends, including William Cazneau and their nephew John M. Baldwin.

As early as the spring of 1854, William Walker, in California after a disastrous filibuster to the Baja, spoke at length with Byron Cole, owner of the San Francisco *Commercial Advertiser* and an avid supporter of a filibuster to Nicaragua. Within a year, Walker and his band of fifty-eight mercenaries, whom he called the Immortals, landed at Realejo on Nicaragua's northern Pacific coast. A summer of frustrating negotiations and poorly executed attacks across Nicaragua nevertheless ended with the successful capture of Granada on October 11 and the declaration of Walker as president of the new republic by the end of the year. In February, 1856, Walker made two errors that cost him his position: the badly led negotiations with neighboring Costa Rica, which led to a counterrevolution against him; and the nationalizing of Commodore Cornelius Vanderbilt's Accessory Transit Company, railroad, steamers, and property. Infuriated, Vanderbilt underwrote an economic and paramilitary offensive that forced Walker back onto the battlefield in March and April.[20]

In need of additional support and money, Walker sent Col. S. A. Lockridge to Galveston to rally the Americans behind him. E. H. Cushing, a Walker follower and publisher of the Houston *Telegraph,* was already advocating the enterprise on his editorial page. And Chappell Hill physician R. J. Swearingen returned from Nicaragua to report on the latest news at a Galveston rally. On May 24 and again two days later, supporters of the filibuster held public meetings in Galveston. McLeod spoke fervently at both meetings on behalf of Walker and was seconded by General Sherman, Galveston Mayor John Henry Brown, Caleb G. Forshey, director of the Rutersville Military Institute, and other prominent Texans. The ad hoc committee passed resolutions published by Cushing that called for "aid to the patriots in Nicaragua" and "taking the isthmus from the imbecile race which controlled it."[21]

A key element in the support for Walker, a diminutive, soft-spoken man who exuded a remarkable charisma, was his belief in the reintroduction of African slavery in Central America. The divine institution, as he called it, would be an integral part of his republic. This stance beckoned to southerners like McLeod, who once had their eyes on Cuba as the center of a trans-Gulf slaveholding empire, and who distrusted the growing northern abolitionist movement. Lockridge's arrival in Galveston further stirred the revolutionary juices, and weekly meetings were held to raise money and recruit volunteers. Cazneau signed on and contracted to lead a thousand men. He also agreed to find and keep an eye on Baldwin, McLeod's twenty-six-year-old nephew, who was already fighting in Nicaragua. Baldwin, born in Texas, raised in New Orleans, and living in the McLeods' home, had leapt at the opportunity for adventure a year earlier, accompanying the first recruits who shipped off for the isthmus. Walker promoted him on the field of battle to captain in October, 1855, and he served as Walker's adjutant for the next six months. Walker and several international reporters noted Baldwin's resourcefulness, and his efforts in the defense of the makeshift hospital camp on Omhetepe Island branded him a hero as far away as New York City.[22]

McLeod continued fund-raising for the filibuster. He helped welcome and fete Col. G. W. Crawford, one of Walker's Rangers, upon his return to Texas in January, 1857, and was instrumental in organizing a grand reception and ball in February at the Methodist Church and the Tremont Hotel for returning heroes. McLeod poured money into the recruiting effort and served on a welcoming committee when Rangers from San Antonio, Corpus Christi, Austin, and Gonzales rendezvoused before heading south. He supported Will Richardson in the newspaper war against the Quitman *Free Press,* which claimed that Walker was a slaver, not a liberator. He helped orchestrate the schedule in March and April that sent off three more companies of recruits, and he arranged for Francis R. Lubbock to speak to Galveston citizens that spring.[23]

In late March, just as the First Company made preparations to sail, news arrived from Nicaragua of the catastrophic defeat of Lockridge and his Texas Rangers. More news dribbled in: the situation on the isthmus was deteriorating rapidly, and Walker had lost control of his army. The volunteers were on the run, chased to the borders by a coalition of Costa Ricans, Guatemalans, and Nicaraguans armed and equipped thanks to Vanderbilt's unlimited wealth. The volunteer companies left Galveston anyway but soon reported that they found the Nicaraguan situation in disarray. In

May the first ships laden with survivors struggled into the harbor. Part of Lockridge's regiment returned, including a badly shaken Baldwin, and the Galveston *News* reported Captain French's company in a destitute condition. Crawford, in New Orleans, wrote a letter to the newspapers vindicating Walker in the massive defeats and announcing his permanent retirement from filibustering. Walker escaped Nicaragua and was in New Orleans by July.[24]

In August the indefatigable Walker sent Lockridge back to Galveston to raise another army for a Nicaraguan invasion. Richardson once again supported the effort on his newspaper editorial page. McLeod had traveled to Austin in July to speak to the Masons on behalf of the filibuster, and he joined in the efforts of recruiters John Waters and W. R. Henry to promote the cause at home. The Galveston *News* compared Walker to Moses Austin: "The most conservative and prudent among our people are now convinced that the last hope of the South is in the Central American cause. We believe that slavery must be seriously affected by events in Central America. We bespeak from our citizens a hearty welcome to [the volunteers]."[25]

In October, 1857, the efforts of McLeod, Sherman, Henry, and other civic leaders seemed to succeed. Five hundred men set off from Galveston aboard the steamer *Mexico* in early November. Three more companies arrived on the island by the end of November, with the promise of four more on the way from Louisiana and elsewhere in Texas. In mid-November Walker headed south with another three hundred men under his command, arriving near Greytown in early December.

Growing concern in the United States about Walker's antics and the escalating support he was receiving prompted U.S. Navy Commander Hiram Paulding, who was patrolling the Central American waters, to take unauthorized action. Marines went ashore and demanded that Walker surrender and agree to be escorted from Nicaragua without resistance. Walker complied peacefully and was returned to the United States. The second filibustering attempt had been foiled. Not to be outdone, and actively supported across the South, Walker called for a third attempt in late 1858. McLeod and Richardson rose to the occasion once more, although editorials seemed to be less fervent and the rallies less well attended.[26] Still, steamers headed south in the winter of 1859. This time the cause did not evoke the necessary enthusiasm, and Walker's enterprise was essentially over. A final attempt in August, 1860, resulted in Walker's arrest and summary execution, and filibustering in Nicaragua ended.

McLeod stood fast behind Walker through it all. His speeches and fundraising letters bespoke his enduring support for the cause, reminiscent of

Santa Fe and the Republic of the Rio Grande. He endorsed Mirabeau B. Lamar as U.S. envoy to Nicaragua in 1857, believing that the old expansionist would keep the fires burning. In July, 1859, Sam Houston reversed his position on Walker and declared in a speech: "I am no friend of filibustering as the term is understood. I am opposed to resistance to the laws, whether it be the African Slave Trade Law, the Fugitive Slave Law or the Dred Scott Decision. When the laws are no longer regarded, liberty is at end." McLeod must have considered this a betrayal of the South itself.[27]

McLeod's words rang clear on the subject when he spoke to Masons in Austin on December 28, 1857: "For years the pulpits of the Northern States have uttered unwarranted attacks against our Southern system of negro slavery, the most humane and beneficent institution for social, material, and religious development, in its proper zone, that Heaven vouchsafed to man." He added that all men must defend the long-standing traditions that "the Southern Christian is sworn to uphold against the pious folly of our age. Truth has often been baffled by her professed guardians, and her worshippers have been fanatical." In sweeping and paradoxical histrionics, he concluded: "It is the individual battle of life that is the history of the human race since man's creation, the history of the struggle between truth and error. . . . Let us hope that charity will yet uproot fanaticism. If the South should, at this crisis, prove recreant to her true self and let the only barrier now left on Earth, against the desolating system of capital and wages, sweep over her, she will see her religion, her civilization, her republican government and her household goods adrift on the torrent. Her very race will be extinguished in that noche triste, or beg their bread in other lands. . . . But we shall not fall alone—the world unwittingly is involved in our destiny."[28]

McLeod believed in the southern way of life. The northern abolitionist movement would ultimately destroy the slave-labor cotton and tobacco regions of the South. The owner of eight slaves, McLeod never wavered in his condemnation of northern hypocrisy or his devout belief in slavery. If the North-controlled federal government ever pressed the issue beyond the Republican Party's insistence of free soil in the West, a last measure of response might lead beyond the Calhoun doctrine of nullification to secession. McLeod would not discount such a decision for Texas.[29] The second alternative—the establishment of a slaveholding empire based in Havana—was promulgated throughout the 1850s. George W. L. Bickley called for "a new Rome" and an "Empire of the Gulf," an echo of ideas belonging to men such as Cordova and Carbajal. As a precursor to this empire, Bickley organized a secret fraternal organization known as the Knights of the Golden Circle. Promoted as a defense against the evils of northern abolitionism, the Knights established "castles" in towns and districts from Texas to Virginia, unabashedly mixing Roman and Arthurian metaphors in their secret rituals and offices.[30]

By 1858 Texas had thirty castles established along the coast and inland to the Sabine River. The *Texas State Gazette* gave its support to the general cause: "Shall we not go in the attempt to acquire Cuba, and thus prepare the way for an inevitable decree of destiny in the final annexation of the rest of the Antilles?"[31] Texans such as John Littleton, N. P. Luckett, and J. A. Wilcox spoke out in support of the Knights. Thomas S. Lubbock presided over the castle in Independence. In 1859 Bickley announced the Knights' general support for Miguel Miramón and Benito Juárez's filibustering efforts in Central America. By 1861 the Knights had melted into the secessionist cause. Sixty avowed Knights served in the state legislature, and many of the delegates who went to Birmingham led castles in Texas.[32]

In Galveston the Knights established a castle through the already well established Galveston City Guard, whose honorary captain commandant since 1854 had been McLeod. In 1857 the City Guard merged with a new organization, the Lone Star Rifles, and became the Galveston Artillery Company. A. C. Crawford served briefly as captain but soon retired and was replaced by McLeod. Ardent secessionists James Wrigley and John T. Holt served as McLeod's lieutenants in the volunteer company.[33] The company's unpublished records, lost during the Civil War when much of the unit enlisted as a regiment in the Confederacy's First Texas Regiment, might have revealed any official connection to the Knights. If McLeod became a Knight, he was probably initiated as a 2nd Degree Knight of the True Faith, the title given to members who supported the organization financially instead of militarily. No records or correspondence indicate his position, but it is likely that the proslavery, pro-South man of many causes would have enjoyed involvement in a group such as the Knights.

McLeod continued to practice law, although the issues of the day kept him largely distracted. In the fall of 1858 he intervened in a celebrated lawsuit involving acquaintances Col. John Forbes, Maj. James M. Wells, and Dr. Nicholas D. Labadie. Forbes and Labadie had been at each other for years over Ladabie's accusations of serious improprieties by Forbes following the 1836 battle of San Jacinto. McLeod had accepted Forbes's offer to mediate the Nacogdoches case, but his attempts went awry. In a December 26 letter to Judge Charles S. Taylor, McLeod tried to explain: "My friendship for Major Wells, as a [West Point] classmate, and the recollection of pleasant intercourse with Col. Forbes' family in old times, made it a duty, in my estimation to assuage, if I could not heal, the angry feelings. . . . I have not only failed, but if possible drawn some portion of Dr. Labadie's culpability upon myself." He concluded, "I still hope that when Col. Forbes' friends consult on the eve of the vexatious and irritating suit, they will be willing to act with more judgment than I think they are now inclined to do." McLeod's tone may be what exacerbated the situation in the first place.[34]

By 1859 the McLeods were recognized as leaders of their island community. Living in a substantial home on an estate that encompassed a city block at Broadway and Twenty-sixth Avenue, the influential and popular couple continued to make astute investments in the cotton and railroad industries. Baldwin, the twenty-nine-year-old great-nephew of the late James F. Perry, had again come to live with them, as had his aunt Eliza a decade earlier. The McLeods kept close ties to the Perry family after Perry's death in 1852, purchasing molasses from their Brazoria estate and corresponding often with his son, Stephen, about affairs of the day. In one letter McLeod referred to a war in Europe and its practical consequence: "The last Italian news is a tremendous fight— 400,000 men engaged & losses in proportion. Cotton is dull but if England and Germany keep out of the fray, it will rise higher than before."[35]

McLeod and James Perry bartered slaves between Brazoria and Galveston, including a slave named William. Nine years earlier McLeod had written Perry about "a negro boy about 10 to 11 years old—who is so fond of running about Town, that I am at a loss what to do with him—owning his whole family—father & mother—I dislike to part them, but I am compelled to place him somewhere to reform him." McLeod offered to lend him to the Perrys "to use him on your stock farm . . . for three or four years, and have him taught all that can be learnt in the way of ploughing." The deal was eventually struck, and William spent some time in Brazoria before returning to the Galveston estate. In the spring of 1859 the McLeods decided to sell William. "I can get, I am told by the negro brokers, $2000 for him at New Orleans," McLeod wrote Stephen Perry, "but you know my wife's objections to separating families. You have tried him and know his qualities . . . and we will take $1600 if you will buy him now." He added, "William will go cheerfully to you, and his mother is satisfied with that arrangement." But three months later McLeod wrote: "I presume of course by your silence that the report of William's stealing the bridle at the river turns out either untrue or unexplained. . . . All negroes will take things under temptation. The fellow has an affectionate disposition, and you can take him a month on hire, for trial . . . to revive his old attachment to you. And I suppose it is a point gained, to get such tempers among plantation negroes. . . . Martha, William's mother, has got reconciled to his being sold, as she knows you and can hear of him often." A later contract shows a purchase amount of $1,300.[36]

As 1860 approached and the presidential elections took on the dangerous look of real confrontation between the North and South, the inevitability of secession charged the political debates in Galveston and every major city in America. McLeod was ready for the moment, and he knew that Texas Gov. Sam Houston would once more oppose him. Already, McLeod rooted for any editorial or speech that castigated the governor. "Have you seen Sherman's pamphlet?" he wrote to Stephen Perry. "[And] Austin's letter is the fullest in its details of any. I think it will do much towards flooring Houston."[37]

Before the year began, however, McLeod had the sad duty of burying his great friend and ally Mirabeau Lamar, who died December 19. The two had worked and schemed together for twenty-one years, and their personal relationship went back to Columbus and Macon, Georgia. The Masonic service was held in Richmond, where the ex-President of the Republic of Texas was buried. Only forty-five years old, McLeod had outlived nearly all of his political cronies, although his great enemy stood as strong and defiant as ever.

CHAPTER 16

Secession and War

On September 1, 1859, McLeod voted for Hardin Runnels as governor of Texas and Francis Lubbock as lieutenant governor. Galveston chose for Runnels by a hundred votes over Sam Houston, and a higher plurality chose the ardent secessionist Lubbock. But statewide McLeod's old nemesis won the day. The issues of states' rights and secession loomed on the horizon. Unionist and secessionist divided at every turn, a schism that affected Texas as much as or more than any other state. Compromise had been tossed to the wind for a decade, and as abolitionism spread its influence above the Mason-Dixon line, political pressures on both sides pointed to the critical presidential elections a year away. An early November ice storm that struck Galveston may have been an eerie warning of the political air of 1860. "The North will not yield an inch," declared a prominent Texas senator.[1]

The Democratic state convention met in Galveston on April 2, 1860, and the issue of secession was foremost on everyone's mind. Willard Richardson's Galveston *News,* the voice of the city's proslavery faction, argued that "Texas possessed the full right, as a sovereign State, to annul the compact and to resume her former place among the powers of the earth."[2] Six weeks later, when news reached the island that the Republican Party had nominated free-soiler Abraham Lincoln as its presidential candidate, McLeod and other leading secessionists hosted an impromptu rally in the market to reiterate their support for the Breckinridge-Lane ticket and form a Breckinridge club. By the end of the summer Unionists and conservatives across the city had formed Bell and Everett clubs under the leadership of William Pitt Ballinger, A. C. McKeen, and Andrew Neill. Ferdinand Flake, a German Unionist and newspaper editor, endorsed the Stephen Douglas ticket as "the only real and regular candidate of the Democracy," arousing the support of the handful of German Texans on the island.[3]

Hamilton Stuart, Charles McCarthy, and McLeod stirred a large crowd of Breckinridge supporters at a September 1 rally. Stuart spoke for calm in the coming electioneering days but was effectively shouted down by the audience in favor of the more inflammatory McCarthy and McLeod. Ballinger noted in his diary that "they gave him [Stuart] the very devil."[4] Lubbock roused the secessionist crowds again on October 23, and the *News* outdueled Stuart's Galveston *Civilian* and Flake's *Woehentliche Union* in the newspaper wars.

On November 6, election day across the nation, 954 ballots cast in Galveston resulted in an overwhelming local win for Breckinridge (684 votes to Bell's 205 and Douglas's 65). Lincoln, not on the island's ballot, received no votes there but won the presidency. Two days later the Lone Star flag was hoisted above Galveston. The November 13 *News* editorial turned somber with the news of "the election of a Black Republican president" and indicated that "the hour of waiting was past. Every precinct, ward, town, or county meeting, at which citizens of all political opinions should attend, must let the sentiments of the people be frankly expressed."[5]

Moderates and some conservatives, southern Democrats above all else, began to join the fire-eater secessionists. McKeen spoke at a November 12 meeting, and old-timer Judge Henry Thompson stood alongside him. Two days later the largest public meeting in Galveston's thirty-year history ensconced the secessionists in political control for the months that lay ahead. McLeod spoke for a defense of the southern way of life. His nominee for temporary chair of the proceedings, William T. Austin, won the straw vote easily and took the makeshift podium. Conservative voices were soon drowned out, and one wrote later: "I cannot disguise from myself the deep apprehension, if not the positive conviction that our government will be overthrown and the Union dissolved. Several Southern States will secede. The employment of force to subdue them is so opposed to the spirit of our government that it will be worse than even disunion."[6]

In preparation for the coming events the ad hoc assembly agreed to create a Committee on Public Safety and Correspondence, no doubt hearkening back to the minutemen of America's revolutionary days. The thirteen members included McLeod, Austin, Sydnor, and General Sherman, with Judge James P. Cole as chairman. Col. Thomas M. Jack took over leadership when Cole became ill soon after. All thirteen were secessionists. McLeod was quoted after the organizational meeting as saying, "We expected that immediately upon the inauguration of Mr. Lincoln, the devil would be to play, and we wanted to be prepared to meet the devil."[7]

Even before news of South Carolina's formal secession from the Union reached Galveston, the committee set to work to promote Texas independence. A December 3 meeting at Morian Hall called for the reorganization of the Galveston City Guards and an immediate recruitment program. Within a week more than a hundred Galvestonians joined up and the Galveston Lone Star Rifle Company was born. The Lone Star Minute Men Club assembled, as did the Lone Star Flag Club. The Wigfall Guards organized on December 8 in a Market Street saloon. A local printer prepared Lone Star crests and sold them to groups and individuals across the city. Against the grain, Oscar Farish organized the Lone Star Association, which called for Texas to remain independent from both Union and Confederacy.

On December 8 Houston made a surprise visit to Galveston, where he spoke with Stuart and a handful of conservative Unionists. He did not confront his political enemies, but he did grant an interview with Richardson. The Galveston *News* reported that the governor said "he had found Texas in a very bad condition a number of times, out of which he had gotten her, but that she was now old enough to take care of herself, and if she was bent upon her own destruction by secession, he would not go with her."[8]

Members of the Committee on Public Safety and Correspondence looked for support from local religious leaders as well as orators and editors. McLeod wrote Rev. J. E. Carnes on December 5, inviting him to speak to the citizens "upon the duty of the Southern states in the present crisis . . . as the impending danger threatened to subvert religion, as well as government and society, and involve all in common ruin" without a resounding affirmation from Providence. Nine others cosigned the letter. One week later Carnes delivered a diatribe in support of the Texas secessionist cause.[9] The secessionists held two large gatherings on December 16 and 20. Judge R. C. Campbell, Gen. E. B. Nichols, and John Muller, a German with pro-slavery sympathies, were elected to represent Galveston at a state convention, should one be called. A General Bradford from Alabama spoke to the crowds, criticizing Houston as "being laggard in this crisis." Members of the Knights of the Golden Circle arrived from Texas and Louisiana castles to recruit initiates and keep an eye on the Unionists.[10]

News of South Carolina's formal secession closed the year with apprehension and celebration; the die was cast, and Texas would not be far behind if the fire-eaters had their way. The *Woehentliche Union* published a scathing attack on South Carolina's decision, and on the night of January 3, 1861, a mob broke into the offices of Flake's Unionist newspaper and ransacked it. Richardson commented, "Our German fellow-citizens ought to look out for gentle persuasion." But the German printer had anticipated such a reaction and set up another press nearby to distribute the paper.[11]

Cole called for a city polling on January 8 to formally elect three delegates to the state convention scheduled for January 28. Not surprisingly, Campbell, Nichols, and Muller were selected; their names were the only ones on the ticket for the 1,022 who voted. The delegates arrived in Austin for the weeklong convention, at which Judge Oran M. Roberts was elected chairman. John Ford chaired the statewide Committee on Public Safety, and John Reagan, Louis T. Wigfall, John Hemphill, T. N. Waul, John Gregg, W. S. Oldham, and William Ochiltree went as delegates to the Montgomery, Alabama, convention to help organize the Confederate States of America. McLeod received votes on the first three ballots but was removed from consideration before the fourth. On February 1 the convention voted 166–7 for secession, and Roberts adjourned the meeting on February 5 with these words: "Let us go home and appeal to the people to sustain our action by their votes; and when we reassemble on the 2nd of March let us bring back with us the voice of a united people, in favor of an immediate action to sustain the rights of the people of Texas and of the South at all hazards, and to the last extremity." [12] On February 23 Texans voted 46,129–14,697 in favor of the Ordinance of Secession. In Galveston the fire-eaters won, 765–33.

In Galveston preparations were already under way for participation in the statewide efforts and for a defensive posture against the hostilities sure to come after Lincoln's inauguration as U.S. president. Ironically the U.S. Congress appropriated $80,000 in 1859 for the defense of Galveston, and those monies could now be utilized on behalf of the Confederacy instead. Sherman and Capt. John C. Moore supervised the work. Fortifications on Pelican Spit were improved. Fort Magruder, the South Battery, and Fort Point were erected around the edges of the harbor, and Fort Moore was established on the Gulf Beach. In addition more than eight hundred men volunteered to defend the city under Nichols's command. [13]

Ford contacted McLeod immediately after the convention's adjournment on February 5. On February 16 McLeod and Nichols prepared to depart Galveston as officers of the Rio Grande Regiment, which included most of the Galveston Lone Star Rifles and the accompanying Galveston Artillery Company. On February 20 McLeod, Nichols, and B. F. Terry embarked on the schooners *General Rusk* and *Shark* with five hundred men, arriving late the following afternoon at Brazos Santiago, an outpost on the north end of Brazos Island. There U.S. troops under the command of 1st Lt. James Thompson, Second Artillery, surrendered the tiny fort without resistance. A thirty-three-gun salute accompanied the lowering of the American flag, and another twenty-two guns heralded the raising of the Lone Star banner. Ford reported that "a high-toned courtesy seemed to prevail throughout." [14]

McLeod accompanied Ford, Nichols, and H. B. Waller to Brownsville to assess the situation at Fort Brown. Capt. B. H. Hill stood defiantly awaiting orders from his superior officer, Gen. David E. Twiggs, commander of U.S. troops in Texas. "He refused to acknowledge me," Ford reported, "taunting, threatening, and insulting in the course of the interview I had with him."[15] As the situation grew tense at Fort Brown, Ford ordered McLeod back to Brazos Santiago to reenforce that outpost. McLeod may have received his commission here as lieutenant colonel in the Texas Confederate army, as the rank is used in subsequent reports.

McLeod spent the next twenty days at Brazos Santiago. On February 24 W. W. Reynolds was appointed quartermaster and charged with establishing a commissary and receiving area for supplies. Reynolds, McLeod, and Nichols posted a $10,000 bond to the State of Texas "to receive and take charge of the government stores and supplies now on Brazos Island."[16] By February 26 Nichols had reported to Ford that "three hundred shovels were being diligently applied" and that "all are happy, with plenty to eat and plenty to do." Nichols returned to Galveston to meet reinforcements, leaving McLeod in sole command.[17] On March 3 the U.S. steamer *Daniel Webster* arrived at Brazos Santiago, carrying Maj. Fitz-John Porter, assistant adjutant general of the Union army. By this time McLeod commanded more than four companies of volunteers—about six hundred men. Porter seemed intent on settling the situation without bloodshed, especially now that word of Twiggs's compliance with the Confederate conditions for surrender had been received.

Captain Hill at Fort Brown remained unyielding, however. On March 4 he ordered a salute fired in honor of Lincoln's inauguration, touching off a dangerous situation. Confederates took up arms at the sound. McLeod conferred with Nichols, who had just returned from Galveston, and with Terry, and sent a hurried message to Ford, who was headquartered in Brownsville. It read: "The firing at Brownsville has been heard here and has excited this command. The troops interpret it as a menace. You know their character. . . . They feel that a salute fired by the garrison at Ft. Brown . . . dishonors this command and through them the State of Texas. . . . I beg that you will reply that the firing of to-day is not of an insulting or hostile character to the State, or your regiment will be in full march on to-morrow to settle the question with the U.S. troops in the field."[18]

Violence was averted by cooler heads, including Capt. George Stoneman of the Second U.S. Cavalry, who intervened and convinced Hill to surrender without further agitation. Ford and Nichols also recognized McLeod later for his calm restraint. Ford reported on March 6 that McLeod "has been very actively and assiduously employed in drilling the men and rendering the command efficient. He has erected temporary earth-works and placed heavy pieces at serviceable points to protect our position on

Brazos Island and to defend the harbor and the roadstead."[19] Apparently McLeod's drilling exercises fared better than they had in Kiowa country twenty years earlier. For the next three days Union troops left the Rio Grande valley; by design, McLeod's Confederates were kept away from the roads to avoid confrontation.

With the situation well in hand, McLeod grew anxious to find another way to participate in the coming war. On March 10 he resigned his post at Brazos Santiago, receiving Ford's formal thanks, and returned to Galveston four days later on the *General Rusk*. Ford wrote a personal letter of gratitude to his friend on March 20—the day the last Union soldiers departed—expressing satisfaction with the Galveston contingent's help in ensuring a smooth transition.[20] McLeod stayed in Galveston for four weeks, assisting Sherman and Moore with reinforcement efforts around the island. He suggested the addition of tracks to BBB&C rails to link several garrisons together, and he supervised the construction of additional shore batteries. He asked his nephew, John Baldwin, who had been working for the BBB&C since his return from Nicaragua, to take charge of the railroad work.

But McLeod still wanted to fight. When news of the firing on Fort Sumter reached Texas in April, he left for Montgomery, Alabama, to offer his services to President Jefferson Davis. After he left, Rebecca, wanting to help, wrote a letter to Texas Gov. Edward Clark on her husband's behalf. "My husband has left for Montgomery," she explained, "[but] in consequence of his service to the State on the Rio Grande many applications are before him [that is, in front of him] and it may be that he will be disappointed . . . should he fail in obtaining a suitable position in the Confederate Army." Rebecca also asked the governor to consider Baldwin for a captaincy: "He is an educated man with good habits, speaks French and Spanish and possesses all the qualifications for a soldier and desires to be employed in the defense of his country." She listed Nichols and Guy Bryan as references, and reminded Clark that Baldwin had been a hero in Nicaragua and "heralded throughout the United States at the time."[21] Baldwin went to war as 3rd lieutenant of Company L in the First Texas Regiment, was wounded at Second Manassas, and was transferred to Hood's Engineer Corps in 1863 as a captain. In 1864 he returned to Texas and directed railway shipping for the Confederacy until the war ended.[22]

Hamilton Stuart visited his old friend Sam Houston late in March, after the governor had resigned his post rather than sign the Ordinance of Secession. In ill health, Houston became upset when he heard of the preparations for war. As Stuart prepared to leave for Galveston, Houston vowed to travel there as he soon as he felt able. "Say I wish them well," Houston told Stuart before he left Cedar Point, "and hope that God will prosper them; but tell Colonel Hugh McLeod that old Sam Houston is not dead yet, and will yet outlive him."

On April 19 Houston arrived in Galveston by steamer. A committee led by Nichols met him at the docks to dissuade him from speaking. But the aging Texan would have none of it. Stuart and other Union sympathizers escorted him to Masonic Hall, but it had been locked by his adversaries. Moving to the Tremont Hotel, Houston climbed the back stairs to reach a balcony that overlooked the street. Hundreds had flocked to the spot by this time with catcalls and jeers, and M. H. Royster summarily kicked a man who attempted to climb the stairs after Houston. Houston spoke slowly but powerfully for several minutes, interrupted by shouts until Mayor Sydnor impolitely told the crowd to shut up. A traveler at the Tremont recorded some of Houston's remarks: "Will you now reject these last counsels of your political father, and squander your political patrimony in riotous adventure, which I now tell you, and with something of prophetic ken, will land you in fire and rivers of blood?" He concluded, "Let me tell you what is coming on the heels of secession. The time will come when your fathers and husbands, your sons and brothers, will be herded together like sheep and cattle at the point of a bayonet; and your mothers and wives and sisters and daughters will ask, 'Where are they?' and an echo will answer, 'Where?'"[23] Houston made his way through the crowds and back to the harbor. He may have glanced over the faces for his old nemesis McLeod, who had missed the moment. He was in Alabama waiting for word of a commission in the army. What a remarkable, poignant confrontation might have taken place if the two warriors had faced off one last time.

Lt. Col. McLeod returned to Galveston in May without a higher commission, but he was appointed aide-de-camp of the Third Military District of Texas, which encompassed Galveston and three counties on the mainland. Moore replaced the ailing Sherman as commander of the Galveston defenses. A quasi-military organization calling itself the Worthy and Ancient Order of J.O.L.O. volunteered to conduct a twenty-four-hour harbor watch for the coming naval blockade, which paid off in May with the capture of the *Nueces* and the *Nebraska,* two barks loaded with northern goods. On July 2 a midsummer squall lashed the island, and when it subsided in late morning the J.O.L.O. belatedly spotted the USS *South Carolina* taking up a position in the harbor, six 42-pounders pointed strategically from her broadsides. The Union blockade immediately took its toll, sinking or seizing a dozen ships in July alone. The shore batteries fired on the cruiser once, on August 6, but the *South Carolina's* return fire devastated the docks and discouraged further artillery battles.[24]

Of more pressing concern was the Galveston civilians' safety. McLeod was less than optimistic about the city's defenses. "No other county is situated as we are. Our city is literally in the sea and may be approached by ships with heavier caliber weapons than any of ours," he had warned in June.[25] Families began heading for the mainland in July, and the retreat continued through the fall. The city lay abandoned except for soldiers and a few wives who stayed to provide medical care and emotional support. Rebecca resolved to stay, although she was concerned for fourteen-year-old Caz. Never shy about speaking her mind, she wrote a June 24 letter to Charles Mason to be forwarded to the governor's office, spelling out her own plan by which Texas could "borrow military supplies from Louisiana, Alabama, Georgia, and South Carolina, for as many arms as they can part from each State, giving them security for the payment of the same . . . [else] our disaster will be theirs and will cost them ten-fold." Rebecca sent the letter "as the suggestion of a woman who fears for Texas though she has strong faith in the Confederacy—God has manifested by His providence, that He is with us not only in fruitful seasons, but also in the madness which has characterized the counsels of our enemies. . . . We cannot expect a continuance of His blessing if we fail to do our part."[26]

By the end of July the first Texas troops in the Galveston area were prepared to leave for Virginia to join the Confederate defense. News of the battle at Manassas had reached Texas, and the soldiers were eager to get into the war. The Lone Star Rifles organized as Company L of the First Texas Regiment and departed on August 2, commanded by McKeen and accompanied by McLeod. The sixteen-day trip took the company to New Orleans, and then by train up the Mississippi valley and east from Corinth to Virginia via Knoxville. A turn from the main rails onto the Danville-Richmond track brought the Texans to the Confederate capital on August 18, where they were welcomed by General Wigfall, who had preceded them by several months and had been at Fort Sumter in April.[27]

On August 20 McLeod received his commission as major in the Confederate army and was assigned to the First Texas Infantry. Thirteen days later, in a command shift, he was promoted to lieutenant colonel and sent with the Texas troops to a camp just below Rocketts on the York Railroad line. On September 12 Davis personally welcomed him and his troops, and the bivouac was renamed Camp Texas. These troops had seen no action, although reports of a move up to the Potomac River to establish a battery against roving Yankee schooners seemed imminent. McLeod met frequently with the other Texas regiment officers, including John B. Hood of the Fourth Infantry, Thomas Jefferson Green of the Fifth Cavalry, and his good friend B. F. Terry, who was commanding the Eighth Cavalry. He probably made contact with the large Georgia forces in the vicinity, which would have included visits with old acquaintances Col. Howell Cobb of the 16th Georgia Infantry and in-law Lt. Col. Charles A. L. Lamar of the Seventh Battalion.[28]

In mid-September the First Texas Regiment was ordered to move north to Dumfries, where it would join other Confederate forces in an ongoing defense of the lower Potomac. The first participation in battle occurred on September 25 at the Freestone Point battery. Wigfall filed a report of the action, in which "an armed tug fired ten shots into the point occupied by Hampton's battery before they were returned. The battery then drove her off." This divided the Union forces, some above and some below the batteries at Powell's Run. "The infantry supports are active and ready," Wigfall reported, in reference to McLeod's troops. "If the enemy land, our knowledge of the ground will make us equal to ten times our numbers. All are cheerful."[29]

Powell's Run saw no action, and for the next several weeks the Texas troops continued to dig in along the west banks, reinforcing batteries and building a permanent base camp and headquarters. On September 29 John Marshall wrote his Austin home from a barracks he called Camp McLeod near Dumfries.[30] There, "Wigfall's Mess" hosted most of the officers' staff meetings. In October Gen. E. K. Smith took command of the Fourth Division in Virginia and reorganized the troops, forming the Texas Fifth Brigade out of the first, fourth, and fifth regiments. The 18th Georgia Regiment under W. T. Wofford was later added. Wigfall took command of the brigade, and McLeod was promoted to colonel to lead the First Texas Regiment. An apparent falling-out between Wigfall and other regimental officers suggests that some objected to McLeod's promotion, although he was certainly in line for the command.[31]

Meanwhile the naval blockade at Galveston finally drove Rebecca and Caz away from their home. On September 10, 1861, they went to Houston and took the train to Savannah. That rail trip was more difficult than the more traveled route to Richmond and included overland stage between Montgomery and Columbus, Georgia. The McLeods left behind all but essential baggage and distributed the slaves in the care of the few neighbors who remained. Rebecca was especially concerned about "dearest Eleanor," her daughter Chloe, and Phillis, who was having trouble at the time with her fiancé, Henry. Caz left his considerable boy's library behind along with his most prized possession, a Mexican saddle his father had given him years before. Rebecca missed her new sewing machine and regretted leaving behind her husband's two favorite portraits, one of George Washington and the other of Stephen F. Austin in frontiersman apparel.[32]

They did not know they would never see Galveston again, nor that another tragic trip awaited them.

On November 5 Wigfall's brigade received orders from Richmond to move farther up the Potomac and reestablish headquarters. By now the weather had deteriorated to constant cold and rain, and the Texas and Georgia soldiers did not fare well. On November 8 additional brigade troops boarded trains in Richmond and rode to Fredericksburg. From there they marched to Dumfries to join the rest. Chaplain Nicholas A. Davis, assigned to regimental headquarters, noted that "our whole camp is in a mess." Of his first sight of the enemy, he wrote: "The roar of the cannon was terrific. Oh what a pity that a nation once so proud & happy must now be torn & rend from one end to the other, & overrun with fire & sword."[33]

On November 14 the regiments of Wigfall's brigade came together southwest of Neabsco Creek, and two days later they were situated on Occuquan Creek along the Potomac. The regiments were to construct a bridge over the creek and shore up the batteries still firing away at occasional Union vessels steaming southward. During this stage of operations, controversy about Wigfall led him to resign for a position in the Davis administration. For the moment, the brigade belonged to McLeod.[34] Most of the soldiers could hardly function in the inclement weather and the illnesses it spawned. Pneumonia and influenza were rampant. An outbreak of measles and "camp fever of a typhoid character" left more than three hundred men sick at the end of October and about two-thirds of the brigade ill at the end of November. John B. Hood came down with a severe case of diarrhea in Richmond in October.[35] When the first freezing storms swept down from the Shenandoah in December, the situation became critical. Secretary of War J. P. Benjamin wrote later that "humanity requires that I should try some way to prevent suffering and mortality among these troops just called from a southern clime and weakened by disease. . . . Try to relieve this regiment from exposure and picket duty till the men have well recovered from the effects." The construction of wood cabins in the Occuquan camp helped, but most of the cabins became hospital huts and morgues by Christmas. A hefty ration of whiskey got many men through the holiday, although "the next day headaches were both epidemic and contagious."[36]

Late in November McLeod began to suffer from a bad cold that quickly turned into pneumonia. The forty-seven-year-old Texan, weakened already by the heavy marching and vulnerable after a year of relentless activity and travel, fell desperately ill and was moved to the Wigfall Mess building, where he was under constant medical care. Fearing the worst, Chaplain Davis rushed a telegram to Savannah, where it found its way to Rebecca.

She and Caz hurried to Virginia and were escorted over the difficult last miles to the Dumfries camp in late December.

They spent New Year's Day, 1862, huddled together in the uncomfortable mess hall, with Hugh nearly incoherent from a rising fever and clogging lungs. Outside the freezing rain had turned to snow. Sometime during the early hours of January 3, with Rebecca and Caz at his bedside, Hugh McLeod died.[37]

The body of Hugh McLeod was transported back to Richmond, and his family accompanied the simple oak coffin. A train bound for New Orleans carried the body, along with that of fellow Texan Judge John Hemphill, who had died in Richmond on January 2. The train stopped in Knoxville on January 11, and a telegram was sent to Governor Lubbock in Austin: "Coming bodies of Hemphill, McLeod. Provide transportation at Brenham to Austin." In New Orleans both bodies lay in state on January 15 at the local Masonic Hall before continuing the journey. The next stop was Houston, where Lubbock met the train only days after burying his brother, Thomas, who had been killed on December 27. Once again, the Masonic lodge, Turner Hall, housed the two Texas leaders for crowds who came to pay their respects. The Galveston newspapers reported McLeod's death on January 14.[38]

The final destination was Austin. On February 1 services were held in the rain on a hill east of the capitol. The governor and dozens of congressional dignitaries stood in the cold drizzle to hear Episcopal Bishop Alexander Gregg's eulogy for the two statesmen. An honor guard fired a salute as the coffins were lowered to their resting places in the Texas State Cemetery.[39]

Afterword

Hugh McLeod's widow always signed her letters, whether business or personal, "R. J. McLeod." After McLeod's death and the short trip to Richmond, his widow and son remained behind in Virginia and did not accompany the body back to Texas. Instead they returned to Savannah and the comfort of family, living most of the time with Rebecca's brother George W. Lamar.

Always fiercely independent, Rebecca took charge of her late husband's estate even though she never returned to Texas. In April she wrote William T. Austin and Jonathan S. Beers, engaging them as her agents and lawyers. She gave instructions for care of the slaves left behind; they were to be placed in responsible homes in the Galveston-Houston area. Beers and his family moved into the McLeod home on Twenty-sixth Street. By December, 1862, Rebecca had given detailed instructions to Beers for selling off all of the belongings "except Caz' books and furniture," and the dividends from the BBB&C railroad stocks were forwarded to Savannah. Her investments in the cotton business also helped her over the years. An interest in a Georgia guano fertilizer company proved profitable until the federal government froze all Confederate assets. In 1866 Rebecca traveled to Washington, D.C., to speak personally with President Johnson regarding those assets.

Rebecca remained in Savannah at least through April, 1864, and then made her way to Richmond, Virginia, several months ahead of General Sherman's March to the Sea. She was back in Augusta in February, 1865. Her first cousin and close friend Charles Augustus Lafayette Lamar, another survivor of the *Pulaski,* was killed by a Union soldier on April 16 while trying to surrender. Devastated by the news, Rebecca took his widow, Caroline ("Caro"), under her wing, and the two were inseparable for the next thirty years.

Between 1865 and 1875 Rebecca occasionally traveled, mostly to Virginia to see Caz and once to Canada and to Allegheny Springs with her son for health reasons. In the 1870 U.S. Census she is listed as living in Savannah in the home of George and Sarah Lamar and their two sons. She continued to correspond with Beers, keeping up with estate sales and the other property she owned in Texas, at one time worth more than $80,000. Most of the property had been sold by 1880, leaving Rebecca to struggle financially in her last years.

She moved to Roanoke County, Virginia, in 1880 to live with Caro on the grounds of Hollins Institute, a young women's academy of more than a hundred students, including Caroline's great-niece. Rebecca became intensely religious in her later years, as evidenced in some of the last letters she wrote to friends and family. She fretted over her son's continuing poor health and wrote to her brother Gazaway often about issues of the day and the conditions of her world. At some point she moved to Richmond to live with Caz and Virginia. She died in their home on January 19, 1891, at the age of seventy-nine.

In 1863, sixteen-year-old Cazneau went back to Richmond to attend the University of Virginia. At the end of the first year he dropped out to serve in the Confederate army. He enrolled in a school for cadets and was still there when the war ended in 1865. By 1867 he was back in school in Virginia. He graduated with a law degree in the summer of 1870, married Virginia Marshall, and eventually went to work in Richmond as a city engineer. He and Virginia raised four children—Hugh, Lamar, Alfred, and Virginia. Caz died on December 31, 1899, and was buried in Richmond's Hollywood Cemetery next to his mother.

The general's first grandson and namesake may have had a similar personality to the old Texas adventurer. He went to the U.S. Military Academy but dropped out after a year and wandered west. He embroiled himself in the excitement and danger of the Montana mining industry at the turn of the century and finally settled down in North Carolina. His son and a grandson, both named Hugh McLeod, had careers in the U.S. Army. The most direct descendants of Hugh and Rebecca are Sally McLeod Knox's children in Florida and the LaMarche family on the West Coast. Sally's mother, Sarah Mathews McLeod, died in Newton, North Carolina, in 1997.

Although she seldom mentioned her husband in later letters, Rebecca spoke affectionately and respectfully of him as "a kind and honorable man." She believed in the causes for which Hugh McLeod fought and died and underscored his life's passions in 1861, when she assured the Texas governor, "His sword will doubtless be at the service of Texas."

How did McLeod's sword serve Texas? He joined forces with the political alliance of Mirabeau Lamar and David Burnet before he left Georgia in the fall of 1835. His friendship with Lamar extended into his support for the western faction when he took on Sam Houston two years later. Although the two political foes came close to reconciliation after the Caddo Wars in 1839, the incident surrounding Chief Bowl's hat destroyed the possibility. Instead the two faced off in verbal duels for the next twenty-one years.

McLeod was a leading voice in Texas politics in the 1840s and 1850s. Speeches at Masonic gatherings, building dedications, railroad rallies, and barbecues included his assaults on Houston's leadership and character. McLeod's two unsuccessful runs for U.S. Congress carried similar political emotions. His popularity as a public speaker overcame the failures of the 1841 Santa Fe expedition, and only history's fickle pen has erased his contributions in favor of blame for his failed command.

McLeod spent most of his public career supporting various causes. He may not have been the same visionary as Bickley, Carbajal, or Walker, but he situated himself as a spokesman for their revolutionary causes. He used his popularity in fund-raising efforts and enlistment rallies with consistent success. His downfall, in history's eyes, was the failure of every cause he celebrated, save the Texas Revolution itself. Lamar's Pacific empire never materialized. Carbajal gave up trying to establish a Republic of the Rio Grande. Bickley's Cuba-based slave state foundered, as did Walker's efforts in Nicaragua. And the South's attempt at secession led to McLeod's death in the Civil War.

A reporter wrote in 1839 that McLeod in battle on the Neches River seemed "like a meteor glancing," and there are no truer words about his life. He spent his last twenty-five years bounding from cause to cause, from office to office, and even from rank to rank in four armies. He failed to accomplish his objectives in nearly every enterprise, but he deserved better than the phrase "commander of the ill-fated Santa Fe Expedition." The people who knew McLeod and heard him regale his impassioned beliefs respected him. Even his political foes took him seriously at every turn. In his lifetime he ranked among the great voices of Texas—Houston, Lamar, and Rusk. History should find a place for him that reflects his ebullient life in enervating times.

Notes

INTRODUCTION

1. *The Papers of Mirabeau Buonaparte Lamar,* vol. 4, 1, no. 2410, pp. 208–209.

2. *Houston Telegraph and Texas Register,* July 28, 1841.

3. Claude Elliott, review of *The Texas Santa Fe Trail,* by Horace Bailey Carroll, *Southwestern Historical Quarterly* 66 (1952): 333–35.

CHAPTER I

1. Passenger lists for the *James Madison,* 1818, New York City to Savannah, Ga. William Bixby, *South Street,* p. 20.

2. Letter of Virginia McLeod Marshall, 1927. McLeod family papers.

3. John William Leonard, *History of the City of New York, 1609–1909,* pp. 322–28.

4. Caroline Price Wilson, ed., *Annals of Georgia,* vol. 3, p. 137. McLeod is listed as a carpenter. Records in the Old Cemetery indicate that he may have been buried in New York. Also, E. Merton Coulter, "The Great Savannah Fire of 1820," *Georgia Historical Quarterly* 23 (1939): 1–5.

5. Henry Southerland, Jr., and Jerry E. Brown, *The Federal Road through Georgia, the Creek Nation, and Alabama, 1806–1836,* pp. 60–75. Also, Elbert W. G. Boogher, *Secondary Education in Georgia, 1732–1858,* p. 78.

6. Martha Lou Houston, *The Land Lottery of Georgia, 1827,* p. 82.

7. Southerland and Brown, *Federal Road through Georgia,* p. 74. Also, John C. Butler, *Historical Records of Macon and Central Georgia,* pp. 91–93. The General Catalogue of the University of Pennsylvania's Medical Department lists Daniel's 1832 thesis paper, *"Trismus nascentium,"* about lockjaw in infants. Daniel became an assistant naval surgeon on Feb. 8, 1832, served in the Florida Seminole Wars aboard the USS *Albany,* and rose to the position of surgeon on July 23, 1841. Edward Callahan, ed., *List of Officers of the Navy of the United States, 1775 to 1900,* p. 372.

8. Boogher, *Secondary Education in Georgia,* p. 79; Butler, *Historical Records of Macon and Central Georgia,* pp. 94–96.

9. Robert M. Myers, ed., *Children of Pride: A True Story of Georgia and the Civil War,* p. 181.

10. Military Records of Hugh McLeod, 1832–1835. United States Military Academy, West Point, New York.

11. Butler, *Historical Records of Macon and Central Georgia*, p. 96. Also, Harold LeMar, *History of the Lamar or Lemar Family*, pp. 91–95.

12. McLeod to H. G. Lamar, Dec. 8, 1829. Military Records of Hugh McLeod.

13. Ibid., Mar. 24, 1831.

14. George W. Cullum, *Biographical Register of the Officers and Graduates of the United States Military Academy at West Point, New York*, pp. 82–87.

15. Ibid., pp. 21–25.

16. *Official Register of the Officers and Cadets of the United States Military Academy 1832*, pp. 17–22.

17. Stephen E. Ambrose, *Duty, Honor, Country: A History of West Point*, pp. 107–108. Also, Leonard D. White, *The Jacksonians: A Study in Administrative History, 1829–1861*, pp. 208–12.

18. McLeod speech in Austin, May 17, 1851, as printed in *Texas State Gazette*, May 24, 1851.

19. W. A. Croffut, ed., *Fifty Years in Camp and Field: The Diary of General Ethan Allen Hitchcock, U.S.A.*, pp. 65–68.

20. *Official Register of Officers and Cadets*, pp. 6–7.

21. Report of the Superintendent, June 3, 1835, in Military Records of Hugh McLeod. Thayer considered Gridley Tavern a nuisance.

22. Report of the Board of Visitors, Sept. 3, 1835, Official Papers of the United States Military Academy, West Point, New York.

23. Cullum, *Biographical Register*, p. 492.

24. LeMar, *History of the Lamar or Lemar Family*, pp. 110–13.

25. George F. Pearce, *The United States Navy in Pensacola: From Sailing Ships to Naval Aviation, 1825–1930*, p. 28.

26. Claude Elliott, "Georgia and the Texas Revolution," *Georgia Historical Quarterly* 28 (1944): 236.

27. Macon *Messenger*, Nov. 12, 1835. In John H. Jenkins, *Papers of the Texas Revolution*, vol. 2, p. 236, no. 1174 (hereafter cited as *PTR*).

28. Ibid., p. 370.

29. Elliott, "Georgia and the Texas Revolution," p. 237.

30. Jenkins, *PTR*, vol. 2, p. 494, no. 1276.

31. Elliott, "Georgia and the Texas Revolution," p. 240.

32. Ibid., p. 242.

33. Jenkins, *PTR*, vol. 2, p. 382, no. 1673. Most biographical sketches of McLeod indicate that he resigned and came to Texas on June 30, 1836; however, this was the date his resignation was accepted, not the day he crossed the Sabine River and headed for Nacogdoches. In *Bounty and Donation Land Grants of Texas, 1835–1888*, T. L. Miller shows that McLeod received 1,280 acres "for service 7 March 1836–21 December 1837" (p. 482).

CHAPTER 2

1. Muster Rolls, U.S. Army, 1835–36, Fort Jesup, La., 3rd. Reg., Co. B. Bill and Marjorie Walraven, *Magnificent Barbarians: Little-Told Tales of the Texas Revolution*, pp. 116–19.

2. James Gaines to J. W. Robinson, Gaines Ferry, Jan. 9, 1836, Jenkins, *PTR*, vol. 2, p. 236, no. 1174.

3. Eugene C. Barker, *Papers of Stephen F. Austin*, vol. 3, p. 385ff.

4. Anna Muckleroy, "Indian Policy in the Republic of Texas," *Southwestern Historical Quarterly* 26 (1922): 6.

5. Report of James W. Robinson, in Jenkins, *PTR*, vol. 3, p. 399, no. 2146.

6. A. J. Houston to Sam Houston, in Thomas M. Marshall, *A History of the Western Boundary of the Louisiana Purchase, 1819–1841*, p. 146. Henry Teal was killed in Mexico later that year.

7. Archie McDonald, in *Nacogdoches: Wilderness Outpost to Modern City, 1779–1979*, mentions Arnold's volunteers (p. 45). Arnold's company is also listed, however, at San Jacinto, in William C. Binkley, *Official Correspondence of the Texas Revolution*, vol. 1, p. 485.

8. Muster Rolls, U.S. Army, Fort Jesup, La., Mar., 1836.

9. House of Representatives of the Republic of Texas Official Records and Journal. Executive Documents, 12:332, 777–80.

10. Juan Almonte, "A Statistical Report on Texas, 1835," *Southwestern Historical Quarterly* 38 (1934): 217f.

11. Lois Blount, "A Brief Study of Thomas J. Rusk through the Letters to His Brother David," *Southwestern Historical Quarterly* 36 (1930): 191.

12. John T. Lamar to Sam Houston, Mar. 16, 1836; Ira Ingram to Sam Houston, Apr. 5, 1836; John Darrington to David Burnet, Apr. 10, 1836, nos. 323 and 350, Papers of Andrew Jackson Houston.

13. Marshall, *History of the Western Boundary*, p. 149; Muckleroy, "Indian Policy," pp. 6–7.

14. Elizabeth Brooks, *Prominent Women of Texas*, pp. 20–21; Mrs. Rusk to McLeod, *Southwestern Historical Quarterly* 34 (1930): 141.

15. Andrew Jackson Houston Papers, Apr. 13, 1836, no. 365; House of Representatives of the Republic of Texas, Official Records and Journal, Executive Documents, 6:256, 56. Marshall, *History of the Western Boundary*, p. 156.

16. Diary of Michael Costley, *Robert Bruce Blake Nacogdoches Papers*, vol. 53, no. 355–64. Also, Douglass, Texas, in *New Handbook of Texas*.

17. R. L. and Pauline Jones, "The Occupation of Nacogdoches," *East Texas Historical Journal* 4 (1966): 24–26.

18. Eugene C. Barker, "The United States and Mexico, 1835–1837," *Mississippi Valley Historical Review* 1 (1914): 26–27.

19. Jones, "Occupation of Nacogdoches," p. 28; Marshall, *History of the Western Boundary*, pp. 180–81.

20. Jones, "Occupation of Nacogdoches," pp. 28–29.

21. Muster Rolls, U.S. Army, Fort Jesup, La., July, 1836; Marshall, *History of the Western Boundary,* p. 146.

22. Marshall, *History of the Western Boundary,* pp. 149–50.

23. Jones, "Occupation of Nacogdoches," p. 30; Marshall, *History of the Western Boundary,* p. 184. Also, Joseph Milton Nance, *After San Jacinto: The Texas-Mexican Frontier, 1836–1841,* p. 16.

24. T. J. Chambers to David Burnet, Feb. 22, 1836, in Jenkins, *PTR,* vol. 7, no. 3308, p. 48.

25. Ibid., vol. 8, no. 3835, p. 78.

26. Ibid., vol. 8, no. 3867, p. 115; vol. 7, no. 3308, p. 48.

27. Jan. 8, 1837, in T. J. Chambers, "Diary of T. J. Chambers," *Southwestern Historical Quarterly* 50 (1946): 167. Sylvester was noted as one of the captors of General Santa Anna after San Jacinto. In fact, Santa Anna was accompanied to Washington, D.C., over a similar route during this period, raising the possibility that McLeod had some contact with the group, which included Gen. Sidney Sherman.

28. Jenkins, *PTR,* vol. 9, no. 4330, pp. 113–35.

29. Chambers, "Diary of T. J. Chambers," p. 168.

30. Jack Ramsay, Jr., *Thunder beyond the Brazos: Mirabeau B. Lamar, A Biography,* pp. 50–51. Also, *Lamar Papers,* nos. 550–99, for correspondence while Lamar was in Georgia that summer.

31. Ramsay, *Thunder beyond the Brazos,* pp. 52–53. Also, Marquis James, *The Raven: A Biography of Sam Houston,* pp. 295–99.

32. Georgia Marriages and Deaths, May 17, 1827, for marriage of Robert Brower and Isabella McLeod in Savannah; *Census of the United States, State of Georgia, 1840,* the Browers and Isabella.

33. Miller, *Bounty and Donation Land Grants of Texas, 1840.* Hugh McLeod, "Pre-October 1, 1837: Single, Class 2, 640 acres, Galveston County." Also, Gifford E. White, *First Settlers of Galveston County, Texas,* pp. 2, 27, 30. Also, James, *Raven,* pp. 281–84.

34. Philosophical Society of Texas, in *New Handbook of Texas.*

35. *Official Records of Freemasonry in Texas,* p. 181.

36. Records of the Office of Adjutant-General of the Republic of Texas. Most biographical sketches of McLeod mention his service under Lamar, which began with his reappointment in December, 1838. But McLeod followed Edwin Morehouse (1801–49). McLeod was also appointed inspector-general by Lamar in 1840.

CHAPTER 3

1. Report of the Adjutant-General, Government of the Army of the Republic of Texas, 1839, Adjutant-General Records.

2. McLeod to Sam Houston, Apr. 18 and 20, 1838, Andrew Jackson Houston Papers.

3. Noah Smithwick, *Evolution of a State, or, Recollections of Old Texas Days,* p. 99. Houston made the statement in a speech to Congress.

4. A. S. Johnston to Barnard Bee, Jan. 14, 1838; Bee to Johnston, Jan. 20, 1838; McLeod to Johnston, Feb. 26, 1838. Papers of Albert Sidney Johnston.

5. McLeod to Lamar, June 25, 1838, *Lamar Papers,* vol. 2, p. 171.

6. McLeod to N. B. Charlton, Nacogdoches, Aug. 5, 1838, *Probate Records of San Augustine County, Texas.*

7. McLeod to Jacob Snively, Nacogdoches, Aug. 31, 1838, Adjutant-General Records. Snively later served as acting adjutant general while McLeod was engaged in the Cherokee Wars of 1839.

8. Dianna Everett, *The Texas Cherokees: A People between Two Fires, 1819–1840,* pp. 90–94.

9. McLeod to Lamar, Nacogdoches, Aug. 26, 1838, *Nacogdoches Papers,* vol. 65, pp. 10–11.

10. Sam Houston to McLeod, Nacogdoches, Aug. 11, 1838, Amelia C. Williams and Eugene C. Barker, eds., *Writings of Sam Houston,* vol. 4, p. 63.

11. McLeod to Lamar, Aug. 4 and 26, 1838, *Lamar Papers,* vol. 2, pp. 196–97, 209–10.

12. Burton to Lamar, Nacogdoches, Aug. 25, 1838, *Lamar Papers,* vol. 2, p. 208.

13. McLeod to Lamar, Nacogdoches, Aug. 4, 1838, *Lamar Papers,* vol. 2, p. 197; Rebecca Lamar McLeod, "The Loss of the Steamer Pulaski," *Georgia Historical Quarterly* 3 (1919): 64–95. Also, Eugenia Price, *To See Your Face Again.*

14. McLeod to Lamar, Aug. 26, 1838, *Lamar Papers,* vol. 2, p. 209.

15. Jack Moore, *The Killough Massacre,* pp. 4–20.

16. McLeod to Lamar, Oct. 22, 1838, *Nacogdoches Papers,* vol. 55, pp. 20–23.

17. Houston to Thomas J. Rusk, Oct. 10, 1838, Williams and Barker, *Writings of Sam Houston,* vol. 2, pp. 288–89; also, Everett, *Texas Cherokees,* pp. 96–97.

18. McLeod to Lamar, Oct. 22, 1838, Williams and Barker, *Writings of Sam Houston,* vol. 2.

19. McLeod to Lamar, Oct. 25, 1838, *Nacogdoches Papers,* vol. 65, p. 26.

20. Ibid., pp. 29–30. McLeod to Lamar, Nov. 16, 1838.

21. Ibid., p. 33. McLeod to Lamar, Nov. 20, 1838.

22. McLeod to Lamar, Port Caddo, Nov. 23, 1838, *Lamar Papers,* vol. 2, p. 302.

23. McLeod's Report to Ashbel Smith, Oct., 1838, Papers of Ashbel Smith.

24. McLeod to Lamar, Port Caddo, Nov. 21, 1838, *Lamar Papers,* vol. 2, pp. 296–99.

25. Ibid., p. 308f. McLeod to Lamar, near Port Caddo, Dec. 1, 1838.

26. McLeod to Lamar, "25 miles west of Clarksville," Dec. 20, 1838, *Nacogdoches Papers,* vol. 65, pp. 37–38.

27. McLeod to Lamar, below Clarksville, Jan. 9, 1839, *Lamar Papers,* vol. 2, p. 406.

28. Ibid., vol. 65, pp. 39–40. McLeod to Lamar, Jan. 18, 1839.

29. McLeod to William Redd, Austin, Mar. 23, 1839, Adjutant-General Records. Also, Apr. 4 and 11 letters indicate recruiting along the Red River as per orders of the secretary of war.

30. Valentin Canalizo to Manuel Flores, Feb. 27, 1839, quoted in Everett, *Texas Cherokees,* pp. 101, 148 n. 7.

31. Lamar to Chief John Bowl, May 26, 1839, in *Texas Indian Papers,* ed. Dorman H. Winfrey and James M. Day, vol. 1, pp. 64–65.

32. John H. Reagan, "The Expulsion of the Cherokees from East Texas," *Southwestern Historical Quarterly* 1 (1897): 38–46.

33. Mary Whatley Clarke, *Chief Bowles and the Texas Cherokees,* pp. 96–106. Also, Everett, *Texas Cherokees,* p. 105.

34. Reagan, "Expulsion of the Cherokees," pp. 38–46. Kelsey Douglass to A. S. Johnston, July 16, 1839, *Lamar Papers,* pp. 46–47.

35. Battle sites today are located just outside Chandler, north of Lake Palestine.

36. *Houston Telegraph & Texas Register,* July 28, 1841, as quoted in Gertrude Burleson Blake, "The Public Career of General Hugh McLeod" (master's thesis, University of Texas, 1932), pp. 20–21. McLeod's horse was killed under McNeely. See also the article portraying McLeod as a heroic Indian fighter in the *Natchitoches Herald,* reprinted in the *Macon (Georgia) Telegraph* on Nov. 27, 1838.

37. Thomas J. Rusk to Kelsey Douglass, July 18, 1839, Letters and Papers of Thomas Jefferson Rusk.

38. J. W. Wilbarger, *Indian Depredations in Texas,* p. 172. Also, "Medical Report of L. B. Brown," July 16, 1839, *Lamar Papers,* vol. 3, p. 44. In other reports McNeely is listed as "Mcnelly" and even "O'Neil."

39. Reagan, "Expulsion of the Cherokees," p. 46. See also Albert Woldert, "The Last of the Cherokees in Texas, and the Life and Death of Chief Bowles," *Chronicles of Oklahoma* 1 (1921): 210–12.

CHAPTER 4

1. Report of the Adjutant-General, Nov., 1839, printed by Act of the Congress, Adjutant-General Records.

2. Supplemental Documents A, B, and C to the 1839 Annual Report of the Adjutant-General, Adjutant-General Records.

3. Box 1306, Adjutant-General Records.

4. Report of Hugh McLeod, Adjutant-General, Dec. 10, 1840, *Nacogdoches Papers,* vol. 65, p. 171.

5. Certification by Hugh McLeod, Nov. 14, 1840, Adjutant-General Records.

6. Llerena B. Friend, *Sam Houston, The Great Designer,* pp. 95–96.

7. R. L. Biesele, "The San Saba Colonizing Company," *Southwestern Historical Quarterly* 33 (1930): 171.

8. See *New Handbook of Texas* for articles on Reuben Ross, Richard Roman, Samuel W. Jordan (who tried to kill Houston with an axe in 1840 and committed suicide in 1841), Antonio Canales Rosillo, Antonio Zapata, and José Maria Jesus Carbajal. Also, see articles about Willard Richardson, B. F. Hill, and Ewen Cameron, who were involved in the auxiliary.

9. Mirabeau B. Lamar, Message to the House of Representatives, Jan. 13, 1839, *Lamar Papers,* vol. 5, pp. 389–90. Also, David M. Vigness, "Relations of the Republic

of Texas and the Republic of the Rio Grande," *Southwestern Historical Quarterly* 57 (1954): 312f.

10. Nance, *After San Jacinto,* pp. 168–73, 186–88.

11. Juan Pablo Anaya to Editor, *Houston Telegraph & Texas Register,* Sept. 20 and 25, 1839, in Vigness, "Relations of the Republic of Texas," p. 314 n. 7.

12. Nance, *After San Jacinto,* p. 190 n. 57. Sam Houston Dixon, *Romance and Tragedy of Texas History,* vol. 1, p. 258.

13. Mirabeau B. Lamar, Proclamation Warning and Admonishing Citizens of the Republic Taking Up Arms against the Mexican Government, City of Austin, Dec. 21, 1839, *Austin City Gazette,* Jan. 1, 1840.

14. Nance, *After San Jacinto,* pp. 240–41. Nance details the Federalist War on pp. 142–377.

15. Reuben Ross, in *New Handbook of Texas.* Ross and Ben McCulloch dueled over a private issue, and Ben was wounded. At a Christmas party, Ben's brother, Henry, challenged the drunken Ross to a duel and killed him. Nance, *After San Jacinto,* p. 235 n. 136.

16. Vigness, "Relations of the Republic of Texas," p. 318.

17. José Maria Jesus Carbajal to Lamar, July 27, 1840, *Lamar Papers,* vol. 3, p. 424.

18. Ibid., p. 437. McLeod to Lamar, Aug. 21, 1840.

19. Ibid.

20. Ibid., p. 439. McLeod to Lamar, Aug. 28, 1840.

21. William Preston Johnston, *The Life of General Albert Sidney Johnston,* p. 115.

22. Walter Prescott Webb, *The Texas Rangers: A Century of Frontier Defense,* pp. 54–57; Wilbarger, *Indian Depredations in Texas,* pp. 160–69.

23. H. W. Karnes to A. S. Johnston, Jan. 10, 1840, *Records Relating to Indian Affairs.*

24. McLeod to Lamar, San Antonio, Mar. 17, 1840, *Lamar Papers,* vol. 3, p. 354.

25. The following is a compilation of three eyewitness reports: Hugh McLeod, Adjutant and Inspector General, San Antonio, to His Excellency M. B. Lamar, Mar. 20, 1840, *Journal of the House,* 5th Congress, Appendix, pp. 136–39; Rena Maverick Green, ed., *Memoirs of Mary A. Maverick, arranged by Mary Maverick and her son;* Letters of Captain George T. Howard to Lieutenant Colonel William S. Fisher, recounted in John Henry Brown, *Indian Wars and Pioneers.*

26. *Texas (Austin) Sentinel,* Apr. 15, 1840.

27. Jo Ella Powell Exley, *Texas Tears and Texas Sunshine: Voices of Frontier Women,* pp. 92–98. Judge Thompson, nominated by Lamar to be Texas' emissary to Belgium, had come to San Antonio shortly after encountering Indians, as evidenced by several arrows through his coat.

28. Brown, *Indian Wars and Pioneers.* McLeod says there was one Indian in the kitchen house; Mary Maverick said two, and Brown said several.

29. Sylvia Van Voast Ferris and Eleanor S. Hoppe, *Scalpels and Sabers,* pp. 133–34.

30. Mildred P. Mayhall, *Indian Wars of Texas,* pp. 25–29, attributes the quote to Booker L. Webster, a captive boy.

31. For a complete account of the Linnville Raid and the Plum Creek Fight, see Donely E. Brice, *The Great Comanche Raid: Boldest Indian Attack of the Texas Republic.*

32. McLeod to A. S. Johnston, Austin, Aug. 19, 1840, Albert Sidney Johnston Pa-

pers. McLeod sent orders to Edward Burleson to prepare the frontier guards "to be in readiness to join you and in case of invasion." John H. Jenkins and Kenneth Kesselus, *Edward Burleson: Texas Frontier Leader.* Those orders were countermanded three days later, but preparations continued.

CHAPTER 5

1. Manning, William Ray, *Early Diplomatic Relations between the United States and Mexico,* pp. 286–87.

2. Stephen F. Austin to Henry Austin, Aug. 27, 1829, Austin Papers.

3. *Texas Congress, House Journal,* 1 Congress, 1 Session, pp. 256–57.

4. Ibid., p. 247.

5. *Houston Telegraph & Texas Register,* Dec. 23, 1837. Also, *Texas Congress, House Journal,* 2 Congress, 2 Session, p. 101.

6. James Webb to Richard C. Dunlap, Mar. 13, 1839, in George Pierce Garrison, *Diplomatic Correspondence of the Republic of Texas,* vol. 2, pp. 368–72.

7. David Burnet to James Treat, Aug. 9, 1839, in Garrison, *Diplomatic Correspondence,* vol. 2, pp. 470–71.

8. President Lamar to the Citizens of Santa Fe, Apr. 14, 1840, Papers of the Santa Fe Expedition, 1841–1842.

9. W. Jefferson Jones to Lamar, Feb. 8, 1839, *Lamar Papers,* no. 1049, vol. 2, p. 427.

10. Both rebellions were put down by the Mexican government, harshly and with a clear message to the people regarding future uprisings. See also, A. K. Christian, "Mirabeau Buonaparte Lamar," *Southwestern Historical Quarterly* 23 (1921): 89. For the fur trade, see Eugene C. Barker, "A Glimpse of the Texas Fur Trade, 1832," *Southwestern Historical Quarterly* 29 (1916): 279–82.

11. Lamar's Address to the Harrisburg Volunteers, Mar., 1839, *Lamar Papers,* vol. 2, p. 474.

12. William G. Dryden to Lamar, Apr. 29, 1840, *Lamar Papers,* vol. 3, p. 385.

13. Ibid. Mar. 10, 1841, no. 2070, vol. 3, p. 556.

14. *Texas Congress, House Journal,* 5 Congress, 1 Session, p. 45.

15. McLeod to Judge John Baldwin, Dec. 14, 1840, *Lamar Papers,* vol. 3, p. 475. McLeod sent this letter of introduction to his friend, who would act as Lamar's host during his convalescence in New Orleans.

16. Burnet's Message to Congress, Dec. 16, 1840, *Texas Congress, House Journal,* 5 Congress, 1 Session, pp. 292–93.

17. Felix Huston to Branch T. Archer, Dec. 23, 1840, Army Papers of the Republic of Texas.

18. *Texas Congress, House Journal,* 5 Congress, 1 Session, p. 723.

19. T. J. Powell to Lamar, Mar. 17, 1841; George Fisher to Lamar, Mar. 25 and Apr. 6, 1841; James Love to Lamar, Apr. 13, 1841, *Lamar Papers,* pp. 499–506.

20. Lamar's Message to Congress, Nov. 3, 1841, Executive Records of President Mirabeau B. Lamar of the Republic of Texas, Book 39, p. 284. Lamar's defense of his

actions earlier that year fell on the deaf ears of an angry Congress upon their return to session.

21. William Cazneau to Robert S. Neighbors, Apr. 8, 1841, Records of the Quartermaster-General of the Republic of Texas.

22. Thomas J. Green to J. Waddy Thompson, Apr. 26, 1842, in George Wilkins Kendall, *Narrative of the Texan Santa Fe Expedition and Capture of the Texans*, vol. 1, p. 14.

23. *Austin City Gazette*, Apr. 28, 1841. In *The Texan–Santa Fe Pioneers*, Noel M. Loomis notes that the announcement was not prominent in that day's edition, but somehow the word spread across central Texas rapidly (pp. 3–4).

24. Military Rolls VI-1, Adjutant-General Records.

25. Albert Sidney Johnston to Lamar, Aug. 6, 1840, *Lamar Papers*, vol. 3, p. 427.

26. George S. Pierce, "The Military Road Expeditions of 1840–41," *Texas Military History* 6 (1967): 115. McLeod and Lindsay reported surveying and marking a fort site on the San Marcos River on Oct. 21, 1840. See also, McLeod to Lamar, San Marcos Spring, Oct. 21, 1840, *Lamar Papers*, vol. 3, p. 462.

27. James Durst to Lamar, Angelina, Apr. 24, 1841, *Lamar Papers*, vol. 3, p. 514; McLeod to Lamar, June 17, 1841, vol. 3, p. 538.

28. Kendall, *Narrative*, vol. 1, pp. 71–72. See also, H. Bailey Carroll, *The Texan Santa Fe Trail*, p. 11 n. 27. The numbers on this expedition have been a source of debate ever since the Pioneers made camp, varying from over 400 to just over 300. The numbers 320 or 321 are usually accepted. The question speaks to the problems of organization from the outset, although exact numbers for such a march would not be altogether critical to the organizers in those days.

29. Acting Secretary of State Roberts to Cooke, Navarro, Brenham, and Dryden, June 15, 1841, in Garrison, *Diplomatic Correspondence*, vol. 2, pp. 738–42.

30. Thomas Falconer, *Letters and Notes on the Texan Santa Fe Expedition, 1841–1842*, pp. 12–13; Kendall, *Narrative*, vol. 1, pp. 53–56.

31. Loomis, *Texan–Santa Fe Pioneers*, p. 202ff.

32. Kendall, *Narrative*, vol. 1, pp. 29–39.

33. Rupert Richardson, *The Frontier of Northwest Texas, 1846–1876*, pp. 39–41. "They were victims of their own ignorance and of the poor Indian relations of their government. . . . Mares' map . . . would have been of priceless value to the wanderers. With that in hand they would have known that their Mexican guide was either a spy or an ignorant knave."

34. Kendall, *Narrative*, vol. 1, pp. 60–62.

35. Loomis, *Texan–Santa Fe Pioneers*, pp. 210–11.

36. George W. Grover, "Minutes of Adventure from June 1841"; Peter Gallagher, "Diary"; and Peter Gallagher, "Journal of the Santa Fe Expedition," as edited by Stephen Hoyle (hereafter cited as Gallagher-Hoyle journal), in Santa Fe Papers. Clayton Erhardt wrote his memoirs of the expedition, but not until 1882 when he was quite old.

37. William Cazneau to Branch T. Archer, Oct. 1, 1841, Army Papers. See also, *Houston Telegraph & Texas Register*, Sept. 29, 1841, where the total appears as $89,549.69.

38. Carroll, *Trail*, pp. 14–16.

39. *Austin City Gazette*, Apr. 28, 1841.

40. Special Order no. 1, June 1, 1841. In Virginia Taylor, ed., *Order Book of General H. McLeod: Santa Fe Expedition.*

41. Special Order no. 4, June 5, 1841, Taylor, *Order Book.*

42. Special Order no. 3, June 4, and Special Order no. 6, June 13, 1841, Taylor, *Order Book.* Also, Kendall, *Narrative,* vol. 1, pp. 85–86.

43. Special Order no. 7, June 19, 1841, Taylor, *Order Book.*

44. Carroll, *Trail,* 16.

45. *Austin City Gazette,* June 16, 1841. The editors also argued that the only expenses they had seen for the march totaled a meager $2,397.25.

46. Ibid., June 17, 1841. Signed, "A Citizen of Washington County." This may have been McLeod's old friend James F. Perry.

47. Kendall, *Narrative,* vol. 1, p. 70.

48. Samuel A. Roberts to William Cooke, June 15, 1841, in Garrison, *Diplomatic Correspondence,* vol. 2, pp. 737–43.

49. Kendall, *Narrative,* vol. 1, p. 70.

CHAPTER 6

1. Carroll, *Trail,* pp. 17–19. Again, there is unresolved debate about the exact day of departure. All but Gallagher wrote their journals as recollections, and they seem to have remembered different dates—June 19, 20, or 21. Carroll prefers the earliest date, but a Sunday morning departure (June 20) would have been appropriate both to the schedules described in most of the diaries and as a traditional way to invoke the blessing of providence on such a journey.

2. The *Austin City Gazette,* June 23, 1841, refers to a Sunday departure.

3. Loomis, *Texan–Santa Fe Pioneers,* p. 23. Loomis admits that the description of the band and banners may have been a later embellishment by storytellers on the frontier.

4. Kendall, *Narrative,* vol. 1, pp. 74–75.

5. Carroll, *Trail,* pp. 27–28. Also, Lucy A. Erath, "Memoirs of Major George Bernard Erath," *Southwestern Historical Quarterly* 9 (1906): 31–32.

6. Gallagher-Hoyle journal, p. 1. Also, Special Order no. 8, June 21, 1841, Taylor, *Order Book.*

7. Kendall, *Narrative,* vol. 1, pp. 76–80.

8. Kendall, *Narrative,* vol. 1, p. 72; Loomis, *Texan–Santa Fe Pioneers,* pp. 26–30.

9. Kendall, *Narrative,* vol. 1, pp. 91; Gallagher-Hoyle journal, p. 1.

10. Special Order no. 9, June 24, and Special Order no. 10, June 26, 1841, Taylor, *Order Book.*

11. Special Order no. 11, June 26, 1841, Taylor, *Order Book.*

12. Kendall, *Narrative,* vol. 1, p. 71.

13. Peter Gallagher's "Diary" is the only detractor of several accounts of the reason for McLeod's leave of absence. The others refer to an illness, but Gallagher notes: "26th.

Killed one buffalo. Same day General McLeod left for the settlement sick with fever. Too much whiskey." Or is this Gallagher?

14. Kendall, *Narrative,* vol. 1, p. 85.

15. Ibid., p. 86.

16. Gallagher-Hoyle journal, p. 1.

17. Special Orders no. 12 and 13, July 1, 1841, Taylor, *Order Book.*

18. Grover's "Minutes"; Kendall, *Narrative,* vol. 1, p. 105; Carroll, *Trail,* pp. 39–41. Acting President Burnet approved a law in Dec., 1840, providing for the appointment of spy companies on the frontier. Howard clearly used this directive as an excuse to assert his authority.

19. Batte, Lelia, *The History of Milam County, Texas,* pp. 47–48.

20. Kendall, *Narrative,* vol. 1, p. 101.

21. General Order no. 11, July 3, 1841, Hubert Howe Bancroft Papers.

22. Kendall, *Narrative,* vol. 1, p. 91.

23. Ibid., pp. 92–94.

24. Ibid., pp. 95–98.

25. Carroll, *Trail,* pp. 55–57.

26. Gallagher-Hoyle journal, p. 2.

27. Kendall, *Narrative,* vol. 1, p. 103. Kendall estimated the revised distance to be 700 miles—still a serious underestimate.

28. Gallagher-Hoyle journal, p. 2; also, Carroll, *Trail,* pp. 59–68.

29. Carroll, *Trail,* p. 70.

30. Gallagher-Hoyle journal, p. 4.

31. John Pope, *Explorations and Surveys for a Railroad Route from the Mississippi River to the Pacific Ocean,* vol. 2, p. 40. Also, Kendall, *Narrative,* vol. 1, pp. 110–11; Carroll, *Trail,* pp. 71–73. Ironically, McLeod had been in the area more than two years earlier, chasing Caddoes out of East Texas. In Jan., 1839, he wrote Lamar that these "cross timbers are the finest portions of Texas, as a body—and its bottoms are equally as fine as the Brazos." He probably wanted to change his assessment after the expedition.

CHAPTER 7

1. Falconer, *Letters,* p. 80; Kendall, *Narrative,* vol. 1, pp. 110–12, with, he concludes, "every attempt to find a passage out proving futile."

2. Grover's "Minutes."

3. Gallagher-Hoyle journal, p. 3.

4. Falconer, *Letters,* p. 80.

5. Excerpts from "Notes on the Santa Fe Expedition," Hubert Howe Bancroft Papers, pp. 712–13; Gallagher-Hoyle journal, p. 3.

6. Hugh McLeod, *Texas State Gazette,* May 24, 1851, from his speech made in Austin a week earlier while he was running a campaign for the Western District of Texas House seat in Washington, D.C.

7. Blake, "Public Career of General Hugh McLeod," pp. 65–66.

8. *Texas State Gazette,* May 24, 1851. As McLeod told the story later, Cooke chose this inopportune moment to "go fishing," thus rendering himself neutral in the argument, much to McLeod's anguish. "The man I most loved and trusted had failed me in my need," McLeod said.

9. Army Papers of Texas, Texas State Library.

10. Special Order no. 14, July 25, 1841, Taylor, *Order Book.*

11. General Order no. 12, July 25, 1841, H. E. Bolton Transcripts, pp. 10–11. Also, Carroll, *Trail,* pp. 75–76.

12. Carroll, *Trail,* p. 76.

13. Kendall, *Narrative,* vol. 1, p. 113–15.

14. Gallagher-Hoyle journal, p. 3.

15. Kendall, *Narrative,* vol. 1, p. 116.

16. Falconer, *Letters,* p. 80.

17. Kendall, *Narrative,* vol. 1, pp. 108–109.

18. Ibid., p. 119.

19. Carroll, *Trail,* pp. 78–79.

20. Loomis, *Texan–Santa Fe Pioneers,* p. 42.

21. Kendall, *Narrative,* vol. 1, p. 121.

22. Ibid., pp. 123–26. This story became one of the favorites in the later newspaper reports, and by storytellers on the Texas frontier.

23. Ibid., pp. 129–30.

24. General Order no. 14, Hubert Howe Bancroft Papers, pp. 715–19.

25. Loomis, *Texan–Santa Fe Pioneers,* p. 45. These Indian dogs, probably left behind at the Waco village when it was hastily abandoned, trailed along to the Llano, often serving as guard dogs when they caught scent of Indians in the shadows, and, sadly, sometimes becoming a meal for starving Pioneers.

26. Gallagher-Hoyle journal, p. 4.

27. Carroll, *Trail,* pp. 84–85. General Orders no. 13 and 14, Hubert Howe Bancroft Papers, pp. 713–15, are dated at "Camp on Wichita."

28. Falconer, *Letters,* p. 81; Kendall, *Narrative,* vol. 1, pp. 140–44; and Gallagher-Hoyle journal, p. 9.

29. Loomis, *Texan–Santa Fe Pioneers,* p. 46.

30. Ibid., p. 235.

31. Grover's "Minutes," as quoted at length in Carroll, *Trail,* p. 88.

32. Loomis, *Texan–Santa Fe Pioneers,* p. 50.

33. Kendall, *Narrative,* vol. 1, p. 162.

34. Falconer, *Letters,* p. 82.

35. General Order no. 16, Hubert Howe Bancroft Papers, pp. 721–23.

36. Loomis, *Texan–Santa Fe Pioneers,* p. 249. He says Sutton, a merchant with a large load of merchandise, was anxious to join the safety of the larger wagon train on its way west.

37. Kendall, *Narrative,* vol. 1, p. 162.

38. Ibid., p. 163.

39. Special Order no. 15, Aug. 11, 1841, Taylor, *Order Book.*

40. Carroll, *Trail,* pp. 99–100.

41. Kendall, *Narrative,* vol. 1, pp. 177–82. Also, Falconer, *Letters,* p. 82; Gallagher's "Diary"; and Carroll, *Trail,* p. 172. Kendall notes that he did not recognize his new friend and fellow traveler Falconer; most of Falconer's hair was gone, and his eyebrows had been singed off. Falconer was bothered by these injuries for the remainder of the trip and pointedly does not mention them when he describes the prairie fire's destruction.

42. Kendall, *Narrative,* vol. 1, pp. 185–86.

43. Ibid., p. 187.

44. Ibid., p. 183.

45. Loomis, *Texan–Santa Fe Pioneers,* p. 58.

46. Kendall, *Narrative,* vol. 1, p. 205.

47. Loomis, *Texan–Santa Fe Pioneers,* p. 58.

48. Gallagher's "Diary" and Grover's "Minutes." Also, Carroll, *Trail,* p. 111. Loomis thinks Dr. Brashear may be J. H. L. Brashear (*Texan–Santa Fe Pioneers,* p. 271).

49. Special Order no. 16, Aug. 18, 1841, Taylor, *Order Book.*

50. Carroll, *Trail,* pp. 112–13.

51. Kendall, *Narrative,* vol. 1, pp. 189–95.

52. Ibid., pp. 196–97.

53. Gallagher-Hoyle journal, pp. 12–13.

54. Falconer, *Letters,* p. 84; Kendall, *Narrative,* vol. 1, pp. 204–205.

55. Carroll, *Trail,* p. 124. Today the campsite is located two miles south of the town of Quitaque and east of Texas Hwy. 1065, at the junction of three counties: Briscoe, Floyd, and Motley. There are freshwater springs a few hundred yards south of where Los Lingos Creek joins the Quitaque.

CHAPTER 8

1. Kendall, *Narrative,* vol. 1, p. 206; also Loomis, *Texan–Santa Fe Pioneers,* p. 62.

2. Gallagher-Hoyle journal, p. 8; also, Falconer, *Letters,* pp. 84–85; and Kendall, *Narrative,* vol. 1, pp. 207–209. This was the most dramatic event of the expedition.

3. Carroll, *Trail,* p. 130 n. 43; and Loomis, *Texan–Santa Fe Pioneers,* p. 64 n. 15.

4. Kendall, *Narrative,* vol. 1, pp. 211–12. McLeod's resolve may have been re-awakened. Certainly his experience—and famed exploits—dealing with Indians on the frontier gave him the skills to deal with this crisis; he knew what he was doing, and his leadership changed because of it.

5. Grover's "Minutes."

6. Loomis, *Texan–Santa Fe Pioneers,* p. 65.

7. Falconer, *Letters,* p. 132. Also Grover's "Minutes" and Garrison, *Diplomatic Correspondence,* p. 778, which quotes the later Brenham-Cooke Report.

8. General Orders, recorded Sept. 1, 1841, the day after McLeod gave the speech, in "Speech of General McLeod"; also quoted in Blake, "Public Career of General Hugh McLeod," pp. 67–69.

9. Carroll, *Trail,* pp. 134–43.

10. Kendall, *Narrative,* vol. 1, pp. 269–70. There is some suggestion that a sixth rider, "a Mexican," may have gone along with this party, perhaps as an interpreter.

11. Ibid., pp. 280–85.

12. Thomas S. Lubbock, Houston, May 9, 1842, in "Recollections of Thomas S. Lubbock," *Texana* 6 (1968): 166–71. Lubbock never finished his account.

13. Falconer, *Letters,* pp. 40–41.

14. Special Orders no. 18 and 19, Sept. 1, 1841, Taylor, *Order Book.* These are the final entries made by McLeod and Sevey in the official orders book.

15. Gallagher's "Diary," p. 13.

16. Falconer, *Letters,* p. 106. On Dec. 2, 1882, in an interview for the Galveston *Free Press,* Pioneers survivor C. Erhard said, "General McLeod drilled us, a thing a frontiersman despises; he is hard to keep under discipline, and believes in a free fight on his own hook, not in regular battle order."

17. Falconer, *Letters,* p. 40.

18. Ibid., pp. 108–109.

19. General Order no. 21, Hubert Howe Bancroft Papers, pp. 734–35.

20. Falconer, *Letters,* p. 108.

21. Ibid.

22. Gallagher's "Diary," pp. 15–18.

23. Loomis, *Texan–Santa Fe Pioneers,* p. 102.

24. Hugh McLeod, *Texas State Gazette,* May 24, 1851, from an Austin speech.

25. Gallagher-Hoyle journal, p.10.

26. Ibid., p. 11; also, Falconer, *Letters,* pp. 110–11.

27. Loomis, *Texan–Santa Fe Pioneers,* p. 110.

28. Falconer, *Letters,* pp. 134–35; Josiah Gregg, *Commerce of the Prairies,* p. 317 n. 4. "The Laguna Colorado is twelve miles west of Mount Tucumcari."

29. Gregg, *Commerce of the Prairies,* p. 317 n. 115. Falconer makes no comment on this conversation, saying only that the healthier men went ahead with Cooke and that the "discussions ended in the general conviction that a surrender was inevitable." However, more than six years later, Charles Burgess argued that Cooke, Howard, Hudson, and other officers conspired to take command from McLeod; that dividing the party was never McLeod's choice; and that the healthier men going ahead further weakened any defense the soldiers at Camp Resolution could have mustered. The letter, though persuasive, seems politically motivated. Burgess to Lamar, July 21, 1848, Santa Fe Papers.

30. Gregg, *Commerce of the Prairies,* 44, 116. Also, Loomis, *Texan–Santa Fe Pioneers,* p. 113 n. 28. Archuleta filed his own report of the proceedings, omitting the number of men he had captured but listing thirty-four horses, three mules, and an undetermined head of cattle as part of the booty.

CHAPTER 9

1. Kendall, *Narrative,* vol. 1, p. 365.

2. Ibid.

3. Webb, *Texas Rangers,* for the battles against the Comanches along the upper Colorado River and the San Saba River; also, Wilbarger, *Indian Depredations in Texas.*

4. Nance, *After San Jacinto,* p. 544, on Lipans as guides and scouts into South Texas in 1842.

5. Loomis, *Texan−Santa Fe Pioneers,* p. 102.

6. Kendall, *Narrative,* vol. 1, p. 365.

7. Ibid., vol. 2, p. 18.

8. Ibid., vol. 1, p. 366.

9. Ibid.

10. Loomis, *Texan−Santa Fe Pioneers,* p. 99 n. 4, quoting an anecdote from J. Evetts Haley's *Charles Goodnight: Cowman and Plainsman* (Boston, Mass.: Houghton Mifflin, 1936, p. 89) and indicating figures of 15 pounds of beef per man and oxen dressing out at 430 pounds, and so on. Haley writes, "McLeod had made strenuous efforts to conserve the beef herd, and this new development—the butchering and eating seven oxen—must have been a serious blow."

11. Kendall, *Narrative,* vol. 1, p. 365.

12. Ibid., p. 366.

13. Ibid.

14. Blake, "Public Career of General Hugh McLeod," pp. 57−58, quoting W. C. Binkley, "New Mexico and the Santa Fe Expedition," *Southwestern Historical Quarterly* 27 (1924): 90f. In 1839 Armijo filed a report with Mexico City that concluded, "It seems, therefore, that unless definite evidence to the contrary is brought to light, the conclusion must stand that in 1840−41 a large part—just how large it is not possible to say— of the people of New Mexico are regarding with favor the possibility of commercial and political relations with Texas" (p. 107).

15. W. C. Binkley, *The Expansionist Movement in Texas, 1836−1850,* pp. 83−88.

16. Kendall, *Narrative,* vol. 1, p. 366.

17. Anson Jones to Mrs. Mary Jones, Jan. 3, 1842, Papers of Anson Jones. "Now ask for all that crowd, of fools and knaves and flatterers of power who basked in the smiles of executive influence, and where are they. Gone and scattered for ever. Some are dead, others doomed to hopeless misery and to spend the remainder perhaps of a cheerless existence, in the mines of Mexico, the rest powerless, weak—accursed and despised and wishing themselves with the others."

18. Andrew Jackson to Sam Houston, May 25, 1842, in Henderson Yoakum, *History of Texas,* vol. 2, p. 329. "The wild-goose campaign was an ill-judged affair."

19. Binkley, *Expansionist Movement,* p. 93.

20. Houston speech, May 8, 1848, in Marshall, *History of the Western Boundary,* p. 259. See Watt Goodwin Hill, "Texan Santa Fe Expedition of 1841: A Visionary Dream" (master's thesis, St. Mary's University, San Antonio, 1965), pp. 117−18.

21. Binkley, *Expansionist Movement,* p. 75.

22. Mexican Vice-President Viddauri to Governor Arista, May 5, 1841, Bolton Transcripts; also, Kendall, *Narrative,* vol. 1, p. 71.

23. Felix Huston to Branch T. Archer, Dec. 23, 1840, Army Papers; Burnet's Message to Congress, Dec. 16, 1840, *Texas Congress, House Journal,* 5 Congress, 1 Session, pp. 292–93.

24. James T. DeShields, *Border Wars of Texas,* pp. 338–39, 362. McLeod was not Lamar's brother-in-law, but he married Mirabeau's first cousin Rebecca. Rebecca did not marry a man named Johnston, as DeShields claims. John T. Lamar was more of a father figure to McLeod than he was like a brother.

25. Binkley, *Expansionist Movement,* pp. 68–69.

26. Lamar's Message to Congress, Nov. 3, 1841, Executive Records of President Mirabeau B. Lamar of the Republic of Texas, Book 39, p. 284.

27. Loomis, *Texan–Santa Fe Pioneers,* pp. 116–17.

28. Binkley, *Expansionist Movement,* p. 67.

29. McLeod's promotion did not take effect until June 17. Until then, and when he signed the initial orders earlier in June, he was commissioned as colonel commanding. Loomis, *Texan–Santa Fe Pioneers,* p. 10 n. 21.

30. Lewis and McLeod were fellow Masons, along with Cooke and several other principal figures, including Lamar and Santa Anna. In fact, Lewis, McLeod, and Cooke all belonged to Lodge No. 12 in Austin, originally founded by McLeod. Lewis's betrayal struck these men, who had shared the secrets of the Freemasonry, hard.

31. "Resolution of February 5, 1842," Castle of San Christopher, Santa Fe Papers.

CHAPTER 10

1. Kendall, *Narrative,* vol. 1, p. 300.

2. Loomis, *Texan–Santa Fe Pioneers,* p. 76.

3. Ibid., p. 79.

4. Kendall, *Narrative,* vol I, pp. 301–303.

5. George Nielsen, "Mathew Caldwell and the Santa Fe Expedition," *Southwestern Historical Quarterly* 64 (1961): 491–93.

6. Ibid, pp. 581–83. Caldwell to Hannah Caldwell, Feb. 10, 1842.

7. McLeod to Armijo, Oct. 8, 1841, in Falconer, *Letters,* pp. 134–35.

8. Spruce M. Baird to Texas Governor George Wood, 1848, in Paul Horgan, *Great River: The Rio Grande in North American History,* vol. 2, p. 799.

9. Ibid., pp. 116 n, 117 n.

10. Kendall, *Narrative,* vol. 1, p. 403 n.

11. Ibid., pp. 510–11.

12. Falconer, *Letters,* p. 136.

13. Kendall, *Narrative,* vol. 2, pp. 14–17.

14. It is difficult to determine exactly how many men were left behind in hospitals,

clinics, and homes between Paseo del Norte and Jalapa. Besides the forty who remained in Vera Cruz, perhaps three dozen more stayed in Mexico past the summer of 1842. One of those was Archibald Fitzgerald, at Hacienda Salado. One year later, mixed in with the Mier prisoners, he died of wounds sustained when he joined the famous Feb. 2 escape attempt.

15. Valentine Bennet to Family, Feb. 3, 1842, in Marie Bennet Urwitz, "Valentine Bennet," *Southwestern Historical Quarterly* 9 (1906): 151–53. Bennet was renowned in Oct., 1835, as one of Gonzales's "Old Eighteen" defenders.

16. Kendall, *Narrative*, vol. 1, pp. 323–25.

17. Ibid., vol. 1, p. 398.

18. Ibid., vol. 2, p. 79.

19. Ibid., pp. 34–39; Briefs 104A–104N, Bolton Transcripts.

20. Loomis, *Texan–Santa Fe Pioneers*, p. 126.

21. Kendall, *Narrative*, vol. 2, pp. 66–67.

22. George F. Ruxton notes that it was not unusual for girls to bathe with strangers (*Adventure in Mexico and the Rocky Mountains*, p. 59). When the men leered or came too close, the girls laughed and called them *sinverguenzas*, or shameless ones. "A fitting punishment," Loomis says *(Texan–Santa Fe Pioneers*, p. 126 n. 9). See also, Kendall, *Narrative*, vol. 2, pp. 54–55, 144–45.

23. Loomis, *Texan–Santa Fe Pioneers*, p. 126.

24. Ibid., p. 228.

25. Manning, *Early Diplomatic Correspondence*, vols. 8 and 12.

26. Gallagher's "Diary" and itinerary, in Carroll, *Trail*, p. 179.

27. Guy M. Bryan to James F. Perry, Jan. 8, 1842, Papers of James F. Perry and Stephen S. Perry. Bryan's life (1821–1901) spanned decades of political and military service to Texas.

28. Joseph Martin Dawson, *José Antonio Navarro, Co-Creator of Texas*, p. 75.

29. J. J. McGrath and Wallace Hawkins, "Perote Fort: Where Texans Were Imprisoned," *Southwestern Historical Quarterly* 48 (1945): 340–45; Llerena B. Friend, "Sidelights and Supplements on the Perote Prisoners," *Southwestern Historical Quarterly* 68 (1965): 366–74.

30. Alvarez to Daniel Webster, Feb. 2, 1842, *Consular Dispatches*, vol. 1, Santa Fe. Pioneer John Rowland's brother Tom was robbed in San Miguel by Armijo's soldiers, and a Frenchman was killed as a Texas sympathizer. Gregg, *Commerce of the Prairies*, pp. 162–63.

31. Loomis, *Texan–Santa Fe Pioneers*, p. 228.

32. Lubbock, "Recollections," quoted in Loomis, *Texan–Santa Fe Pioneers*, p. 128. Commodore Moore of the Texas Navy reported seeing Lubbock aboard the *San Antonio* in April. Alexander Dienst, "The Navy of the Republic of Texas," *Southwestern Historical Quarterly* 13 (1909): 43.

33. Loomis, *Texan–Santa Fe Pioneers*, p. 131. Two years later, in attempts to obtain the release of Navarro, McLeod refuted a claim that a British flag had been surrendered to the Mexican army by the expedition (presumably by Tom Falconer). "No British flag

there," he asserted. McLeod to British Chargé D'Affaires Charles Elliot, Nov. 26 and 29, 1843, in E. D. Adams, ed., "British Correspondence Concerning Texas," *Southwestern Historical Quarterly,* 17 (1914): 425.

34. McLeod to A. J. Donalson, U.S. Chargé D'Affaires, Jan. 21, 1845, printed in *Texas National Register,* Feb. 1, 1845. "To express my gratitude to the brave old warrior, is beyond my powers of language. May he long enjoy a green old age, to realize the grateful reward a patriot can receive—the voluntary homage of a nation of freemen, whose history he adorns."

35. Loomis, *Texan–Santa Fe Pioneers,* p. 127. Hargous argued more than a decade later that he had never been repaid the $2,000 he loaned to McLeod and Cooke. McLeod was very clear that the money had been sent long before, through the efforts of Gazaway Bugg Lamar of New York City and J. Waddy Thompson. See "Joint Resolution Acknowledging the Claims of L. S. Hargous and Others," in *Laws of the Republic of Texas,* Special Session, 2:1203, June 24, 1845; also, Waddy Thompson to Gazaway Lamar, Oct. 5, 1855, Papers of James Britton.

36. Kendall, *Narrative,* vol. 2, pp. 306–10.

37. Waddy Thompson to Daniel Webster, June 20, 1842, in Manning, *Early Diplomatic Correspondence,* p. 499. "General McLeod says that his prisoners were well treated, he does not deny that they were made to labor and in chains. . . . I state these facts with no view to disparage General McLeod, but to justify myself for an interference which the letter of McLeod would seem to represent as both causeless and officious."

38. J. Waddy Thompson, *Recollections of Mexico,* p. 74.

39. Falconer, *Letters,* p. 141.

40. Thompson, *Recollections,* p. 92.

41. Kendall, *Narrative,* vol. 2, pp. 355–56; Jacob DeCordova, *Biography of José Antonio Navarro, written by an old Texan,* pp. 19–25.

42. Loomis, *Texan–Santa Fe Pioneers,* p. 132.

43. W. Eugene Hollen and Ruth L. Butler, eds., *William Bollaert's Texas, 1836–1846,* pp. 130–32.

44. Julia Lee Sinks, "Original Sketch for the *Fayette County News* of the Santa Fe Prisoners," *Southwestern Historical Quarterly* 64 (1961): 514–16. R. L. Duffus considered Kendall's book "the 'Uncle Tom's Cabin' of the Mexican War. Its delineation of the character of the Mexican governing classes . . . stirred up resentment far beyond the boundaries of Texas." R. L. Duffus, *The Santa Fe Trail,* p. 184.

CHAPTER 11

1. Letters and Papers of Julia Lee Sinks. See *New Handbook of Texas* for additional information on Dancy and Jones.

2. Paula M. Marks, *Turn Your Eyes toward Texas: Pioneers Sam and Mary Maverick,* pp. 102–104.

3. Paul N. Spellman, "Zadock and Minerva Cottle Woods, American Pioneers" (master's thesis, University of Texas, 1987), pp. 94–96, 121–22.

4. Marks, *Turn Your Eyes toward Texas*, pp. 105–106.

5 Joseph Milton Nance, *Attack and Counter-Attack: Texas-Mexican Relations, 1842*, pp. 335–63. Also, Marks, *Turn Your Eyes toward Texas*, p. 106; and Spellman, "Zadock and Minerva Cottle Woods," pp. 127–37.

6. Nance, *Attack and Counter-Attack*, pp. 364–81.

7. Seymour V. Connor, *Adventure in Glory: The Saga of Texas, 1836–1849*, p. 184.

8. Hollen and Butler, *William Bollaert's Texas*, p. 156.

9. Fascinated by the newspaper business since his Georgia days, when Mirabeau B. Lamar ran a paper there, McLeod would later try his hand at editing and publishing. Teulon may have had some influence, along with Kendall of the New Orleans *Picayune*.

10. George Teulon to William Cooke, Sept. 28, 1842, Adjutant-General Records.

11. Charles DeMorse, John S. Bell, and James S. Mayfield to McLeod, Oct. 3, 1842, Papers of Hugh McLeod.

12. Friend, *Sam Houston*, p. 108.

13. L. W. Kemp, "Mrs. Angelina B. Eberly," *Southwestern Historical Quarterly* 36 (1933): 196–97; also, Hope Yager, "The Archive War in Texas" (master's thesis, University of Texas, 1939), p. 67.

14. *Houston Telegraph & Texas Register*, Jan. 4, 1843; also, Henry Gillett to Ashbel Smith, Jan. 10, 1843, Ashbel Smith Papers.

15. *Laws of the Republic of Texas*, Seventh Congress, 2:838, Jan.14, 1843.

16. "Hugh McLeod, for service 7 March 1836–21 December 1837," in Miller, *Land Grants of Texas*, p. 462.

17. Rebecca Lamar McLeod was born Dec. 22, 1811. She wrote an account of the shipwreck in the 1840s, "The Loss of the Steamer Pulaski," which appeared in the *Georgia Historical Quarterly* (vol. 3, 1919) twenty years after her death. Also, see LeMar, *History of the Lamar or Lemar Family*, pp. 111–15. Rebecca's exploits are even recounted in Eugenia Price's contemporary romance novel, *To See Your Face Again*.

18. Connor, *Adventure in Glory*, pp. 201–203.

19. *Houston Morning Star*, May 9, 1843.

20. Daniel C. McLeod was promoted to surgeon on July 23, 1841. Callahan, *Officers of the Navy*, p. 372.

21. Charles W. Hayes, *Galveston: A History of the Island and City*, p. 713.

22. Tom Henderson Wells, *Commodore Moore and the Texas Navy*, pp. 161–65.

23. Connor, *Adventure in Glory*, p. 199.

24. Adams, ed., "British Correspondence Concerning Texas," 423–25.

25. Marks, *Turn Your Eyes toward Texas*, pp. 113–17; also, Rena Maverick Green, *Samuel Maverick, Texan, 1803–1870*, pp. 155–75.

26. Hayes, *Galveston*, pp. 459–60. The *Texas Times* closed down shortly thereafter. Marilyn McAdams Sibley, *Lone Stars and State Gazettes: Texas Newspapers before the Civil War*, pp. 174–75.

27. Representatives of the Republic of Texas Official Records and Journal. Roll of the Members of the Ninth Congress.

28. Reily to Starr, Aug. 5, 1844, Papers of James Harper Starr; McLeod to Thomas J. Rusk, July 16, 1844, Thomas Jefferson Rusk Papers.

29. W. P. Ballinger, "Reminiscences," Galveston *News*, June 3, 1882; also in the Papers of Edward S. Burleson.

30. Groves H. Cartledge, *Presbyterian Churches and Early Settlers in Northeast Georgia*, p. 32. Reverend Dod was described by his parishioners as "not a man of much noise, but his sermons were very lucid, pointed, and effective."

31. McLeod to Editor, *Texas National Register*, Dec. 28, 1844. McLeod wrote on Dec. 19 that he had a pleasant crossing from the island four days earlier, thanks to the ship's captain, who ferried him to Houston.

32. *Laws of the Republic of Texas*, vol. 2, p. 1066.

33. John S. Oates, ed., *Memoirs of John S. "Rip" Ford*, p. 49. "These were able and influential men in both Houses who could not have been satisfied by anything short of a full acceptance of the terms [for annexation] offered."

34. House of Representatives of the Republic of Texas Official Records and Journal. Ninth Congress, Jan. 20, 1845. Also in the *Texas National Register*, Feb. 1, 1845.

35. *Laws of the Republic of Texas*, vol. 2, p. 116, Feb. 3, 1845.

36. House of Representatives of the Republic of Texas Official Records and Journal. Ninth Congress, Jan. 22, 1845.

37. *Laws of the Republic of Texas*, vol. 2, p. 1155; also, Hayes, *Galveston*, p. 719.

38. *Laws of the Republic of Texas*, vol. 2, p. 1068, Jan. 20, 1845.

39. *Telegraph & Texas Register*, Feb. 12, 1845.

40. *Texas National Register*, Mar. 15, 1845.

41. Ibid.

42. William Beck Ochiltree to Oran Roberts, Dec. 17, 1844, Papers of Oran Roberts; in Friend, *Sam Houston*, p. 146 n.

43. Friend, *Sam Houston*, pp. 152-54.

44. *Texas National Register*, July 3, 1845; also in Blake, "Public Career of General Hugh McLeod," pp. 99-100.

45. *Texas National Register*, July 10, 1845; also in Blake, "Public Career of General Hugh McLeod," pp. 102-103.

CHAPTER 12

1. Lamar to James Knox Polk, Oct. 17, 1845; J. M. Storms to Lamar, Mar. 27, 1846, *Lamar Papers*, vol. 4, p. 130.

2. Hayes, *Galveston*, p. 713.

3. Ibid., pp. 471-72.

4. Ibid., p. 470.

5. Rebecca McLeod to J. S. Beers, June, 1866, Papers of J. S. Beers.

6. Census of Texas, 1846; Miller, *Land Grants of Texas*, p. 462.

7. Hayes, *Galveston*, pp. 477–78.

8. Hugh McLeod, "An Address on Temperance," Apr. 1, 1846, H. E. Huntington Library, San Marino, Calif.

9. Hugh McLeod to Rebecca McLeod, Point Isabel, May 4, 1846, Hugh McLeod Papers.

10. Lota M. Spell, *Pioneer Printer: Samuel Bangs in Mexico and Texas*, pp. 125–28.

11. Ibid., p. 129.

12. Hayes, *Galveston*, pp. 464–65.

13. John S. D. Eisenhower, *So Far from God: The U.S. War with Mexico, 1846–48*, p. 75. Also, Henry W. Barton, *Texas Volunteers in the Mexican War*, pp. 22–24. There seems to have been some criticism of those coming to the fray before Taylor's call for volunteers. McLeod probably accompanied these first volunteers, who made their way down the coast on the rickety barque *Blaze*, the only vessel available in Galveston harbor when they were ready to depart.

14. Hayes, *Galveston*, p. 476.

15. Sibley, *Lone Stars and State Gazettes*, p. 202. Dryden is not listed in any other writings as being in Matamoros during this time.

16. David M. Pletcher, *The Diplomacy of Annexation: Texas, Oregon, and the Mexican War*, pp. 462–63.

17. Spell, *Pioneer Printer*, pp. 130–32.

18. Horgan, *Great River*, vol. 2, pp. 703–704.

19. J. H. Smith, "La Republica de Rio Grande," *American Historical Review* 25 (1920): 666.

20. Pletcher, *Diplomacy of Annexation*, p. 463. One copy of the second edition of McLeod's paper is the McLeod Papers in Austin.

21. Eisenhower, *So Far from God*, p. 101 n.

22. Smith, "La Republica de Rio Grande," p. 667 n.

23. Lota Spell, "The Anglo-Saxon Press in Mexico, 1846–1848," *American Historical Review* 38 (1932): 22. Spell says that McLeod later became one of the owners of the San Antonio *Ledger* (p. 31). This is incorrect; the owner in question was Aeneas Macleod, no known relation. See also, Sibley, *Lone Stars and State Gazettes*, p. 215.

24. Gen. John Sibley wrote Lamar on Aug. 13, 1846, regarding a mule of his in General McLeod's possession. The mule's whereabouts were unknown, but McLeod had returned to Galveston. *Lamar Papers*, vol. 4, p. 135.

25. Gazaway Bugg Lamar to Mirabeau B. Lamar, May 14, 1846, *Lamar Papers*, vol. 4, p. 134; and McLeod to Mirabeau Lamar, Nov. 10, 1846, vol. 4, p. 144.

26. Hayes, *Galveston*, pp. 466–67. The lavish banquet was held in the Tremont House and "eclipsed anything that had ever been attempted before (in Galveston)." The invitations were handwritten, not engraved, and many of the regular soldiers from the island were honored, as were Sherman, Wood, McLean, and Ben McCulloch. The banquet committee included Samuel May Williams, J. C. Watrous, and other dignitaries.

27. Walker was killed on Oct. 9 in battle deep in Mexico. Both Bangs and McLeod wrote articles on the famous Ranger in the summer of 1846. Teulon had left Texas and

the United States disillusioned with the politics of his day; he died of cholera in Asia. See *New Handbook of Texas*.

CHAPTER 13

1. McLeod to Albert Sidney Johnston, Nov. 25, 1848, Albert Sidney Johnston Papers. Also, Johnston, *Life of General Albert Sidney Johnston*, p. 54.

2. McLeod to Johnston, Nov. 25, 1848. It is unclear what other agenda McLeod may have had on this trip, for this writer has not been able to find reference to it elsewhere.

3. Samuel May Williams to McLeod, June 29, 1849, Hugh McLeod Papers. Williams wrote about the "awards" for those who campaign, and about the upcoming election.

4. S. C. Griffin, *A History of Galveston*, pp. 35 – 36. This was a subcommittee of the Chamber of Commerce, whose responsibilities included maintenance of roads and bridges for the island and the city.

5. McLeod to Samuel May Williams, June 20, 1849, Papers of Samuel May Williams. McLeod wrote the letter before his speech that evening and mentioned an editorial in the Victoria paper.

6. *Biographical Directory of Members of the U.S. Congress*, pp. 1218 and 1649; *New Handbook of Texas*.

7. "Relief of the Santa Fe and Mier Prisoners," *Laws of the State of Texas*, Feb. 9, 1850, vol. 3, pt. 1, ch. 127, p. 594.

8. United States Census of 1850, State of Texas, vol. 2, p. 794. The listed ages of the four members of the family were incorrect, as was typical. Hugh was thirty-five, not thirty-four; Rebecca thirty-eight, not thirty; and Cazneau had just turned three, not four.

9. Letters of the McLeod family, June, 1964, in possession of the author.

10. S. G. Reed, *A History of the Texas Railroads and Transportation Conditions under Spain and Mexico and the Republic and the State*, p. 54.

11. Sidney Sherman entry, *Handbook of Texas*. Walter Bate, *General Sidney Sherman, Texas Soldier, Statesman, and Builder*, pp. 190 – 212.

12. Reed, *History of the Texas Railroads*.

13. Sidney Sherman to Andrew Briscoe, Oct.2, 1847, Papers of W. A. Philpott. Sherman added, "To borrow money on Texas securities seems to be entirely out of the question especially in this section of the country" (Bate, *General Sidney Sherman*, p. 195). Cazneau moved to Eagle Pass before the 1850 charter and did not participate again in the corporation.

14. Charter of the Harrisburg City Company, 1848, Harris County Records, Houston. Bate, *General Sidney Sherman*, pp. 197 – 98.

15. Earl F. Woodward, "Internal Improvements in Texas in the Early 1850s," *Southwestern Historical Quarterly* 76 (1972): 161 – 82.

16. *Laws of the State of Texas*, vol. 3, pt. 1, p. 632, Feb. 11, 1850.

17. Reed, *History of the Texas Railroads*, p. 56.

18. 1850 List of Subscribers (23–2391), Samuel May Williams Papers. There are fifty-three people on this list. McLeod is no. 35. Most have $100 next to their names, and the total is $11,700.

19. Reed, *History of the Texas Railroads,* pp. 56–58.

20. Carland Elaine Crook, "Benjamin Theron and French Designs in Texas," *Southwestern Historical Quarterly* 68 (1965): 446. Theron's hard-luck story seemed endless during his years in Texas. He attempted unsuccessfully to seek redress in the courts against the railroad-town company.

21. Reed, *History of the Texas Railroads,* p. 57. B. F. Terry later led the famous Terry's Texas Rangers brigade into the Civil War. He also was present at the 1852 Texas State Fair.

22. Woodward, "Internal Improvements in Texas," p. 175.

23. Reed, *History of the Texas Railroads,* pp. 58–59.

24. Andrew F. Muir, "Railroads Come to Houston, 1857–1861," *Southwestern Historical Quarterly* 64 (1960): 47–50; Bate, *General Sidney Sherman,* p. 209, from recollections in the Galveston *News,* Dec. 6, 1936.

25. Galveston *News,* Sept, 2, 1853. The advertisement was written by John A. Williams as superintendent. Also, see R. G. Ottman, ed., *The Southern Pacific Bulletin* (May–June, 1951), for a summary of the BBB&C's early days.

26. *New Handbook of Texas.* Also, *Houston Telegraph & Texas Register,* Aug. 22, 1851.

27. *Texas State Gazette,* May 24, 1851.

28. Ibid.

29. Ibid., May 17, 1851.

30. Ibid., May 24, 1851. This quote and the following excerpts of McLeod's Austin speech are taken from the complete transcript as printed in the *Texas State Gazette.*

31. McLeod to Thomas Rusk, May 26, 1851, Thomas Jefferson Rusk Papers.

32. Ibid. McLeod to Rusk, June 27, 1851.

33. Thomas Rusk to McLeod, June 17, 1851, Hugh McLeod Papers.

34. *Telegraph & Texas Register,* Aug. 22, 1851, has as complete a listing of the election results as may be available. Howard lost his bid in 1853, left Texas for California, and never returned. *Biographical Directory of Members of the U.S. Congress,* p. 1218.

35. Frank Brown, *Annals of the History of Travis County and the City of Austin,* Book 15.

36. Josiah Tattnall, Commandant of Pensacola Navy Yard, to William A. Graham, Secretary of the Navy, Mar. 3, 1852, Letter of Recommendation, Service Records of Daniel C. McLeod.

CHAPTER 14

1. J. Waddy Thompson to McLeod, Jan. 14, 1852, Hugh McLeod Papers; also, Elizabeth Silverthorne, *Ashbel Smith of Texas,* pp. 119–21.

2. *Texas State Gazette,* Nov. 15 and 22, 1851.

3. H. L. Kinney to McLeod, Jan. 15, 1852, Hugh McLeod Papers; Kinney to Ash-

bel Smith, Mar. 17, 1852, Ashbel Smith Papers. The Merchants' War was a long-standing commercial feud between Brownsville and Matamoros.

4. New Orleans *Daily Picayune,* Nov. 9, 1851; New Orleans *Daily Delta,* May 20, 1852.

5. New Orleans *Daily Delta,* May 20, 1852.

6. *Texas State Gazette,* May 22, 1852.

7. Hortense Warner Ward, "The First State Fair of Texas," *Southwestern Historical Quarterly* 57 (1953): 168–70.

8. Oates, *Memoirs,* pp. 636–44. Also, Silverthorne, *Ashbel Smith,* p. 129.

9. Ward, "First State Fair of Texas," p. 173.

10. *Kinney v. McCleod,* 9 Texas Reports 77–78 (TxSuprCt 1852).

11. Josiah Tattnall to William A. Graham, Secretary of the Navy, Mar. 3, 1852, Records of Daniel C. McLeod.

12. Jeffrey to Josiah Tattnall, Sept. 2, 1852, Records of Daniel C. McLeod.

13. Ibid.

14. Surgeon Daniel C. McLeod, in Callahan, *Officers of the Navy,* p. 372; also, family letter of Hugh McLeod to H. Bailey Carroll, Dec., 1964, in possession of author.

15. Hayes, *Galveston,* pp. 730, 931.

16. P. Debondova (?) to McLeod, Austin, Mar. 24, 1853, Hugh McLeod Papers.

17. Oliver Hunter to McLeod, Savannah, Apr. 15, 1854, Hugh McLeod Papers.

18. *Petitions to the State Congress of Texas,* Oct., 1855; also, family letter from McLeod to Carroll, 1964, in possession of author.

19. Mayor of Galveston and Alderman to Hugh McLeod, Jan. 2, 1855, *Lamar Papers,* vol. 4, no. 2487.

20. Gordon Gillson, "Louisiana: Pioneer in Public Health," *Louisiana History* 4 (1963): 215; DeBow's *Review* 18 (1855): 630. Also, Thomas P. Martin, "Conflicting Cotton Interests, 1848–1857," *Journal of Southern History* 7 (1941): 18 n. 74.

21. John S. Ford to McLeod, Austin, Jan. 14, 1855, Hugh McLeod Papers.

22. John Sidney Thrasher to McLeod, New Orleans, Jan. 24, 1855, Hugh McLeod Papers.

23. George Howard to McLeod, Zurich, Mar. 29, 1855, Hugh McLeod Papers. This long and newsy letter speaks of Howard's raising money for the troubled Galveston-Houston-Beaumont Railroad Company, and inquires about Cordova as well.

24. William Cazneau to McLeod, Austin, Feb. 12, 1855, Hugh McLeod Papers. Written the day after McLeod's speech to Lodge No. 12 and consigned by fourteen others.

25. Jonathan Fay Barrett to McLeod, Oct. 19 and Nov. 5, 1855; Aug. 3, 1856; Oct. 25, 1857, Hugh McLeod Papers.

26. Barnard Bee and William Beck Ochiltree to McLeod, Austin, Aug. 23, 1856, Hugh McLeod Papers.

27. Citizens of Union Hill to McLeod, Aug. 4, 1856; Bryan Supporters to McLeod, Aug. 10, 1856, Hugh McLeod Papers.

28. Hayes, *Galveston,* pp. 748–59.

29. McLeod to Committee, Macon, Nov. 10, 1856; Herschel Johnson to McLeod,

Milledgeville, Nov. 14, 1856; T. Patrick Collins to McLeod, Nov.15 and 17, 1856, Hugh McLeod Papers.

30. Charleston *Mercury*, Dec. 9, 1856. "An estimated one thousand delegates, including a large representation of Southern Fire-Eaters, will be attending the commercial convention next week."

31. Herbert Wender, "The Southern Commercial Convention, 1856," *Georgia Historical Quarterly* 15 (1931): 183–85.

32. DeBow's *Review* 221 (1857): 216; Richmond *Enquirer*, Dec. 17, 1856; Savannah *Daily Republican*, Dec. 15, 16, 17, 18, 22, 23, 1856.

CHAPTER 15

1. *Texas State Gazette*, June 13, 1854.

2. Burnet to McLeod, Aug. 13, 1855, Hugh McLeod Papers.

3. James Harper Starr to McLeod, Austin, Sept. 4, 1855, Hugh McLeod Papers.

4. Friend, *Sam Houston*, p. 238.

5. Williams and Barker, *Writings of Sam Houston*, vol. 6, pp. 192–99.

6. McLeod to Lamar, Sept. 15, 1855, *Lamar Papers*, vol. 4, p. 28.

7. Hayes, *Galveston*, p. 695. Cronican had served on the city council several times in the previous decade. Corsicana *Prairie Blade*, Oct. 22, 1855.

8. McLeod to John Grant Tod, Austin, Nov. 19, 1855, Papers of Robert S. Tod.

9. Dorman Winfrey, "Julien Sidney Devereux and His Monte Verde, Texas, Plantation," *East Texas Historical Journal* 5 (1967): 90. Brown, *Austin and Travis County*, vol. 17, p. 26.

10. Nov. 23, 1855, Williams and Barker, *Writings of Sam Houston*, vol. 6, pp. 209–34.

11. *Texas State Gazette*, Dec. 22, 1855.

12. Francis R. Lubbock, *Six Decades in Texas*, pp. 198–99.

13. Friend, *Sam Houston*, p. 243 n, from E. W. Winkler, *Platforms of Political Parties in Texas*, 68.

14. Litha Crews, "The Know-Nothing Party in Texas" (master's thesis, University of Texas, 1925); also, Ralph A. Wooster, "An Analysis of the Texas Know-Nothings," *Southwestern Historical Quarterly* 70 (1967): 414–23.

15. Galveston *News*, Oct. 14, 1856.

16. Mary Starr Barkley, *History of Travis County and Austin, 1839–1899*, p. 75.

17. Lubbock, *Six Decades in Texas*, pp. 233–35, tells this entire story in detail.

18. Earl W. Fornell, *The Galveston Era: The Texas Crescent on the Eve of Secession*, pp. 189–92.

19. Galveston *News*, May 21, 1857.

20. Edward S. Wallace, *Destiny and Glory*, pp. 162–73.

21. Earl W. Fornell, "Texans and Filibusters in the 1850s," *Southwestern Historical Quarterly*, 54 (1956): 415.

22. Charles H. Brown, *Agents of Manifest Destiny: Lives and Times of the Filibusters*, pp. 397–400.

23. William Crites, "The Grey-Eyed Man of Destiny," *American West* 9 (1972): 4–9.

24. Fornell, *Galveston Era*, pp. 206–10.

25. Galveston *News,* Sept. 5, 1857.

26. Fornell, *Galveston Era*, p. 214.

27. Williams and Barker, *Writings of Sam Houston,* vol. 7, p. 262. McLeod to T. J. Green, Feb. 25, 1857, *Lamar Papers,* vol. 4, no. 2510.

28. Speech of Gen. Hugh McLeod to the officers of Masonic Lodge No. 12, Dec. 28, 1857, copy in the possession of author.

29. *U.S. Census, Galveston, Texas, 1860,* p. 508. This entry, made on July 8, also lists John M. Baldwin as a resident of this address. McLeod is listed as a Know-Nothing Party member, in Wooster, "Texas Know-Nothings," p. 419f.

30. Ollinger Crenshaw, "The Knights of the Golden Circle: The Career of George Bickley," *American Historical Review* 47 (1941): 23–50.

31. *Texas State Gazette,* Oct. 12, 1858.

32. Roy Sylvan Dunn, "The KGC in Texas, 1860–1861," *Southwestern Historical Quarterly* 70 (1967): 548; also James Farber, *Texas, CSA: A Spotlight on Disaster,* pp. 18–19.

33. Hayes, *Galveston,* pp. 484–86.

34. McLeod to Judge Taylor, Charles S. Taylor Letters and Papers. The case was not settled until 1867.

35. McLeod to James F. Perry, Feb. 7, 1850; McLeod to Stephen S. Perry, Apr. 23, 1859, Perry Papers.

36. McLeod to Stephen S. Perry, July 11, 1859, Perry Papers.

37. Siegel, Stanley, *Poet President of Texas: The Life of Mirabeau B. Lamar, President of the Republic of Texas,* pp. 156–58.

CHAPTER 16

1. Lubbock, *Six Decades in Texas,* pp. 303–304.

2. Galveston *News,* Apr. 10, 1860.

3. Fornell, *Galveston Era*, p. 276.

4. William Pitt Ballinger's diary, Sept. 2, 1860, in Fornell, *Galveston Era*, p. 277.

5. Galveston *News,* Nov. 13, 1860.

6. Fornell, *Galveston Era*, pp. 280–81.

7. Hayes, *Galveston,* p. 481.

8. See also *The Texas Republican,* Dec. 15, 1860.

9. Fornell, *Galveston Era*, p. 282 n. McLeod wrote to J. E. Carnes on Dec. 5; Carnes responded on Dec. 8. The text was titled, "Address on the Duty of the Slave States in the Present Crisis: Delivered in Galveston, December 12, 1860, by Special Invitation of the Committee of Safety and Correspondence, and Many of the Older Citizens of Galveston."

10. C. A. Bridges, "The Knights of the Golden Circle: A Filibustering Fantasy," *Southwestern Historical Quarterly* 44 (1941): 286–302.

11. Galveston *News,* Jan. 22, 1861; also Hayes, *Galveston,* p. 488.

12. Anna Irene Sandbo, "The First Session of the Secession Convention in Texas," *Southwestern Historical Quarterly* 18 (1914): 194.

13. Bill Winsor, *Texas in the Confederacy: Military Installations, Economy, and People,* p. 59.

14. John Ford to J. C. Robertson, Feb. 22, 1861, *War of the Rebellion: A Compilation of the Official Records of the Union and Confederate Armies,* ser. 1, vol. 53, p. 651; also, ser. 1, vol. 1, pp. 535−40.

15. E. B. Nichols to Sterling Robertson, Feb. 26, 1861, *War of the Rebellion,* ser. 1, vol. 53, p. 620.

16. E. W. Winkler, ed., *Journal of the Secession Convention,* pp. 355−56.

17. Nichols to Ford, Feb. 26, 1861, *War of the Rebellion,* ser. 1, vol. 53, p. 620.

18. McLeod to Ford, Brazos Santiago, Mar. 4, 1861, Winkler, *Journal of the Secession Convention,* p. 359.

19. Ford to Robertson, Mar. 6, 1861, *War of the Rebellion,* ser. 1, vol. 53, p. 652.

20. Ford to McLeod, Mar. 20, 1861, Hugh McLeod Papers.

21. Rebecca J. McLeod to Governor Edward Clark, Apr. 23, 1861, J. S. Beers Papers. This letter also proves that McLeod could not have been in the city when Houston arrived and made his famous speech from the Tremont Hotel balcony.

22. Harold Simpson, *Hood's Brigade: A Compendium,* p. 78.

23. Hayes, *Galveston,* pp. 488−89; Gary Cartwright, *Galveston: A History of the Island,* pp. 92−93.

24. Winsor, *Texas in the Confederacy,* p. 60; Cartwright, *Galveston,* pp. 96−100. No one ever found out the meaning of the J.O.L.O. acronym. Cartwright also points out that the watch was never overly disciplined; it was more often a way for young men and women to be together out on the harbor shores.

25. McLeod report to the city council, June 26, 1861. McLeod Papers, Rosenberg Library.

26. R. J. McLeod to Charles Mason, June 24, 1861, J. S. Beers Papers.

27. All of the rail lines are listed in George T. Todd, *First Texas Regiment,* p. 31 n. 6.

28. Adjutant and Inspector General's Office, Richmond, Report for Dec. 13, 1861, *War of the Rebellion,* ser. 1, vol. 5, pp. 788−90.

29. Louis T. Wigfall to Jefferson Davis, Sept. 25, 1861, *War of the Rebellion,* ser. 1, vol. 5, p. 215.

30. Letter of John Marshall, Sept. 29, 1861, in Larry Jay Gage, "The Texas Road to Secession and War," *Southwestern Historical Quarterly* 62 (1958): 196.

31. Diary of E. O. Perry, 1st Texas Infantry, in Simpson, *Hood's Brigade,* p. 72 n.

32. R. J. McLeod to J. S. Beers, Sept. 1, 1862; Dec. 19, 1862; June, 1866; and June, 1869, in J. S. Beers Papers.

33. Donald E. Everett, ed., *Chaplain Davis and Hood's Texas Brigade,* pp. 10−14.

34. Richard M. McMurry, *John Bell Hood and the War for Southern Independence,* pp. 30−31.

35. Ibid., p. 31; also, Everett, *Chaplain Davis,* pp. 11−13.

36. W. P. Benjamin to Major-General Holmes, Jan. 5, 1862, *War of the Rebellion,* se-

ries 1, vol. 5, p. 1020; also, Jefferson Davis, *The Rise and Fall of the Confederate Government*, pp. 212–13.

37. McLeod family letter of Virginia McLeod Marshall, 1927, in possession of the author; also, Mrs. A. V. Winkler, *The Confederate Capital and Hood's Texas Brigade*, pp. 31–41. She mentions McLeod as being "brave, and his death mourned by his men and those who knew him."

38. Lubbock, *Six Decades in Texas*, p. 380.

39. Dudley G. Wooten, *A Comprehensive History of Texas*, vol. 2, pp. 651–53; also, E. W. Winkler, ed., "Checklist of Texas Imprints," *Southwestern Historical Quarterly* 52 (1948): 80, 210; and the Galveston *News*, Feb. 8, 1862.

Bibliography

MANUSCRIPTS AND COLLECTIONS

Army Papers of Texas. Texas State Library, Archives Division, Austin.

Bancroft, Hubert Howe. Papers. University of California, Berkeley.

Beers, J. S. Papers. Rosenberg Library Archives, Galveston, Tex.

Bell, W. H. "The Knights of the Golden Cross in Texas." Master's thesis, Texas A&I University, 1965.

Blake, Gertrude Burleson. "The Public Career of General Hugh McLeod." Master's thesis, University of Texas, 1932.

Bolton, H. E. Santa Fe Papers. Transcripts. Texas State Library, Austin.

Britton, James. Papers. San Jacinto Museum, Houston, Tex.

Brown, Frank. "Annals of Travis County and the City of Austin: From the Earliest Times to the Close of 1875." Typescript. Center for American History, University of Texas, Austin.

Burleson, Edward S. Papers. Barker Texas History Center, Austin.

"Consular Dispatches, Santa Fe." National Archives, G.S.A., Washington, D.C., 1961.

Crews, Litha. "The Know-Nothing Party in Texas." Master's thesis, University of Texas, 1925.

Erhard, Clayton. Papers. University of Texas, Austin.

Frantz, Joe B. "Newspapers in the Republic of Texas." Master's thesis, University of Texas, 1940.

Grover, George W. "Minutes of Adventure from June 1841." Texan–Santa Fe Expedition Papers. Texas State Library, Archives Division, Austin.

Hill, Watt Goodwin. "Texan Santa Fe Expedition of 1841: A Visionary Dream." Master's thesis, St. Mary's University, San Antonio, 1965.

Houston, Andrew Jackson. Papers. San Jacinto Museum and Archives, San Jacinto Battlefield.

Johnston, Albert Sidney. Papers. Barret Collection. Tulane University Archives. New Orleans, La.

Jones, Anson. Papers. Barker Texas History Center, Austin.

Kreneck, Thomas H. "Lone Star Volunteers: History of Texas Participation in the Mexican War." Master's thesis, University of Houston, 1973.

Lamar, Mirabeau B. Executive Records of President Mirabeau B. Lamar of the Republic of Texas. Texas State Library, Austin.

McLeod, Daniel C. Service Records. National Archives, Washington, D.C.

McLeod, Hugh. Family Papers. Philip LaMarche, Grass Valley, Calif.

McLeod, Hugh. Military Records, 1832–1835. United States Military Academy, West Point, N.Y.

McLeod, Hugh. Papers. Texas State Archives, Austin.

Muir, Andrew Forest. "The Buffalo Bayou, Brazos, and Colorado Railway Company, and Its Antecedents." Master's thesis, Rice University, 1942.

Office of Adjutant-General of the Republic of Texas. Records. Texas State Archives, Austin.

Official Papers of the United States Military Academy. West Point, N.Y.

Perry, James F. and Stephen S. Papers. University of Texas, Austin.

Petitions to the State Congress of Texas, 1855. Texas State Archives, Austin.

Philpott, W. A. Papers. Private Collection, Dallas, Tex.

Records Relating to Indian Affairs. National Archives, G.S.A., Washington, D.C., 1929.

Republic of Texas. Army Papers. Texas State Library, Austin.

———. House of Representatives Official Records and Journal. Texas State Archives, Austin.

———. Records of the Quartermaster-General. Texas State Archives, Austin.

The Robert Bruce Blake Nacogdoches Papers. Stephen F. Austin State University, Nacogdoches, Tex.

Roberts, Oran. Papers. University of Texas, Austin.

Rusk, Thomas Jefferson. Letters and Papers. Stephen F. Austin State University Archives, Nacogdoches, Tex.

Santa Fe Expedition, 1841–1842. Papers. Texas State Archives, Austin.

Sinks, Julia Lee. Letters and Papers. University of Texas, Austin.

Smith, Ashbel. Papers. University of Texas, Austin.

Spellman, Paul N. "Zadock and Minerva Cottle Woods, American Pioneers." Master's thesis, University of Texas, 1987.

Starr, James Harper. Papers. Barker Texas History Center, Austin.

Stuart, Benjamin. Rosenberg Library Archives, Galveston, Tex.

Taylor, Charles S. Papers and Letters. Center for American History, Austin, Tex.

Tod, Robert S. Papers. Rosenberg Library Archives, Galveston, Tex.

Williams, Samuel May. Papers. Rosenberg Library Archives, Galveston, Tex.

Yager, Hope. "The Archive War in Texas." Master's thesis, University of Texas, 1939.

BOOKS AND ARTICLES

Almonte, Juan. "A Statistical Report on Texas, 1835." Southwestern Historical Quarterly 38 (1934): 206–17.

Ambrose, Stephen E. *Duty, Honor, Country: A History of West Point.* Baltimore, Md.: Johns Hopkins University Press, 1966.

Barker, Eugene C. "A Glimpse of the Texas Fur Trade, 1832." *Southwestern Historical Quarterly* 19 (1916): 279–82.

———. "The United States and Mexico, 1835–1837." *Mississippi Valley Historical Review* 1 (1914): 3–30.

———, ed. *The Austin Papers.* Washington, D.C.: GPO, 1924–28.

Barkley, Mary Starr. *History of Travis County and Austin, 1839–1899.* Austin, Tex.: n.p., 1963.

Barton, Henry W. *Texas Volunteers in the Mexican War.* Waco, Tex.: Texian Press, 1970.

Bate, Walter N. *General Sidney Sherman, Texas Soldier, Statesman, and Builder.* Waco, Tex.: Texian Press, 1974.

Batte, Lelia. *History of Milam County, Texas.* San Antonio, Tex.: Naylor Publishing Company, 1956.

Biesele, R. L. "The San Saba Colonizing Company." *Southwestern Historical Quarterly* 33 (1930): 169–83.

Binkley, W. C. "New Mexico and the Santa Fe Expedition." *Southwestern Historical Quarterly* 27 (1924): 85–107.

Binkley, William C. *The Expansionist Movement in Texas, 1836–1850.* Berkeley: University of California, 1925.

———. *Official Correspondence of the Texas Revolution.* New York: Appleton-Century, 1936.

Biographical Directory of the United States Congress, 1774–1989. Washington, D.C.: GPO, 1989.

Bixby, William. *South Street.* New York: D. McKay, 1972.

Blount, Lois. "A Brief Study of Thomas J. Rusk through the Letters to His Brother David." *Southwestern Historical Quarterly* 36 (1930): 181–93.

Boogher, Elbert W. G. *Secondary Education in Georgia, 1732–1858.* Philadelphia, Pa.: n.p., 1933.

Brice, Donely E. *The Great Comanche Raid: Boldest Indian Attack of the Texas Republic.* Austin, Tex.: Eakin Press, 1987.

Bridges, C. A. "The Knights of the Golden Circle: A Filibustering Fantasy." *Southwestern Historical Quarterly* 44 (1941): 287–301.

Brooks, Elizabeth. *Prominent Women of Texas.* Akron, Ohio: Werner Co., 1896.

Brown, Charles H. *Agents of Manifest Destiny: Lives and Times of the Filibusters.* Chapel Hill: University of North Carolina Press, 1980.

Brown, John H. *The History of Texas, 1685–1892.* 1892. Reprint, Austin, Tex.: Pemberton, 1970.

———. *Indian Wars and Pioneers.* Austin, Tex.: Ben Jones Co., 1890.

Buenger, Walter L. *Secession and the Union in Texas.* Austin: University of Texas Press, 1984.

Butler, John C. *Historical Records of Macon and Central Georgia.* Macon, Ga.: n.p., 1879.

Callahan, Edward, ed. *List of Officers of the Navy of the United States, 1775 to 1900.* New York: Haskell House, 1901.

Carroll, Horace Bailey. *The Texan Santa Fe Trail.* Canyon, Tex.: Panhandle-Plains Historical Society, 1951.

Carter, James D., ed. *Masonry in Texas.* Waco, Tex.: Masonic Education Service, 1955.

Cartledge, Groves H. *Presbyterian Churches and Early Settlers in Northeast Georgia.* Athens: University of Georgia Press, 1960.

Cartwright, Gary. *Galveston: A History of the Island.* New York: Macmillan, 1991.

Census of Texas, 1846. Austin, Tex.: G. White, 1846.

Chambers, T. J. "Diary of T. J. Chambers." *Southwestern Historical Quarterly* 50 (1946): 112–73.

Christian, A. K. "Mirabeau Buonaparte Lamar." *Southwestern Historical Quarterly* 23 (1921): 89, 153–70.

Clarke, Mary Whatley. *Chief Bowles and the Texas Cherokees.* Norman: University of Oklahoma Press, 1971.

Connor, Seymour V. *Adventure in Glory: The Saga of Texas, 1836–1849.* Austin, Tex.: Steck-Vaughn, 1965.

Coulter, E. Merton. "The Great Savannah Fire of 1820." *Georgia Historical Quarterly* 23 (1939): 1–5.

Crenshaw, Ollinger. "The Knights of the Golden Circle: The Career of George Bickley." *American Historical Review* 47 (1941): 25–50.

Crites, William. "The Grey-Eyed Man of Destiny." *American West* 9 (1972): 4–10.

Croffut, W. A. *Fifty Years in Camp and Field: The Diary of General Ethan Allen Hitchcock, U.S.A.* New York: Putnam and Sons, 1909.

Crook, Carland Elaine. "Benjamin Theron and French Designs in Texas." *Southwestern Historical Quarterly* 68 (1965): 432–54.

Cullum, George W. *Biographical Register of the Officers and Graduates of the United States Military Academy at West Point, New York.* D. Appleton, 1868.

Davis, Jefferson. *Rise and Fall of the Confederate Government.* 1881.

Dawson, Joseph Martin. *José Antonio Navarro, Co-Creator of Texas.* Waco, Tex.: Baylor University Press, 1969.

De Bow's Review. New Orleans: J. D. B. De Bow, 1853–64.

De Bruhl, Marshall. *Sword of San Jacinto: A Life of Sam Houston.* New York: Random House, 1993.

DeCordova, Jacob. *Biography of José Antonio Navarro, written by an old Texan.* Houston, Tex.: Telegraph Steam Printing, 1876.

Denslow, William R., ed. *10,000 Famous Freemasons.* 4 vols. Trenton, Mo.: Royal Arch Magazine, 1958.

DeShields, James T. *Battle with the Kickapoos.* Houston, Tex.: Union National Bank, 1933.

———. *Border Wars of Texas.* Tioga, Tex.: Herald, 1912.

Dixon, Sam Houston. *Romance and Tragedy in Texas History.* Houston: Texas Historical Publishers, 1924.

Duffus, R. L. *The Santa Fe Trail.* New York: Longmans, Green and Company, 1930.

Dunn, Roy Sylvan. "The KGC in Texas, 1860–1861." *Southwestern Historical Quarterly* 70 (1967): 543–73.

Eisenhower, John S. D. *So Far from God: The U.S. War with Mexico, 1846–1848.* New York: Random House, 1989.

Elliott, Claude. "Georgia and the Texas Revolution." *Georgia Historical Quarterly* 28 (1944): 233–50.

Erath, Lucy A. "Memoirs of Major George Bernard Erath." *Southwestern Historical Quarterly* 26 (1923): 207–33.

Everett, Dianna. *The Texas Cherokees: A People between Two Fires, 1819–1840.* Norman: University of Oklahoma Press, 1990.

Everett, Donald E., ed. *Chaplain Davis and Hood's Texas Brigade.* San Antonio, Tex.: Trinity University, 1962.

Exley, Jo Ella Powell. *Texas Tears and Texas Sunshine: Voices of Frontier Women.* College Station: Texas A&M University Press, 1985.

Falconer, Thomas. *Letters and Notes on the Texan Santa Fe Expedition.* New York: Dauber and Pine, 1930.

Farber, James. *Texas, CSA: A Spotlight on Disaster.* New York: Jackson, 1947.

Ferris, Sylvia Van Voast, and Eleanor S. Hoppe. *Scalpels and Sabers.* Austin, Tex.: Eakin Press, 1985.

Fornell, Earl W. *The Galveston Era: The Texas Crescent on the Eve of Secession.* Austin: University of Texas Press, 1961.

———. "Texans and Filibusters in the 1850s." *Southwestern Historical Quarterly* 59 (1956): 411–28.

Freeman, Martha Doty. *History of Civil War Military Activities at Velasco and Quintana, Brazoria County, and Virginia Point, Galveston County, Texas.* Austin, Tex.: Prewitt & Associates, 1995.

Friend, Llerena B. *Sam Houston, The Great Designer.* Austin: University of Texas Press, 1954.

———. "Sidelights and Supplements on the Perote Prisoners." *Southwestern Historical Quarterly* 68 (1965): 366–74.

Gage, Larry Jay. "The Texas Road to Secession and War." *Southwestern Historical Quarterly* 62 (1958): 191–226.

Gambrell, Herbert P. *Mirabeau B. Lamar, Troubadour and Crusader.* Dallas, Tex.: Southwest Press, 1934.

Garrison, George Pierce. *Diplomatic Correspondence of the Republic of Texas.* II vols. Washington, D.C.: GPO, 1908–11.

Gibson, A. M. *The Kickapoos.* Norman: University of Oklahoma Press, 1963.

Gillson, Gordon. "Louisiana: Pioneer in Public Health." *Louisiana History* 4 (1963): 207–32.

Green, Mary Rena Maverick. *Samuel Maverick, Texan, 1803–1870.* San Antonio, Tex.: Corona, 1952.

Green, Rena Maverick, ed. *Memoirs of Mary A. Maverick, arranged by Mary Maverick and her son.* San Antonio, Tex.: Alamo Publishing Co., 1921.

Gregg, Josiah. *Commerce of the Prairies.* Edited by Max L. Moorehead. Norman: University of Oklahoma Press, 1954.

Griffin, S. C. *A History of Galveston.* Galveston, Tex.: Cawston, 1931.

Gulick, Charles Adams, Jr., ed. *The Papers of Mirabeau Buonaparte Lamar.* 6 vols. Austin, Tex.: Baldwin and Sons, 1922.

Hayes, Charles W. *Galveston: A History of the Island and City.* 1879. Reprint, Austin, Tex.: Jenkins-Garrett, 1974.

Haynes, Sam. *Soldiers of Fortune: The Somervell and Mier Expeditions.* Austin: University of Texas Press, 1990.

Hogan, William Ransom. *The Texas Republic: A Social and Economic History.* Norman: Oklahoma University Press, 1993.

Hollen, W. Eugene, and Ruth L. Butler, eds. *William Bollaert's Texas, 1836–1846.* Norman: University of Oklahoma Press, 1956.

Horgan, Paul. *Great River: The Rio Grande in North American History.* 2 vols. New York: Holt, Rinehart, Winston, 1954.

Houston, Martha Lou. *The Land Lottery of Georgia, 1827.* Columbus: Walton-Forbes, 1929.

James, Marquis. *The Raven: A Biography of Sam Houston.* Indianapolis, Ind.: Bobbs-Merrill, 1929.

Jenkins, John H. *Papers of the Texas Revolution.* 10 vols. Austin, Tex.: Presidial Press, 1973.
———, and Kenneth Kesselus. *Edward Burleson: Texas Frontier Leader.* Austin, Tex.: Jenkins, 1990.

Johnson, Frank W. *A History of Texas and Texans.* Edited by Eugene C. Barker. New York: American Historical Society, 1914.

Johnston, William Preston. *The Life of General Albert Sidney Johnston.* New York: n.p., 1878.

Jones, R. L. and Pauline. "The Occupation of Nacogdoches." *East Texas Historical Journal* 4: 23–43.

Journal of the Texas House of Representatives. Austin, Tex.: Von Boeckmann–Jones, 1945.

Kemp, L. W. "Mrs. Angelina B. Eberly." *Southwestern Historical Quarterly* 36 (1933): 193–99.

Kendall, George Wilkins. *Narrative of the Texan Santa Fe Expedition and Capture of the Texans.* 2 vols. New York: Harper and Brothers, 1856.

Laws of the Republic of Texas. Austin, Tex.: Von Boeckmann–Jones, 1940.

LeMar, Harold. *History of the Lamar or Lemar Family.* Omaha, Nebr.: Cockle Press, 1941.

Leonard, John William. *History of the City of New York, 1609–1909.* New York: n.p., 1910.

Lindheim, Milton. *Republic of the Rio Grande: Texans in Mexico, 1839–1840.* Waco, Tex.: W. M. Morrison, 1964.

Lindley, E. R., ed. *Biographical Directory of the Texan Conventions and Congresses, 1832–1845.* Austin, Tex.: n.p., 1941.

Loomis, Noel M. *The Texan–Santa Fe Pioneers.* Norman: University of Oklahoma Press, 1958.

Lubbock, Francis R. *Six Decades in Texas.* Austin, Tex.: Jones and Co., 1900.

Lubbock, Thomas S. "Recollections of Thomas S. Lubbock." *Texana* 6 (1968): 166–71.

McCaleb, Walter. *The Santa Fe Expedition.* Austin, Tex.: Eakin Press, 1964.

McDonald, Archie. *Nacogdoches: Wilderness Outpost to Modern City, 1779–1979.* Burnet, Tex.: Eakin Press, 1980.

McGrath, J. J., and Wallace Hawkins. "Perote Fort: Where Texans Were Imprisoned." *Southwestern Historical Quarterly* 48 (1945): 340–45.

McLeod, Rebecca Lamar. "The Loss of the Steamer Pulaski." *Georgia Historical Quarterly* 3 (1919): 63–95.

McMurry, Richard M. *John Bell Hood and the War for Southern Independence.* Lexington: University of Kentucky Press, 1982.

Malone, Dumas, ed. *Dictionary of American Biography.* 22 vols. New York: Scribner's Sons, 1928.

Manning, Wentworth. *Some History of Van Zandt County, Texas.* Vol. 1. Des Moines, Iowa: Homestead, 1919.

Manning, William Ray. *Early Diplomatic Relations between the United States and Mexico.* 12 vols. Baltimore, Md.: Johns Hopkins University Press, 1916.

Marks, Paula M. *Turn Your Eyes Toward Texas: Pioneers Sam and Mary Maverick.* College Station: Texas A&M University Press, 1989.

Marshall, Thomas M. *A History of the Western Boundary of the Louisiana Purchase, 1819–1841.* Berkeley: University of California Press, 1914.

Martin, Thomas P. "Conflicting Cotton Interests, 1848–1857." *Journal of Southern History* 7 (1941): 173–94.

Mayhall, Mildred P. *Indian Wars of Texas.* Waco, Tex.: Texian Press, 1965.

Miller, T. L. *Bounty and Donation Land Grants of Texas, 1835–1888.* Austin: University of Texas Press, 1967.

Moore, Jack. *The Killough Massacre.* Jacksonville, Tex.: Kiely Printing, 1966.

Muckleroy, Anna. "Indian Policy in the Republic of Texas." *Southwestern Historical Quarterly* 26 (1922): 1–9.

Muir, Andrew F. "Railroads Come to Houston, 1857–1861." *Southwestern Historical Quarterly* 64 (1960): 42–63.

Myers, Robert M., ed. *Children of Pride: A True Story of Georgia and the Civil War.* New Haven, Conn.: Yale University Press, 1972.

Nance, Joseph Milton. *After San Jacinto: The Texas-Mexico Frontier, 1836–1841.* Austin: University of Texas Press, 1963.

———. *Attack and Counter-Attack: Texas-Mexico Relations, 1842.* College Station: Texas A&M University Press, 1964.

Neighbors, Kenneth F. *R. S. Neighbors and the Texas Frontier, 1836–1859.* Waco, Tex.: Texian Press, 1975.

Nielsen, George. "Mathew Caldwell and the Santa Fe Expedition." *Southwestern Historical Quarterly* 64 (1961): 478–502.

Oates, Stephen B., ed. *Memoirs of John S. "Rip" Ford.* Austin: University of Texas Press, 1963.

Official Records of Freemasonry in Texas. Waco: Masonic Grand Lodge and Museum of Texas.

Official Register of the Officers and Cadets of the United States Military Academy, West Point, N.Y.

Pearce, George F. *The United States Navy in Pensacola: From Sailing Ships to Naval Aviation, 1825–1930.* Pensacola: University of Florida Press, 1980.

Pierce, Gerald S. "The Military Road Expeditions of 1840–41." *Texas Military History* 6: 115–35.

———. *Texas under Arms: The Camps, Posts, and Military Towns of the Republic of Texas, 1836–1846.* Austin, Tex.: Encino Press, 1969.

Pletcher, David M. *The Diplomacy of Annexation: Texas, Oregon, and the Mexican War.* Columbia: University of Missouri Press, 1973.

Pope, John. *Explorations and Surveys for a Rail Road Route from the Mississippi River to the Pacific Ocean.* Richmond, Va.: U.S. Topographic Engineers, 1850?

Price, Eugenia. *To See Your Face Again.* Garden City, N.J.: Doubleday, 1985.

Ramsay, Jack, Jr. *Thunder beyond the Brazos: Mirabeau B. Lamar, A Biography.* Austin, Tex.: Eakin Press, 1985.

Reagan, John H. "The Expulsion of the Cherokees from East Texas." *Southwestern Historical Quarterly* 1 (1897): 38–46.

Reed, S. G. *A History of the Texas Railroads and Transportation Conditions under Spain and Mexico and the Republic and the State.* Houston, Tex.: St. Clair, 1941.

Reports of Cases Argued and Decided in the Supreme Court of the State of Texas, 1846–1962. St. Louis: Gilbert, 1881–1963.

Richardson, Rupert. *The Frontier of Northwest Texas, 1846–1876.* Glendale, Calif.: A. H. Clark, 1963.

Ruxton, George F. *Adventure in Mexico and the Rocky Mountains.* 1855.

Sandbo, Anna Irene. "The First Session of the Secession Convention in Texas." *Southwestern Historical Quarterly* 18 (1914): 41–73.

Sibley, Marilyn McAdams. *Lone Stars and State Gazettes: Texas Newspapers before the Civil War.* College Station: Texas A&M University Press, 1983.

Siegel, Stanley. *Poet President of Texas: The Life of Mirabeau B. Lamar, President of the Republic of Texas.* Austin, Tex.: Jenkins, 1977.

———. *A Political History of the Texas Republic.* Austin: University of Texas Press, 1956.

Silverthorne, Elizabeth. *Ashbel Smith of Texas.* College Station: Texas A&M University Press, 1982.

Simpson, Col. Harold B. *Hood's Brigade: A Compendium.* Hillsboro, Tex.: Hill Junior College, 1977.

———, and Marcus J. Wright. *Texas in the War.* Hillsboro, Tex.: Hill Junior College, 1965.

Sinks, Julia Lee. "Original Sketch for the *Fayette County News* of the Santa Fe Prisoners." *Southwestern Historical Quarterly* 64 (1961): 515–16.

Smith, J. H. "La Republica de Rio Grande." *American Historical Review* 25 (1920): 660–75.

Smithwick, Noah. *Evolution of a State, or, Recollections of Old Texas Days.* Austin, Tex.: Gammel Books, 1900.

Southerland, Henry, Jr., and Jerry E. Brown. *The Federal Road through Georgia, the Creek Nation, and Alabama, 1806–1836.* Tuscaloosa: University of Alabama Press, 1989.

Spell, Lota M. "The Anglo-Saxon Press in Mexico, 1846–1848." *American Historical Review* 38 (1932): 20–31.

———. *Pioneer Printer: Samuel Bangs in Mexico and Texas.* Austin: University of Texas Press, 1963.

Spurlin, Charles, ed. *Texas Veterans in the Mexican War.* Victoria, Tex.: Victoria College, 1984.

Taylor, Virginia, ed. *Order Book of General H. McLeod: Santa Fe Expedition.* Austin: Texas State Library, 1956.

———. *Texas Treasury Papers.* 4 vols. Austin: Texas State Library, 1956.

Thompson, J. Waddy. *Recollections of Mexico.* New York: Wiley and Putnam, 1846.

Thrall, Homer. *Pictorial History of Texas.* St. Louis: n.p., 1879.

Todd, George T. *First Texas Regiment.* Waco, Tex.: Texian Press, 1963.

Tyler, Ron, ed. *New Handbook of Texas.* 6 vols. Austin: Texas State Historical Association, 1996.

Tyson, Carl. N. *The Red River in Southwestern History.* Norman: University of Oklahoma Press, 1981.

U.S. Bureau of the Census. *Census of the United States, 1840 — Georgia.* Washington, D.C.

———. *Census of the United States, 1860 — Galveston, Texas.* Washington, D.C.

Vigness, David M. "Relations of the Republic of Texas and the Republic of the Rio Grande." *Southwestern Historical Quarterly* 57 (1954): 312–21.

Wallace, Edward S. *Destiny and Glory.* New York: Coward-McCann, 1957.

Walraven, Bill and Marjorie. *Magnificent Barbarians: Little-Told Tales of the Texas Revolution.* Austin, Tex.: Eakin Press, 1993.

Walther, Eric. *The Fire-Eaters.* Baton Rouge: Louisiana State University Press, 1992.

Ward, Hortense Warner. "The First State Fair of Texas." *Southwestern Historical Quarterly* 57 (1953): 163–74.

War of the Rebellion: A Compilation of the Official Records of the Union and Confederate Armies. 70 vols. Under the direction of Robert N. Scott, Secretary of War. Washington, D.C.: GPO, 1971.

Warren, Mary B., ed. *Georgia Marriages and Deaths.* Danielsville, Ga.: Heritage Papers, 1968.

Webb, Walter P., ed. *Handbook of Texas.* 3 vols. Austin: Texas State Historical Association, 1952.

Webb, Walter Prescott. *The Texas Rangers: A Century of Frontier Defense.* New York: Houghton Mifflin, 1935.

Weems, John E. *Dream of Empire: A Human History of the Republic of Texas, 1836–1846.* Fort Worth: Texas Christian University Press, 1986.

Wells, Tom Henderson. *Commodore Moore and the Texas Navy.* Austin: University of Texas Press, 1960.

Wender, Herbert. "The Southern Commercial Convention, 1856." *Georgia Historical Quarterly* 15 (1931): 173–91.

White, Gifford E. *First Settlers of Galveston County, Texas.* Nacogdoches, Tex.: Ericson Books, 1985.

White, Leonard D. *The Jacksonians: A Study in Administrative History, 1829–1861.* New York: Macmillan, 1954.

Wilbarger, J. W. *Indian Depredations in Texas.* Austin, Tex.: n.p., 1889.

Williams, Amelia C., and Eugene C. Barker, eds. *Writings of Sam Houston.* 8 vols. Austin, Tex.: Pemberton, 1970.

Williams, John Hoyt. *Sam Houston: A Biography of the Father of Texas.* New York: Simon & Schuster, 1993.

Wilson, Caroline Price, ed. *Annals of Georgia.* Savannah, Ga.: Braid and Hutton, 1933.

Winfrey, Dorman. "Julien Sidney Devereux and His Monte Verde, Texas, Plantation." *East Texas Historical Journal* 5 (1967): 83–93.

Winkler, Mrs. A. V. *The Confederate Capital and Hood's Texas Brigade.* Austin, Tex.: n.p., 1898.

Winkler, E. W. *Platforms of Political Parties in Texas.* Austin: University of Texas Press, 1916.

———, ed. *Journal of the Secession Convention of Texas, 1861.* Austin, Tex., 1912.

Winsor, Bill. *Texas in the Confederacy: Military Installations, Economy, and People.* Hillsboro, Tex.: Hill Junior College, 1978.

Wisehart, M. K. *Sam Houston: American Giant.* Washington, D.C.: R. B. Luce, 1962.

Woldert, Albert. "The Last of the Cherokees in Texas, and the Life and Death of Chief Bowles." *Chronicles of Oklahoma* 1 (1921): 179–226.

Woodward, Earl F. "Internal Improvements in Texas in the Early 1850s." *Southwestern Historical Quarterly* 76 (1972): 161–82.

Wooster, Ralph A. "An Analysis of the Texas Know-Nothings." *Southwestern Historical Quarterly* 70 (1967): 414–23.

Wooten, Dudley G. *A Comprehensive History of Texas.* 2 vols. Dallas, Tex.: n.p., 1898.

Yoakum, Henderson. *History of Texas.* 2 vols. 1855.

Index

223